## Praise for
### *Taking Root: The Girls Write Now 2022 Anthology*

"As a young writer, understanding and believing how important your voice is, how extraordinary and singular it is, and how powerful it is in its capacity to connect to others—it is a gift and a wonder. And all this makes Girls Write Now more vital than ever. We all reap the rewards."

**–MEGAN ABBOTT**, author of *The Turnout*

"The remarkable young voices in this anthology show the brilliance, diversity, and power of the next generation of writers. Girls Write Now is building a brighter literary future for all of us."

**–SUSIE DUMOND**, author of *Queerly Beloved*

"Girls Write Now is overflowing with inspiration. This powerful organization allows young people to know with 100 percent certainty their ideas and minds not only matter but are our future, and a very bright future at that."

**–KALI FAJARDO-ANSTINE**, author of *Sabrina & Corina*

"Read this book as an antidote to dark forebodings; these young thinkers and writers are original, brilliant, and wise."

**–RIVKA GALCHEN**, author of *Everyone Knows Your Mother Is a Witch*

"I am so inspired by the talent, honesty, and creativity in these pages. Girls Write Now mentees show us what writing for the future looks like in this beautiful anthology."

**–REYNA GRANDE**, coeditor of *Somewhere We Are Human*

"I am blown away by the realizations and the sense of self these young writers possess. Their voices are not merely 'unmuted' in this latest anthology but explode off the page with conviction and talent. It's simply joyous."

**–BARBARA HEREL**, contributing author to *Tick Tock: Essays on Becoming a Parent After 40*

"If you need inspiration, if you need hope that the future is in safe and thoughtful hands, dive into the stories of Girls Write Now. Here you will find young writers who share their unvarnished truth and in return offer a glimpse of their world, which we are privileged to see."

**–YVONNE LATTY**, author of *We Were There* and *In Conflict*

"Girls Write Now is about supporting and mentoring young women and gender-expansive youth who are passionate about writing. But it is also about beginning your career journey and beginning to understand the transformative power of the written word."

—JANE LAUDER, executive vice president, enterprise marketing, and chief data officer, Estée Lauder Companies, and Girls Write Now honoree

"As Joan Didion said, 'We tell ourselves stories in order to live.' Girls Write Now blows this wide open, thanks to seasoned mentors helping new writers tell their stories in order to live better. The brave and heartfelt stories in this anthology will help all of us live better. Together."

—LESLIE LEHR, author of *A Boob's Life: How America's Obsession Shaped Me . . . and You*

"Girls Write Now's mission to instill the power of the written word from an early age is a necessary one for young writers. It is my hope that they all carry that sense of power with them into adulthood, and never lose the courage to express themselves."

—MEGAN MARGULIES, author of *My Captain America*

"Even if you think you're a full-blown adult, Girls Write Now work will time-warp you back to your most emotionally intense and vulnerable years—and you'll be so happy it did. Brimming with fresh and unexpected wisdom, the 2022 anthology is a necessary reminder that, no matter how old, we're all always a little bit teenage."

—GRACE PERRY, author of *The 2000s Made Me Gay: Essays on Pop Culture*

"Women have been consistently silenced throughout history by those afraid of the enormous power that their collective voices wield. Girls Write Now provides the invaluable mentorship and guidance girls need to connect with the fire that was always inside of them."

—LIZ PLANK, author of *For the Love of Men: From Toxic to a More Mindful Masculinity*

"Building bridges, unlocking worlds, unleashing hidden potential—all begin with cultivating confidence and expression. Girls Write Now provides a gateway to young writers everywhere to find their words and express their voices for the moment and the future. They are changed. We are changed, all for the better."

—VANESSA RILEY, author of *Island Queen*

"What a gift it is to be able to read young writers while they're developing, to get a glimpse behind the curtain of the creative process and witness the incredibly unique and vibrant voices come into their full power. Girls Write Now is an incredible organization and these literary conversations between established and brand-new writers are a joy to read."

 –DANA SCHWARTZ, author of *Anatomy: A Love Story*

"Girls Write Now inspired me to think of myself as more than someone who writes, but as a writer. My years as a mentee gave me the foundation to be the author I'm proud to be today."

 –JOY L. SMITH, author of *Turning* and Girls Write Now mentee alum

"Some of the young writers I met within the organization Girls Write Now are some of the brightest, most intelligent, and strongest young minds I've encountered in my many, many years of teaching and presenting. I cannot underscore enough the importance of the Girls Write Now organization, which mentors, supports, and empowers these young women. I cannot underscore enough the importance of their voices, voices that are needed to save others and change the course of our troubled nation and world."

 –PAMELA SNEED, author of *Funeral Diva*

"Young women represent the change we would like to see in a world in which half the population is female. Yet their and many other marginalized voices are stifled by lack of educational opportunities due to societal and cultural constraints. Girls Write Now is the beginning of a collective awareness that our youth have something to say, and they have the voices in which to enact those societal changes. Ruth Bader Ginsburg said, 'Never underestimate the power of a girl with a book.' I say, never underestimate the power of the young people who can write those books."

 –KATHY STEARMAN, author of *It's Not About the Gun: Lessons from My Global Career as a Female FBI Agent*

"The work in this anthology is a testament to the importance of the mentorship and support provided by Girls Write Now for young voices. It's so magical and special to see what these writers can do when given a chance to play on the page."

 –KAYLA KUMARI UPADHYAYA, author of *Helen House*

"Girls Write Now is creating a diverse community of future leaders that will guide the next generation on the path to creativity, knowledge, and power. They are changing lives one word and one story at a time."

 –AILEEN WEINTRAUB, author of *Knocked Down: A High-Risk Memoir*

"Literature lives on as the most powerful form of expression. Girls Write Now empowers young women to declare their interpretations of the world and transcend generations to ignite minds."

—ELAINE WELTEROTH, author of *More Than Enough: Claiming Space for Who You Are (No Matter What They Say)*

"As always, I am so thrilled and grateful for what Girls Write Now manages to make. Here, not only poetry and prose, but also we see writers themselves being made, unmade, and made anew. As Tess Nealon Raskin says in 'liar's job,' the writer might be a necromancer, who dances with the things not living, brings them to life, bringing herself to life. The young, very alive writers here make art with language. Yacine Barry moves deftly between forms of language, formal and informal address, into emojis in her 'The Birth of the Rose Flower.' In 'Where Reality Truly Resides?' Fariha Chowdhury moves and changes language, making it sound richer with connection: Bengal tiger, Bengali traders, bargain, bare minimum. These young women make themselves, look back and around at their mothers and sisters, and go forward to make a literature that considers and serves community."

—TIPHANIE YANIQUE, author of *Monster in the Middle*

# Taking Root

## The Girls Write Now 2022 Anthology

# Taking Root

## The Girls Write Now
## 2022 Anthology

FOREWORD BY *Allison Russell*

INTRODUCTION BY *Madeline McIntosh*

Published 2022

Printed in the United States

Print ISBN: 978-0-9962772-6-6

E-ISBN: 9781952177248

Library of Congress Control Number: 2022902220

Cover design by Dominique Jones

For information, write to:

Girls Write Now, Inc.
247 West 37th Street, Suite 1000
New York, NY 10018

info@girlswritenow.org
girlswritenow.org

# Taking Root
## The Girls Write Now 2022 Anthology

Perhaps you've seen a mangrove. These saltwater-loving trees grow thickly along the coastlines of South Florida. They edge the shores in heavy clumps; they huddle in meandering rows. The roots will catch your eye first: a rich reddish-brown color, they grow out of the brackish water like creeping fingers. As a child, I thought the roots were trying to wrench themselves from the sediment—that the mangrove was a tree desperately seeking other waters.

What I didn't know then was that the mangrove had adapted to thrive there. Between twice-a-day tides, the stilt-like roots pull oxygen from the air. The sediment that collects beneath the roots builds the shoreline, and a vibrant community of plants and animals lives on or below the roots. Even the leaves are gifted. Two holes on each pump out the excess salt; it covers the waxy green leaves like crystals.

The young writers of *Taking Root: The Girls Write Now 2022 Anthology* remind me of those red mangroves and their hardy, branching roots. Like the tree, they flourish at the borders, but their roots straddle the prickly border between youth and adulthood. In waters friendly or inhospitable, these writers persevere: always creating, always building, expanding. Through their words they interrogate the world we take for granted, and in their wonderings, propose new Earths to inhabit.

Here's to those brave, beautiful writers and the works that will take them near and far. Deeply rooted in who they are, their words are the salt crystals that adorn the leaves.

---

MORAYO FALEYIMU is a writer of short- and long-form fiction. She works as a professional development writer for Uncommon Schools. Faleyimu is also a Girls Write Now mentor alumna and a co-chair of the Girls Write Now Anthology Committee.

# Anthology Editorial Committee

### Editor

Molly MacDermot

### Committee Co-Chairs

Rosie Black

Morayo Faleyimu

Spencer George

Maya Millett

Carol Paik

### Committee Editors

Nan Bauer-Maglin

Susanne Beck

Shannon Carlin

Mary Darby

Morgan Leigh Davies

Katie Della Mora

Amy Flyntz

Gabriela Galvin

Catherine Greenman

Donna Hill

Becca James

Rebecca Lowry Warchut

Nadine Matthews

Katie McGuire

Nikki Palumbo

Debra Register

Patricia Rossi

Mara Santilli

Hannah Sheldon-Dean

Madeline Stone

Kiki T.

Maryellen Tighe

Lauren Vespoli

Liza Wyles

Sarah Zobel

### Promotions Subcommittee Co-Chairs

Sara Felsentein

Livia Nelson

# Contents

Note: Stories that depict sensitive topics are necessary for many reasons. Shedding light on the darkest part of the human experience can both help others feel less alone and inspire readers to work toward a better future. However, we recognize that certain topics may be distressing when they catch readers off guard. That is why we have included a content warning for some of the stories.

# Foreword

## ALLISON RUSSELL

Never underestimate the power of a story. Stories save lives. Words are infinitely powerful. Words are spells. Words can also kill. How we wield them matters.

For too long over half of the world's one human family has been purposefully silenced, oppressed, repressed, subjected to violence. Words stolen, erased, appropriated.

But times are changing.

Each of the brilliant and brave young womxn and gender-expansive writers in this anthology is changing them.

The visionary programs that Girls Write Now nurtures are changing them.

As a mother, a musician, a writer, a songmaker, as a mixed-heritage queer black womxn, as a new immigrant—a Scottish Grenadian Canadian living in America—as a survivor of more than a decade of severe childhood sexual, physical, and psychological abuse—I feel a profound gratitude for and resonance with these words and works. I believe what Alice Walker wrote: "We Are the Ones We Have Been Waiting For." Each of these young writers is living proof.

I had the surreal honor of being named an Agent of Change by Girls Write Now in 2021, following in Cicely Tyson's footsteps. I found myself weeping more than once during the presentations of each of the Girls Write Now mentees and mentee alumni. Their spells of self-determination, insight, and poetic flight moved me to tears. I was astounded by their confidence and evolved self-love; by the generosity of their spirits and the incisive force of their words. When I was their age, I was barely alive and actively trying to disappear. It took me many, many years to step into my own voice and story consciously and joyfully. I wish there had been an organization like Girls Write Now back then for me.

The stories we choose to inhabit, to support, to amplify—matter. The stories and voices historically and presently suppressed are the very ones we need to hear the most. Every Storyteller Matters.

Girls Write Now understands this.

Each of the Storytellers in this anthology has a unique, inclusive, infinitely powerful voice and perspective.

As the world faces a war, and chasms of iniquity gape wider, as we struggle to overcome insidious, destructive bigotry here in an empathy-impaired America and across the globe, as the pandemics of intergenerational abuse, violence, and silence continue to take their toll—we need these Storytellers more than ever.

We who stand at the intersections of the margins have the clearest view of the page. Our vision is essential. Our stories, told in our own words, are medicine and healing. Our empathy is honed, high-level, hard-won. Our whole lives we've had to see the world through a straight white man's eyes in order to survive. We all hold Ph.D.s in Resilience and Empathy. It's our turn to speak, to write, to lead. We must teach those whose empathy has been stunted and impaired through the false ideologies of bigotry and delusional superiority. We must teach them to see the world in *our* images. In *our* experiences. In *our* hopes and dreams and wishes.

For we are all mentors. And we are all mentees—it's not A or B—not zero-sum, choose one and forever hold your peace. It's *yes*, AND . . . It's *both*, please. It's three or more. It's each one, teach as many as you can and *don't stop*. Listening, learning, transcending—reaching for that deeper understanding. That compassion, that love which grows from empathy and resilience and forgiveness—hard-won. We must learn to rejoice in all our glorious differences and *still* see ourselves in another's crisis. We must find the courage to share ourselves, our minds—unabashedly, unashamedly—just as each of these intrepid mentee writers has done.

So let us learn from them.

I invite you to lose yourself within the pages of this Girls Write Now anthology and find yourself changed.

I have and I will, again and again.

Here's to building the Beloved Community and a better, kinder world one spell, one vital Storyteller, at a time.

May you be immersed, engaged, enraged, galvanized, challenged, comforted, recognized, represented, restored, inspired!

Never underestimate the power of a story.

---

ALLISON RUSSELL is a three-time Grammy-nominated musician and songwriter for *Outside Child*, the author of a forthcoming memoir with Flatiron Books, an anti-bigotry activist, and a Girls Write Now honoree.

# Introduction

## MADELINE McINTOSH

My journey in book publishing started with a temp job after college, and I've never really looked back. But just a few years before that first gig, despite being a dedicated reader, I was barely aware of this industry as a possible professional home. As grateful as I am to have found this path, I hate to think how easy it would have been to miss it altogether.

As loud and proud as publishers are when it comes to putting our authors and their words out into the world, we like to keep a pretty low profile for ourselves. The humility makes for a healthy culture at work, but it's a handicap when it comes to attracting the attention of talented young people of all backgrounds and interests. That's why we so value Girls Write Now—they have been an excellent partner helping to connect us with a richly diverse community of potential employees, authors, and readers.

Reflecting on this organization's mission to help young women and gender-expansive youth strengthen their own voices, I was reminded of a critical early experience of my own.

One day in kindergarten, I was asked to give examples of words to represent each letter of the alphabet. *A* is for *Apple*, etc. At *X*, I of course wrote that *X* is for *Xylophone*. My teacher—let's protect identities here and call her Miss Smith—corrected me that "*Xylophone* begins with *Z*."

Naïve as I was, I thought I was being helpful the next day by bringing in my younger brother's baby book, which of course backed up my crazy idea that *Xylophone* started with *X*. In response, Miss Smith wrote a report that I had an attitude problem and probably couldn't be taught much at all.

Thankfully, my mother would have none of that. My clearest memory of this whole incident is of hiding behind her skirt while she fought my battle for me with Miss Smith.

You won't be surprised to hear that within a year, I'd changed schools and found a place in which the alphabet was less a battleground than the starting point of a life happily immersed in books.

I'm very conscious of the privilege inherent in the story I've just told. Without a parent who not only backed me up but had enough systemic support to be able to change my educational path, I would have had a different life. Not only might I have fallen prey to fake alphabet news, but more important, I might have doubted my own ability to learn and achieve.

For every teen who Girls Write Now helps to find their voice on the page or elsewhere, that's one more young writer who will have confidence in their own ability to learn and achieve and lead. It looks like ours will be a world in which we sorely need new leadership, and I'm so grateful to Girls Write Now for everything they're doing to empower it.

---

MADELINE McINTOSH is the CEO of Penguin Random House U.S. She has worked in publishing for almost three decades, and in that time has held positions in publishing, sales, operations, and audio, and was a pioneer in the early development of online sales and in the digital transition. McIntosh is a Girls Write Now honoree.

# Taking Root
## The Girls Write Now 2022 Anthology

# SANYA AFSAR

**GRADE:** Junior

**BORN:** Jeddah, Saudi Arabia

**LIVES:** Woodside, NY

### MENTEE'S ANECDOTE:

I was grinning from ear to ear during my first meeting with Thérèse. She has such a beautiful, bubbly personality, and I'm so grateful for having such an outstandingly supportive mentor to look up to. Every piece I've shared with her has been received with such praise and applause that I'm incredibly validated in my own talents as a writer, but she knows exactly how to give me the criticism I need to further grow in my skills. I've loved every minute of getting to know her, and I can't wait to continue the journey of our relationship.

---

# THÉRÈSE NELSON

**OCCUPATION:** Chef/Owner

**BORN:** Newark, NJ

**LIVES:** New York, NY

**PUBLICATIONS & RECOGNITIONS:** *The Washington Post, The New York Times, HuffPost, The Get 'Em Girls' Guide to the Power of Cuisine, The Get 'Em Girls' Guide to the Perfect Get-Together*

### MENTOR'S ANECDOTE:

Sanya has floored me since our first conversation. I was so inspired by how clear she was about using the Girls Write Now experience to prepare herself for the words and genres she's yet to write. Her work this year has been deeply rooted in self-discovery. The beautiful stories she's produced have been profoundly vulnerable yet infinitely hopeful. Her work is personal but always in service of the reader and the affirmation they might need, which is the highest aspiration for a writer. It's been an honor to watch her plant the seeds of what I'm sure will be a transformational career.

# all at once

## SANYA AFSAR

*a poem of aching candor narrating the varied, implicit forms of heartbreak*

Sitting in my designated seat
on the floor of my candlelit bathroom
I think about the tragedies of heartbreak

i do not mean the romantic date nights
turned sour breakups
the young puppy love couples
growing up and apart

i don't mean the drunken infidelities
turned shouting competitions
jealousy and duplicity
attracting the end of a long-term relationship

heartbreak is the feeling of isolation
amongst a group of close friends
the continuous fake laughter
i fail to recognize my voice in

or the feeling of disgust
when finding a photo of myself

that i didn't manipulate
to make everything look exactly proportional

it's the feeling of dread
when a teacher hands back a paper
upside down and folded in half
their look of fake encouragement
piercing into my bones

and the feeling of shame
when i watch my grades
turn from blue to green to yellow
the borderline goods
mocking me
and spitting in my face

heartbreak is feeling the drop in my chest
when her tone changes
and her discourse dies down
and the door slams on her way out

it's the feeling of light
at the end of a tunnel
combined with the refusal to nudge
from the glue of the darkness
right at the start

and the feeling of despondency
every weekend and weeknight
for lack of diversion by school
and lack of distraction by noise

heartbreak is when you seek comfort
in all the wrong places

and when you force yourself
to get out of bed every day
for something as desolate
as needing to hide away
in something as meaningless
as numbers on a paper

it's when you look in the mirror
and fail to connect with the person staring back at you
judgment radiating off her body and soul
repulsion sinking deep into your mind and being

it's when your blankets and pillows
are your safest dwellings
your only friends
and your only home

heartbreak is too much
and not enough
it is an understatement
and an exaggeration
all at once

# HAZEL AGICHA

**GRADE:** Sophomore

**LIVES:** Massapequa Park, NY

**BORN:** New Delhi, India

### MENTEE'S ANECDOTE:

My mentor and I are similar people in many senses. We share a love for Angelina Jolie, typewriters, and Marvel. We have a mutual strong dislike too: shoveling snow. They are one of the most supportive people in my life and help me learn how to use my writing as a tool, not an obligation (plus they are funny, which is a bonus).

---

# NIKKI PALUMBO

**OCCUPATION:** Writer and Comedian

**BORN:** Union, NJ

**LIVES:** Brooklyn, NY

**PUBLICATIONS & RECOGNITIONS:** *The New Yorker* Daily Shouts, *Reductress*

### MENTOR'S ANECDOTE:

Hazel is both a perfect mirror of my former self (spooky) and also has the self-reflection of my current self (spookier). Working with someone with such self-possession and awareness is like being in a fun house where sometimes Hazel looks a lot more like the mentor than I do. She's not afraid to ask big questions and actually seems to prefer writing her way toward exploration and curiosity instead of conclusion. What a gift.

# Light-bulb

## HAZEL AGICHA

*Note: Even if you're like me and prefer to read the ending first, surprise!! There's no ending and you'll still be as curious as you were when you started.*

When we hear the phrase "There is light at the end of the tunnel," it brings us relief and hope that maybe if we keep pushing through the hardship and adversity we'll find relief on the other side. We hope that if we work hard enough, grit our teeth, bear everything life throws at us, one day, a door to a magical world will open to reward us for our tenacity. It would be a world where we will never have to feel even one ounce of strain, it will taste exactly like eating that one dish that brings you back, it will feel precisely like touching your dreams and sleeping on a cloud for the rest of your life. But when I hear the phrase, the magical world doesn't exist because I don't think about the light, I think about the tunnel.

I remember when I had a project for my seventh-grade social studies class. It was within my capabilities, but I left it to the last minute (predictable, duh, I was thirteen). I remember working on it until one a.m. and then brewing a pot of coffee, not for me, but for the project. I dipped papers in coffee, stepped on them, and burnt them to match the theme (World War II). I don't remember the final result (except for the fact it was coffee-dipped) or the grade, I just remember making it. For me, it was more about the journey than the destination. I mean, I did care about finishing it, but when I think about it the journey is all I remember.

Personally, it's just the journey that matters, because it's the journey that gets me through, it's the journey that develops me as a character. It's the journey I use to brag. It's the journey that is more exciting to share because I can edit it to highlight my best parts, features, moments (without seeming like a total narcissist). It's the journey that's the story. It's the journey that you get excited to tell children. It's the journey that is used on dates to impress someone else. Joey from *Friends* didn't get girls without his famous fake stories. "Yeah, I hitchhiked to Mexico and had to pee in a bottle because I couldn't find a bathroom" sounds way better than "I went to Mexico," and frankly, it's a way better way to keep the conversation going.

There is *light* at the end of the tunnel . . .

But what about the *tunnel*? The struggle is what I look back on. You don't magically wake up and know that you have reached the end of your tunnel (unless you just graduated from something, but even then, that ending is just the beginning of a new tunnel). And when do I truly know that I know enough? How does one just leave their tunnel and reach the light? What happens when one is in their light? What if there is light in the tunnel but we all just see the brightness outside and overlook the light we have inside?

You can see who I am today, but if you knew how I started my journey, my today makes a lot more sense. It's just like villains in movies. In the end, you see how they grew up to become what they were shown and suddenly it all falls into place. "Oh, no wonder he turned out that way!" Your journey isn't always just positive or negative, you can't sort them into bad or good like you're sorting M&M's. You have to look deep and find the result. That is why in therapy you always start by looking at your past and work from there, because your past makes your present, and your present makes your future.

Do I know what the end result is? No. Who does? I mean, your best friend Sarah from sixth grade may have helped you realize that you trust people too easily and she probably won't be a part of your light—or even seventh grade. I mean, everyone has their own journey and I am an important part of theirs (hopefully), as they are to mine. I don't know if they'll be featured in the end result, but whether you want it or not, they're a part of your journey. Even the stranger that asked you for directions is a part of your journey, albeit a negligible one (whereas you're a more important part of theirs because you literally gave them directions).

The light and the tunnel are complex subjects, with many questions and little to no answers. Sometimes it's better to focus on the light to drive you to finish your "tunnel." But just maybe, have you ever thought about where you are in the tunnel? How fast would you have to sprint to leave the tunnel? Why aren't you looking to see what's in your tunnel? You're probably looking to see the answers to all the questions I proposed in this piece. Yet, you won't find them, because just like me, this piece hasn't reached the end of its tunnel.

# EMMANUELLA AGYEMANG

**GRADE:** Senior

**BORN:** Bronx, NY

**LIVES:** Bronx, NY

### MENTEE'S ANECDOTE:

Grace is the best mentor a mentee could ask for. Her name, Grace, is one of the greatest reflections of her character. She often tells me that she is still going to be there even when I go off to college (we are for life!). I appreciate her because if there is one person that is going to keep it real, it will be her. She may not know it, but I love bragging about her because she is a true inspiration not only to me, but to other women, both old and young.

---

# GRACE ANEIZA ALI

**OCCUPATION:** Curator and Professor

**BORN:** Georgetown, Guyana

**LIVES:** Tallahassee, FL

### MENTOR'S ANECDOTE:

After three beautiful years working with Emmanuella, our writing process is more and more of a collaboration and partnership between two people who absolutely revel in shaping language. We bounce ideas off each other, we laugh at each other and with each other over many of those ideas, and, most important, we elevate each other's writing. We can't wait to get to the editing process, where we chisel and chisel away at the words on the page. And in that process, Emmanuella always reminds me of the joy in the writing process.

# The First Naturalista

## EMMANUELLA AGYEMANG

*This piece was born from a Girls Write Now personal statement
workshop. In this piece, I stumble across the wonders of natural hair
and, after, try to convince my mother to let me go natural.*

### Age 5: "Mommy, this stuff burns."

The chemical relaxer smelled like a combination of Nair, bleach, and rotten eggs, aggravating my tiny nose. I sat on the floor as my mother applied the cream to my roots for the first time. After combing it through with a hair-snapping red wide-tooth comb, she washed it out, and I was left with strands that resembled hairs on a wet rat. For the next ten years, this was a common scene: the never-ending cycle of stinging chemicals met with the constant "Mommy, this stuff burns" complaints from me. My mother adopted the idea of beautiful hair from her family. This made her see straight hair as feminine, ideal, and classy. And natural hair was ugly and time-consuming.

Relaxers were inescapable for the women in my family. My aunts, cousins, and grandmothers were all under the unbreakable spell of what we called the "creamy crack." They were addicted to the substance that gave them their prized straight hair. I think of my seventy-year-old grandmother, who still applies relaxers to hair that is balding and thin, and I ask myself: What hold do relaxers have on Black women to make us use such chemicals even into our old age?

### Age 11: "Mom, can I go natural?"

I encountered a YouTube video about the makeup of natural hair. I stopped scrolling and looked at the video with a raised eyebrow. *What is natural hair?* I asked myself. I clicked on the video and a Black woman with an afro appeared. As she spoke, I began to learn terms like *hair type* and *shrinkage*. I saw images of natural hair that ranged from loose curls to coils. I saw its strands come together to resemble that of a weeping willow tree. After the video, I could not believe that I had been living the straight-hair life for so long. Unlike my chemically straightened hair, natural hair had a unique personality. That same night I asked my mother if I could go natural. With a blank expression, she responded, "No, it's not a good look on you." I frowned and replied, "Okay." I walked back into my room with shoulders slumped and realized this journey to natural hair would be filled with kinks. Despite my disappointment, I wanted to correct the misconception of beauty in my mother's eyes. For the next few years, I found myself pleading with my mother to stop using that god-awful chemical on my hair. I could feel her annoyance and impatience each time she responded with "No!"

### Age 15: "I don't want a relaxer anymore."

After ten years, I had enough. On December 2, 2019, my mother came to my room to remind me it was time for a retouch. Terrified, I took a deep breath and said to my mother, "I don't want a relaxer anymore." I saw my mother's dark brown eyes switch to fiery red. She realized I had come to a point where I wanted to be my most authentic self. Surprisingly, she backed off and instead ranted about my hair-making decision to my father for the next hour.

### Age 17: "Wash-n-go's, twist-outs, and braid-outs!"

I cut off all of my relaxed ends after transitioning my hair to natural for two years. During this time, my hair and combs competed in a boxing match every washday. Now that I have been fully natural for some time, I have been reminding myself to enjoy the process. Sometimes my hair stays in a puff for so long that it gets in a tangled mess. Other times, I can't pass a comb through it. But on my fabulous hair days, I see my wash-n-go's, twist-outs, and braid-outs and remember why I started this journey and how long it took me to get to this place. And I fall in love with my hair all over again. I finally broke the deep-rooted cycle of relaxers within the women in my family. Now I wear the crown as our first naturalista.

# ASMA AL-MASYABI

**GRADE:** Senior

**BORN:** Denver, CO

**LIVES:** Aurora, CO

**PUBLICATIONS & RECOGNITIONS:** *The Ilanot Review, Up North Lit, Navigating the Maze*

### MENTEE'S ANECDOTE:

Meeting Kaci has often felt like winning the lottery. I consider myself lucky to know such a considerate, organized (despite her protests otherwise), and kind person and, what's more, an incredible poet and writer. Her passion for language has helped me expand my own appreciation and abilities, far past what I've thought possible. Our pair sessions are the highlight of my week, a time to swap our favorite poems and stories, share writing prompts, and chat about what's going on in our lives. Learning with Kaci has allowed me to grow beyond my imagination. Moreover, she's simply an awesome friend.

---

# KACI X. TAVARES

**OCCUPATION:** Receptionist

**BORN:** Fuzhou, China

**LIVES:** Shelton, WA

**PUBLICATIONS & RECOGNITIONS:** *University of East Anglia MA Poetry Anthology 2020*

### MENTOR'S ANECDOTE:

Thanks to Asma, Thursday has become my favorite weekday. In each pair session, where we craft 100-word stories, bake chocolate-chip cookies, and share the occasional pet cameo, I get to reunite with and learn from a kind, positive, and bright young woman who is both artist and poet. Asma finds natural musicality and beauty in everything she writes, and her poem "Have You Seen This Word?" is no exception. Each word was considered, every line break questioned. It is a testament to her bilingual experimentation and growth as a writer, both of which I am privileged to witness.

# Have You Seen This Word?

## ASMA AL-MASYABI

*This poem explores the mystery of lost words and where one must go to find them.*

**i.**

I have lost
[ ]
on many occasions. Sunny days
when nothing seems amiss,
and I am just a little hungry.
Or winter ones,
falling
    away
with hollowed longing.
I rarely misplace
رومان
ru'maan.
Sometimes one
helps find the other.
As if searching
for a missing person, I recite to my sister
its picture,
red-stained fingers reaching
for bitter tissue

our father's hands, rounded,
carved jewels between teeth.
I let the curve

ر

of ra linger between us.
*Pomegranate* Have you seen this word?    Sometimes
it is she who asks me. Sometimes
we must figure it out together.
We often lose things
easily retrievable.


**ii.**

Suddenly,
I remember
I have forgotten.
The edges are blurred and though
I feel its outline
on my tongue, I cannot taste it.
[     ]
Cutting cucumbers,
I slice them lengthwise,
once, twice, into wedges. I reach
for fragments—

ا عص

recall its sharp s sound, sa'd, the lengthy        yawn        of 'ayn and alif.
د
Dal resurfaces.
I play anagrams
with echoes of letters, stumble upon
        a name,    a bowl,
happiness. I pierce
the thin flesh of a tomato,
dice it into three,    then four,    then four,

then—
        My knife poses
above lettuce leaves. The blade
slips into green and I snag on
        صداع
        Su'daa—
headache.
I wonder
why words
escape, chew cucumbers
in silence.

# CHARLOTTE ADELE EDLUND ALMOND

**GRADE:** Sophomore

**BORN:** New York, NY

**LIVES:** New York, NY

### MENTEE'S ANECDOTE:

Throughout the writing process, my mentor has been thoroughly supportive. She gave me the tools to take my haphazard thoughts and form them into something that tells a story. And my mentor has not only shown me how to write; she also introduced me to egg curls and to her handsome cat, Stanley! She is the first person I have met who shares my love for *Mamma Mia!*

---

# AMY B. SCHER

**OCCUPATION:** Author

**BORN:** Ojai, CA

**LIVES:** New York, NY

**PUBLICATIONS & RECOGNITIONS:** *The Washington Post, Good Morning America*

### MENTOR'S ANECDOTE:

I love how my mentee and I have traded teaching each other. As she's learned about writing and editing, I've learned all about athletic lingo, bunnies, ABBA, and desserts I'd never heard of.

# Running Towards Self-Care

## CHARLOTTE ADELE EDLUND ALMOND

*This is what an injury taught me about self-care.*

In 2020, I started high school at a small public school in New York City. With dozens of other freshmen, I joined the cross-country running team, made up mostly of boys. I bonded with the few girls over being a minority on the team, and found lasting friendships. But as the trees lost their leaves, I lost them too. By early winter, all of my friends had quit and practices became more intense. I gave up on building relationships with my team-mates and pushed everything into my running. The team that used to be dozens of jogging freshmen became five or ten athletes exploring New York City's parks. As the training progressed, I ran faster and longer than ever before, then walked home and fell asleep a few feet inside the front door, the rough seagrass carpet transforming into a plush heaven. I accepted the exhaustion, assuming it was the natural cost of pushing myself.

While my male teammates discussed the importance of eating enough, they were not the same size or even sex as I was, so I didn't even consider that it would apply to me. A few months into the school year, I broke my toe. I was afraid to acknowledge my injury and appear weak, so I told no one and learned to favor my left leg. I thought I had a responsibility to prove that girls were just as committed and capable as the boys. I blamed myself for not having the willpower to overcome my pain and exhaustion, so I continued to spend two hours every afternoon warming up and running along the oblivious, sparkling Hudson.

After months of keeping up with (and occasionally surpassing) the boys, despite my worsening injury and constant fatigue, I always felt my coach's surprise when I did well. On a chilly winter day in Central Park, the team gathered for practice. The typically gray roads were a deep and reflective black topped with freshly melted snow. Three-foot-high white mounds bordered the roads, indented with the small footprints of children and squashed under the weight of hurried adults. I stepped onto the road with the rest of the freshmen, only to be held back by my coach, because if I slowed the boys down I would ruin the drill. Even though I started thirty seconds after them, I saw them turn a corner just a minute later. I followed them out of sight for a mile, afraid of slowing them down, but eventually I gained confidence and caught up to them. Soon after, I sped ahead and ended the workout sprinting alongside my fastest teammate. A month later, when I was playing Frisbee with twenty boys at the track, my coach commented that I "played well with the boys." I took his compliment as something negative. No matter how well I performed, I was worried my coach saw me as the team's weak link and that his comment showed he didn't think of me as an equal to the boys.

When my coach named me Rookie of the Year during the team's spring end-of-season picnic, I realized that he noticed how hard I worked. To my surprise, my drive and accomplishments were also recognized by my teammates, with my role model telling me that I was "awe-inspiring" and "incredible" at everything I tried. Their support gave me the confidence to connect with my teammates. I started making a conscious effort to eat more, and felt my constant lethargy flicker away. Soon after, during my sophomore year, a dozen more girls joined the team, and I finally felt like a part of it.

A few months into the new season, I was getting injured more than my friends were. During one of my coach's lessons, he mentioned how small imbalances and asymmetries in running form often led to running injuries. I realized that my constant injuries were not random, but caused by a serious running imbalance. I was forced to stop pushing myself during practice and races. I was upset that I couldn't continue running, but I finally gave myself permission to take a break. While my teammates trained for races, I hesitantly switched to yoga with my injured teammates and watched the bags. Instead of running through the beautiful parks of the city, I dutifully pulled out lilac yoga mats from the tightly stuffed classroom shelf, laying them down in a small grassy area nearby. When my teammates and I ran together, we were too out of breath to speak, able to sneak in conversations only when we rested. But the injured group was completely different because there was nothing to do but talk. I wanted to prevent the freshmen from making my same mistakes, so I talked to them about the importance of giving themselves time to heal instead of hoping their issues would disappear.

A month later, I was finally able to compete without injuring myself. I learned that taking time off didn't mean that I was weak, but that I had the maturity and self-respect to realize when I needed to slow down. And the wealth of knowledge my peers held taught me to respect my classmates and teammates. Being on the team gave me more than an extracurricular for applications or physical fitness. It gave me the opportunity to grow in ways I didn't even know I needed to.

# JAMILAH ARAF

**GRADE:** Freshman

**BORN:** Queens, NY

**LIVES:** East Elmhurst, NY

**PUBLICATIONS & RECOGNITIONS:**
*The BaccRag* Newspaper Club

### MENTEE'S ANECDOTE:

Kate has become one of the few people I can truly connect to over writing, as I can talk to her about the highs and lows of writing a piece. Although I have not met her in person, we have connected greatly over our weekly sessions. An hour feels like seconds as we discuss writing, life, and our fandoms. Kate is a bubbly person who always lightens the mood, making weekly meetings one of the best parts of my week. I can't wait to meet her in person so our mentor/mentee relationship can continue to grow.

---

# KATE RILEY

**OCCUPATION:** Manager of
Institutional Giving

**BORN:** Hartford, CT

**LIVES:** Huntington, NY

### MENTOR'S ANECDOTE:

Jamilah may be a mentee, but she is the real writing teacher here. From the jump, we bonded over our *Hamilton* fandom, and she schools me on the Marvel Cinematic Universe. It must be where she picked up her superpower, vanquishing her inner critic. Jamilah is fearless in the face of writing prompts: creating richly developed worlds, characters, and turns of phrase. She is a tenacious, self-possessed, and joyful young woman who inspires me to be playful when I write. I cherish our weekly sessions, and am excited to see her grow as an artist with Girls Write Now and beyond.

# Animal

## JAMILAH ARAF

**Content Warning:** descriptions of wounds/death

*When Evanna finds herself in a snowy forest pursued by a menacing figure with no memory of how she got there, she knows to do only one thing: run.*

I moved as fast as my feet could take me into the woods. I was blindly putting one foot in front of the other, when I brought myself to a sudden stop.

*Why am I running? And when did I start?*

I felt like a windup robot. Someone had twisted my crank and let me roam. I looked at my surroundings. The tall trees reached the clouds and were covered in snow, blocking the moon's light.

It was very quiet. Something was wrong.

I had no clue where I was or where I could go. My gut told me there was danger, so I kept looking. I turned around to find a small cottage. The lights were out. A figure could still be seen lurking, even in the night.

Someone was coming.

I ran, and it wasn't long before I felt the sharp pain of needles in my foot. I kept a steady, relentless pace, looking back once or twice. He was always there, standing a few feet behind me. He never looked tired, as if he had teleported to catch up with me. He had the eyes of a shark, ready for the kill. His wolf always looked the same.

My shoes were coming apart and the snow was now sprinkled with red. I had cramps everywhere, but the fear of this man and his wolf pushed me. I did not realize I had been in a full sprint for hours, with no rest, water, or food. I felt like I had all the energy I needed. And then, I crashed.

I woke up. The snow around my feet was bright red. Facedown, I tried to get up, but I wasn't sure how. I put my hands on the snow, and pushed up. But my hands weren't listening, and pain shot up my right arm. I crashed back down. This time, I tried with my elbows. I put them under my body and pushed up. *I'm doing it!* I was a few inches off the ground when I was immediately pushed down. I heard growling above me. Fear shocked my system like caffeine. The sun was up. My hands were cold. One arm felt broken. And I couldn't feel my feet.

I turned my head quickly to look at my feet, but instead saw the man. In a matter of seconds, I saw he was resting on a tree, his arms loosely by his sides. His eyes were open, looking straight ahead. His face had no expression. His legs were frozen together, he was covered in wounds and blood, and he was dead.

*Oh no oh no oh no.* The murderer was on my back. My first instinct was to roll, slamming the wolf against the snow. It was when I tried to get up that I noticed my feet. They weren't there. I screamed. *My feet are . . . gone. Oh my god that's so disgusting!* At that moment, I should have been focused on the wolf, but I couldn't. The wolf, the woods, the dead man had all faded into the background as I stared at the two stumps that were my feet. Flesh and bone were all that was left. I threw up in my mouth and quickly swallowed it. As it all came back into focus, I became light-headed. I couldn't tell if it was from the loss of blood or the newfound realization that I could not escape. That this wolf would be my end. He was now facing me, only mere inches from my face, revealing his teeth, sharp and red, matching his claws.

I was in pain, and even though I couldn't fight, I still tried. My shaky hands had grabbed his snout, mimicking a gutsy move from a movie I had remembered seeing on my thirteenth birthday.

The wolf was stronger. It escaped my grasp and dragged its claws through my eye socket. I let go to cover my gushing eye. Although pain had clouded my vision, I could see a blurry figure leaping toward the wolf.

A fox, a snowy one, had attacked him, and was winning the fight.

As the world began to come into focus, the fox approached.

"We need to get you home."

The word *home* shocked me more than the talking animal. I couldn't remember a home. I couldn't remember anything but that stupid movie I saw on my thirteenth birthday, and running.

"Home?" I said, on the verge of tears.

The fox stared at me, as if tolerating my confusion. He looked back to the cabin, which was now a dot in the distance, and turned to me. "The cabin will do," he said.

Pain seared through my head as I made the small gesture of looking down. *How am I supposed to get to the cabin in such a weak condition?* The fox grabbed me by the hood and dragged me to the cabin.

Something about this fox felt familiar. I tried searching my brain for memories, but all that came up was the movie. There was no fox in it.

# SHAYLA ASTUDILLO

**GRADE:** Senior

**BORN:** Queens, NY

**LIVES:** Ozone Park, NY

### MENTEE'S ANECDOTE:

Working with Danielle for the past two years has been incredible. Writing is something we both care about deeply. And so, to be able to speak to someone on such a rich level about writing is something that pushes my writing to be more freeing. She has pushed my writing to be much more than honesty, perspectives, or carefulness. It's about writing just so that I can write. Not writing for others or what they need. But writing for myself. And she has taught me that in depth for the past two years, which I am immensely grateful for.

---

# DANIELLE MAZZEO

**OCCUPATION:** Associate Director, Government Relations

**BORN:** Staten Island, NY

**LIVES:** Brooklyn, NY

### MENTOR'S ANECDOTE:

Shayla says what they mean. They write truthfully and bravely and with so much compassion. They write amazing titles. Shayla empathizes, makes art, and speaks up when something isn't fair. They know how to ask questions. They know when passive voice is preferred. Shayla has accomplished so much over the last two years, and I'm so proud of them! Now in the second half of their senior year, I can't wait to see what Shayla does next.

# Stupidly Optimistic.

## SHAYLA ASTUDILLO

*Mental health is often overlooked in society. This poem dives into the mind of a teenager who finally has had enough.*

I think we've forgotten what good mental health looks like as a society.

It's accumulated from various sources.
The panic attacks from homework, the fear of hearing a bang in
the hallway, the homeless people far too cold, and the fear of
getting sick.

I remember watching *Grey's Anatomy* one day, and the main character,
Meredith, stated the following, "You don't know this yet . . . but
life's not supposed to be this hard."
I've never agreed more.
I think
as
a society our mental health has hit a low.
And, especially for teens and kids.
Yet lately, I've noticed teachers, too, and even parents, friends, and
everyone. Just everyone that I could pluck out like a flower that's going
through way too much right now.
It's not supposed to be this hard.
It's just not.
Yet it's become such a norm that some things seem more important
than our mental health.

It's not okay.

I hope we all find some peace.

It may not be today, tomorrow, or a few years from now, but
at some point
we will hear the birds sing in the morning, the sun won't feel too strong,
and we will find some peace.

Maybe that's too optimistic, but it's better than being bitter, I think.

# CLIO BARRETT

**GRADE:** Junior        **LIVES:** Brooklyn, NY

**BORN:** Brooklyn, NY

### MENTEE'S ANECDOTE:

Although my mentor and I have been remote throughout this entire process, I have still been able to connect with them in ways I did not expect possible. I have grown to appreciate their work so much, admiring not only their talent and written words, but the conversations we have. Each meeting is like a life update and a fun workshop of our latest pieces!

---

# NADIA BOVY

**OCCUPATION:** Senior Strategist        **LIVES:** Brooklyn, NY

**BORN:** Marlow, England

### MENTOR'S ANECDOTE:

It's been really wonderful to discover that writing with Clio helps me to let go of my inhibition. Her candor, free-flowing style, and often playful quirks of language and imagery help me let go of pretensions and write from instinct and imagination. I'm so grateful for her beautiful light and energy. She inspires me to show up with energy and curiosity, and recommit to my own work as a writer.

# Snapchat Eulogy

## CLIO BARRETT

**Content Warning:** description of injury and death

*I was scrolling on social media and my eye caught a rather shocking headline. This poem is about the article I read and how very serious news is made palatable.*

Snapchat news titled the story "Man Dies For $2.75" because he broke his neck after propelling himself over the turnstiles of the New York 71st Street station, and because Snapchat is cooler than the snap of someone's vertebrae, even the sudden cutting of one's nervous system needs a catchy headline. The video footage shows him gathering up his momentum before bolstering his legs over the three metal arms and taking a few steps peeled away from gravity, spinning over himself like ragdoll timber. His feet hesitate in midair as if he is trying to walk on water, or else the sewage of the MTA, and dash right up to heaven. His body, folded neatly, was then (and only then) covered in static and content warnings, fuzzy and blurred so as to not give it all away to the readers. I slide my finger up to watch the video in its entirety, but it pauses just as the man tumbles, freezing for a few seconds before the screen goes black. I think about all the dollars and quarters I have not had to pay. How many chances to fold up, shatter like a sheet of porcelain, a paused, omitted neck, a censored hop. I keep scrolling.

# YACINE BARRY

**GRADE:** Senior

**BORN:** Conakry, Guinea

**LIVES:** New York, NY

**PUBLICATIONS & RECOGNITIONS:** Freedom and Citizenship Program, Columbia University; Stand Up Girls; NYPD Explorer

### MENTEE'S ANECDOTE:

My mentor and I meet every Thursday. Usually, we go over any piece of writing that I am working on. Our first meeting was amazing. We got to laugh and share our stories in which we found our mutual appreciation for journalism. I like journaling and so does she. We get along well—I am lucky to have her as my mentor!

---

# KELLY MOFFITT

**OCCUPATION:** Engagement Editor

**BORN:** St. Louis, MO

**LIVES:** Brooklyn, NY

### MENTOR'S ANECDOTE:

Yacine always makes me laugh, which makes sense, because she is a stand-up comic in addition to a poet and budding journalist. I love learning about where Yacine is from. She has made me appreciate so much the special form of writing and communication that flows from a background in several different languages. Great things are coming from this young writer!

# The Birth of the Rose Flower

## YACINE BARRY

*This is a poem about two people who are separated due to circum-stances that are beyond their control. Do you think they will end up together?*

Hello, Fifth of January!
Happy birthday to my Rose flower,
my fragile and gentle Rose,
blooming from a deep stone of coldness,
my heart,
into this warm universe
I have never felt this happy

January Fifth gave birth to a Rose flower
Do you remember what Day it is today?

*Our text messages change*
*From the formal* vous *to the informal* tu
*A bad decision, a good memory*

*Your omg emoji makes me worried*
*Your love emoji makes me smile*
*Your like emoji makes me want to send more*
*When I text you, my heart yearns for your reply,*
*pauses in anticipation,*
*I can't wait for notifications*

*So*
*I chose to stare at your ". . ." looking for an answer.*
*My eyes go dry cuz I can't close them*

Where is your youthful voice now?

Our memory will never fade
If it happens,
I am willing to swim the Atlantic Ocean
to stop it from drowning

The Rose in my heart wanders in a hypnotic dream,
I can't really face my feelings
I can't even see your face
I can't help missing the past
I can't wake up
Because our future only exists in my dream.

Was it love?
Or
might it be anti-loneliness?
Is our friendship pure or artificial?
Is my Rose red? A rosebud? Or a thornless red rose?
Do you think it was the Yellow rose?
How do you identify it?
Cuz, to me, it is and always will be a Red rose.
Why this end?
Can I blame fate?
Am I the only one wandering in old dreams?
Where can I find you?
I have spent months waiting.

What's in my heart is what I can't get over.
For a single glance at a message from you

I wouldn't regret nurturing my Rose alone
Even if you aren't included
The fact The Rose exists is most important

How lucky am I to have you in my life history?

Happy birthday to our Rose Flower
and
Happy birthday to you as well.

# TILDA BARTLETT

**GRADE:** Freshman

**BORN:** New York, NY

**LIVES:** New York, NY

### MENTEE'S ANECDOTE:

I love working with Brandi. She helps me create the best version of my work and pushes me to try new ideas and techniques. While I've been at Girls Write Now only since December, I've already done so much more than I thought I could, thanks to Brandi. I think this submission really demonstrates the value of our work together. My story would not be where it is if she hadn't been there to guide me along the way.

# BRANDI BROXSON

**OCCUPATION:** Features Editor

**BORN:** Brooklyn, NY

**LIVES:** Brooklyn, NY

**PUBLICATIONS & RECOGNITIONS:** *Real Simple*; Meme Queen award, Florida Press Club Travel and Environmental Writing Awards

### MENTOR'S ANECDOTE:

What started as a small idea that Tilda had for this piece expanded into a rich story. Tilda's creativity is apparent in her visual and impactful descriptions. There were many times while reading her draft that I felt like I was sitting in the dark and mysterious Emrys castle. What I most enjoyed about working on this piece with Tilda was how good she was at staying true to her characters. It was a treat to see how this story about family, power, and the pulling of strings came to fruition.

# Puppet Master

## TILDA BARTLETT

**Content Warning:** description of assault

*Estelle had a habit of walking around the castle at night. What she didn't know is that her little habit would change her life forever.*

Estelle Adrienne grew up in a dark room with vast windows overlooking the kingdom of Emrys. If one were to look inside her room they would likely find her surrounded by a pile of books or mixing different vials of various concoctions. Sure, she was a little strange, but she was as normal as she could be for a princess.

The candle painted a haze of yellow light against the dark walls as the floorboards creaked under Estelle's footsteps. The moonlight shone through the slanted windows lining the hall. Whenever Estelle was unable to fall asleep she wandered around the castle in search of secrets that hadn't yet revealed themselves.

Estelle gravitated toward her father's office and heard sharp breaths and whispered shouts. Estelle nudged the door open just a crack. What she saw would stay with her forever. She ran away holding in a stream of her dinner as her father raised a bloodied knife above his head. Its destination: her mother's chest. She had an inkling that her mother was going to be killed by her father, but this was the first time Estelle had seen anything like this.

Months passed and all Estelle could think about was the crimson dagger that held her mother's life. She locked herself in her room and thought about how she could fix her swimming pool of thoughts. It had been days of Estelle doing nothing but pondering solutions to the problem. If we're being honest, Estelle knew what to do the whole time, but it was solidified only as she uttered the words: "I need to kill my father."

Estelle knocked three times on the grand door that held all of the kingdom's secrets behind it.

"Come in," the deep voice of her father answered.

Estelle pushed the door open to reveal the office, clad with dark paneling and three tall windows overlooking the kingdom she so badly wanted to be hers. The walls were lined with leather-bound novels and all sorts of odd trinkets. It was perfect for a monarch.

"You know, I always thought this office would suit me more," Estelle said to her father. She had always imagined herself as queen of Emrys. With her parents in charge she had nothing, no freedom. Her every move was dictated by their needs and "what was good for Emrys." Her parents didn't know what was good for Emrys, not like she did, at least. Estelle needed to be queen.

Her father heaved a great sigh before saying: "Estelle, I am a very busy man, I don't have time for all your little mind games."

Estelle laughed. "What mind games do you mean? The only mind game I play is the game of knowledge."

Her father pushed himself out of the chair behind his desk and walked over to a bookshelf, staring lazily at the tomes. Estelle took this as an opportunity to take his place behind the desk. She swung her feet up and rested them on top of very important-looking documents.

"Estelle, when you were a young girl your mother and I knew you were special. Then one day your nanny approached your mother and I. *'Pardon me, but could I trouble you for a moment of your time? I know you both are very busy but this is very important,'* she said.

"She walked us to your bedroom, where you were playing with a few of your friends. It was strange. You were holding dolls in your hands and the actions of your friends were mirroring the dolls' actions. It was like you were controlling those poor boys and girls.

"That night your mother and I knew what had happened. You see, when you were learning how to walk you fell, knocked your head, and lost consciousness. We thought you had died. But you lived and something deep within shifted that day. Peculiar things started to happen, moments where your mother and I's minds would go blank. It was like we weren't in control."

"You think I don't know this, Father?" Estelle droned. "I remember it all, and trust me, I figured it out long before you two imbeciles did. I knew one day it would come in handy." The king never saw the knife behind Estelle's back.

The king took slow, sharp breaths. "The day your mother died I woke from a trance with a bloody dagger lying in my palms. I didn't know what happened, all I knew was that I killed her. I was scared, Estelle, I had killed the love of my life and I didn't remember it.

"What happened to you?" The king breathed wearily. "I don't know who you are anymore, Estelle." His eyes went blank and his humanity slowly faded until he was just another soul lost to the universe. Another victim to Estelle's thirst for power.

From that day on Estelle sat in that chair, overlooking the kingdom that was now hers. Until she fell and hit her head . . . just like she did all those years ago.

# SHADIYA BECKETT

**GRADE:** Sophomore

**BORN:** Kingston, Jamaica

**LIVES:** Brooklyn, NY

### MENTEE'S ANECDOTE:

I have never met another person that I relate to more than my mentor, Maygen. We have endless conversations about any topic that comes up during our meetings. Throughout the course of this program, she has truly boosted my confidence by always complimenting my writing, while giving me tips to make my work better. With our writing activities, she has helped to expand my imagination and find new ways to reduce writer's block. It has been a great experience getting to know her, and connecting with her in ways that I don't normally connect with many people.

---

# MAYGEN S. TAVARES

**OCCUPATION:** Youth Engagement Counselor

**BORN:** Livingston, NJ

**LIVES:** New York, NY

**PUBLICATIONS & RECOGNITIONS:** "She Was My Mommy Too," *Pride*

### MENTOR'S ANECDOTE:

Shadiya is a breath of fresh air. As a first-time mentor, I wasn't sure what to expect. Since our first meeting every interaction and conversation with Shadiya has been memorable. They have taught me through their words and actions what resilience, creativity, and dedication to hard work look like. They are more mature than I remember being at their age. As a sophomore in high school, Shadiya excels both academically and socially. They are always participating in various extracurriculars and exploring their interests. Mentoring Shadiya has felt more like gaining a friend who is kind, funny, and incredibly brave. They push themselves to continuously try new things, learn a new instrument, and apply for different types of academic programs. Shadiya is the type of person others gravitate toward. A born leader, there is no glass ceiling they will not break. Through adversity and triumphs, their willingness to be vulnerable is one of the qualities I admire most and is a strength many seek to obtain.

# French Messenger

## SHADIYA BECKETT AND
## MAYGEN S. TAVARES

*A sitcom about the McKnight family, who move from Texas to France after Mom is relocated for work with the U.S. military. A heartfelt and witty show where family dynamics and culture clash.*

## CAST

**Alicia McKnight**—Mother, 39; works for the U.S. Military Armory; her job is the reason the McKnights relocate to Gordes, France

**King McKnight**—Father, 38; freelance interior designer

**Richard McKnight**—Oldest son, 19; wants to become a break-dancer; charming; extrovert

**Monét McKnight**—Middle child, only daughter, 16; diva; doesn't have many friends; volleyball player

**Malachi McKnight**—Youngest son, 14; family genius; funny; introvert

**Aunt Gwendolyn**—Alicia's only aunt, 68; witty; doesn't like pets; doesn't take no for an answer; sassy

# PILOT—"SOUTHERN HOSPITALITY"

## SCENE ONE

SET IN ROLLINGWOOD, TEXAS, IN NOVEMBER 2018. ALICIA, KING, MALACHI, MONÉT, AND RICHARD ARE IN A 1990 OLDSMOBILE ON THEIR WAY TO THE AIRPORT. THEIR LUGGAGE IS STRAPPED ON TOP WITH BUNGEE CORDS.

"SWEET CAROLINE" BY NEIL DIAMOND IS PLAYING ON THE RADIO. EVERYONE SINGS ALONG EXCEPT FOR MALACHI, WHO IS ON HIS IPAD AND ROLLING HIS EYES.

"Good times never seemed so good . . ."

> PULL UP TO THE AIRPORT. ALICIA BEGINS UNLOADING SUITCASES AND REALIZES OTIS IS MISSING.

#### ALICIA

Malachi! Where is Otis?!

#### MONÉT

Really, Mama? That's what you worried 'bout?! How 'bout my midlife crisis? I ain't neva gon' see my friends again!

#### KING

*(Gets out of the car and joins Alicia at trunk)*

What's all this commotion 'bout Otis and a midlife crisis?

#### MALACHI

*(Looks in the trunk)*

Oh, man! I forgot to put Otis in the car. I guess he gon' have to live in Texas without us.

ALICIA

Oh, hush, boi! Where's Richard?! Boi, getcha aunt
Gwendolyn on the phone!


**SCENE TWO**

FAMILY AT SECURITY CHECKPOINT PLACING LUGGAGE ON
CONVEYOR BELT. RICHARD ON SPEAKERPHONE WITH AUNT
GWENDOLYN.


AUNT GWENDOLYN

*(Turns key in door and walks into the McKnights'
kitchen, frustrated)*

Ion even like animals and y'all got me here lookin'
for some bunny! He betta hop his way to that airport
if he knows what's good fo' him. Where y'all leave
Otis at?


RICHARD

Ion know! Malachi said Otis was on the kitchen
counter.


AUNT GWENDOLYN

*(Spots Otis in his cage chewing on carrot)*

Ugh! There's that rodent! What'cha expect me to do?
Sell him back to PetSmart?! Ain't nobody gon' pay
for dis.


ALICIA

*(Grabs phone)*

What'chu mean, sell him to PetSmart? Could you
please bring my baby to the airport?

AUNT GWENDOLYN

Girl, you crazy? Alright, fine! But'chu know Social
Security don' pay me enough for gas money! You gon'
owe me big for dis one.

> FAMILY IS HOLDING UP THE LINE AND IS
> FORCED TO GO THROUGH SECURITY. RICHARD
> PUTS PHONE ON CONVEYOR BELT TO GO
> THROUGH METAL DETECTOR.

> AUNT GWENDOLYN HESITANTLY GRABS OTIS'S
> CAGE. DRIVES TO AIRPORT.

## SCENE THREE

AT AIRPORT.

AUNT GWENDOLYN

*(Arguing with security officers inside airport)*

But'chu don' understand! I gotta get this bunny to
my niece. I ain't fit to nor do I have the time or
patience to care for a bunny.

SECURITY OFFICER #1

Ma'am, do you have a flight ticket for dis bunny?

AUNT GWENDOLYN

Ticket?! He ain't holdin' no seat!

SECURITY OFFICER #2

He needs a ticket for public health purposes. I'm
sorry, but I can't let you or this bunny past this
checkpoint without a ticket.

AUNT GWENDOLYN

*(Calls Richard back on the phone and he picks up)*

I got two 10'9" security guards tellin' me I can't get past without a ticket. Looks like I'ma have me a feast of rabbit feet fo' supper tonight!

AIRPORT PA SYSTEM ANNOUNCEMENT

Last call for Flight 2481 to Gordes, France, boarding at Gate 5. Again, all passengers for Flight 2481 make your way to Gate 5 immediately.

MALACHI

(In French)

Allez dépêche-toi.

MONÉT

Boi! What are you even saying?

MALACHI

Get cultured. It means "Come on, hurry up."

> FAMILY GRABS CARRY-ON LUGGAGE, RUNS TO GATE 5, AND BOARDS PLANE.

> MONÉT STRUGGLES TO KEEP UP IN HER 5-INCH STILETTO HEELS.

MALACHI

Girl, ain't nobody tell you to wear twin towers on yo' feet. I hope you fall. Those heels ain't gettin' you no mo' French!

> MONÉT SCOFFS. THE McKNIGHTS BOARD THE PLANE JUST IN TIME.

**SCENE FOUR**

TWO DAYS LATER AT McKNIGHTS' NEW HOME IN GORDES, FRANCE. DOORBELL RINGS.

KING

Malachi! Come open dis door.

MALACHI

Why me?! Richard just standin' there needin' somethin' to do.

KING

(Yelling)

Boy-if-you-don't . . . Ain't nobody else here speak French! Ain't my fault you Einstein.

RICHARD

(Laughing at Malachi)

That's what you get fo' bein' the smart one.

DOORBELL RINGS AGAIN.

MALACHI

(Speaking French)

J'arrive!

(Opens door to Aunt Gwendolyn. She's with Otis's cage and four suitcases)

Auntie! What are you doin' here?! You miss me that much already??

AUNT GWENDOLYN

(Storms in, leaving all of her suitcases outside)

Boi, hush! Y'all know how long I been standin' out there in the cold?! Croissants slowin' you down already?

(Looks over at Richard)

Boi, go get my bags and bring them in here. Otis out there too. I'm movin' in. This is me collectin' my payment.

KING

(Shouting)

Alicia! Come here right now! We done gots ourself one hella surprise!

**END OF EPISODE ONE**

# ALEX BERMAN

**GRADE:** Junior

**BORN:** New York, NY

**LIVES:** New York, NY

### MENTEE'S ANECDOTE:

It's been so wonderful continuing to get to know Jennifer during our second year working together. Every day we build on the shared canon of stories that we love and that inspire our writing. I love hearing about Jennifer's real-life professional writing projects as we work to make my own as real-life professional as we can. It's great to have a mentor who is willing to indulge me as I swing from idea to idea, yet knows when to push me to complete a promising project. Here's to another year of a top-notch writing partnership!

---

# JENNIFER L. BROWN

**OCCUPATION:** Writer, Tutor, College Essay Coach

**BORN:** Suffern, NY

**LIVES:** New York, NY

### MENTOR'S ANECDOTE:

It has been a truly lovely experience working with Alex for a second year. Our shorthand is only getting faster and our exchange of ideas even richer. I love all the energy and creative curiosity Alex brings into our sessions, from sharing new finds (have you heard of this surrealist collagist?) to dissecting old favorites. I love that our vocabularies are expanding together, as Alex bravely explores new genres and forms. In art or writing, Alex continues to wow me. I am so excited to continue working together and see what new semesters may bring.

# It Ends with an Explosion (It Always Does)

## ALEX BERMAN

*Like most stories about friendship, this one involves whale bones.*

I must have loved Caroline once; I don't remember. All I have is her name needle-scratched into ivory, cutting a dark line through the white. She would press her index finger into my palm, and she was the moon, and I was a moon orbiting her moon, infinite recursions and refractions trying to light the India ink sky. She wanted the whole world filled with light, but we could never quite get the corners. Maybe she could have if I were not tracing circles around her like a sick puppy.

Creamer diffuses from a flash-bang into milky tendrils across my coffee. I search for her face in the ribbons during the fleeting moments before the color settles into brown. Caroline took her coffee black. I never had the fortitude to go without creamer, no matter how many times she told me what I was drinking was no longer coffee. I was always dimming things for her, diluting her great plans. She's gone, and my scrimshaw is all that I'm allowed to keep; her name etched into my eye sockets so it's all I see when I sleep.

Her name isn't the only one I've scratched into whalebone, but it's the only one I've carved more than once. I have a wall of Carolines in the shop's backroom. Caroline, scratched into the rib of a minke. Caroline, beached onto a sternum. Caroline, tracing a shoulder blade. C a r o l i n e, separated across phalanges.

If I could Frankenstein together an entire skeleton, she might come back. My coffee is warm but not sweet enough, and the shock of bitterness hitting my tongue feels like skin hitting frigid water the way I imagine whales feel rolling onto the beach.

My town is where whales come to die. They throw themselves onto the sand, and we can do nothing but watch. They are monumental. Too big for the beach. Caroline was always too big for this town. She never said it, but she disapproved of my livelihood, making kitschy whalebone souvenirs to sell to tourists by our grisly landmarks.

*Don't you want to* do *something?* she would say.

I thought I was doing something, but apparently not. She always had dreams of leaving, so I shouldn't have been surprised to wake one day to an empty coffeepot.

Sometimes I see her rowing back to me in a little dory. The boat is made of bones. She is cradled in a blue whale's rib cage. Whenever whales wash up on the beach, I find myself believing she'll be there when they cut them open, safe inside a gargantuan artery. She never is, so I take the bones back piece by piece, up the cobbled path and into the backroom, onto the pile of bones that are not my own.

When we were little, Caroline liked scavenging for bones with me after school. We would go everywhere together. *You two must know each other so well,* people would say. Like it was a good thing.

They never tell you how much it hurts to know someone so well that her hands are your hands. How in every ripple of her voice you sense dissatisfaction, how you will forever trace and retrace the raised bumps the pen made on the note she left, how the space between the letters scales exactly to the miles of ocean now between you.

*I had to leave. I know you understand.* She was always making presumptions about me, and the worst thing is that they were true.

*I couldn't stay any longer.* Caroline moved like her bones might at any moment jump out of her skin.

*I don't know if I'll see you again.* We both knew she wouldn't, but even Caroline wasn't cruel enough to say it outright. She tried to maintain some semblance of politeness, but pretending was hard for her. She's not human like the rest of us. She never once said "I'm sorry" to me, although she danced endlessly around the subject.

Love,

Caroline

The way she tossed love around made me dizzy. *Love you,* as she swept out the door each morning. *Love you,* when she ran across the beach. Always loving away from me. Every time she said it, my world flipped on its axis, but then she would laugh in that way and she was the moon and I was space junk struggling to orbit stupidly, smally around her. I said it back every time.

She's the place I was born, and I desperately want to swim back to her. But I can't. The last thing I want to do is gasp for air at her feet. Besides, I have the shop. My world is smaller than hers, but it's mine. I try to keep it. I drink my coffee with creamer. I hold my home close.

Red hits the window, blotting out the shore.

Did you know that beached whales sometimes explode?

They say it's because of gas buildup in the stomach

but I think

it's because their hearts are too big

to possibly stand it any longer.

# JACQUELINE BERNABE

**GRADE:** Senior

**BORN:** Bronx, NY

**LIVES:** Bronx, NY

### MENTEE'S ANECDOTE:

I remember my first meeting with Marci. It was through a Zoom call and I remember feeling anxious. But by the end of the session those nerves had disappeared and in return came comfort and ease. Every Monday at five p.m. I sit in my room and join the Zoom call, eager to talk and write with Marci. We always share a new piece of media that we like, and in the process have learned each other's favorite songs, articles, books, and shows. But we also learned how to envision our goals and continue growing in our writing journey.

---

# MARCI ALBOHER

**OCCUPATION:** Author and VP, Narrative Change, Encore.org

**BORN:** Brooklyn, NY

**LIVES:** New York, NY

**PUBLICATIONS & RECOGNITIONS:** *The New York Times, Penn Gazette, The Washington Post*

### MENTOR'S ANECDOTE:

After serving on the Girls Write Now board, I was excited to become a mentor. But when meetings went virtual, I feared that it would feel like yet another Zoom room. Scratch that. Jacqueline's intelligence, curiosity, passion, and commitment radiate through the screen. She always shows up on time, keeps track of all program requirements, and makes the most of our regular freewriting—toggling between college application essays and her muse. Her creative-meets-disciplined approach continually inspires me to push myself even when I'm feeling burned out. I'm hoping we'll close out the year with an in-real-life celebration of her graduation!

# Mis Dos Casitas

## JACQUELINE BERNABE

*"Mis Dos Casitas" is a piece that highlights the beauty of my two colorful homes.*

*Mis dos casitas.* My two little homes.

My two little homes, both stained with pink. In New York, it's in the bookbags, pens, pencils, and books I have lying around. All tired from days of constant writing and studying. In El Salvador, it's in the hibiscus drinks, desserts, candies sold in the vendor carts. All tired from days of constant ogling by the local kids.

My two little homes, both stained with green. In New York, it's in the MetroCards my friends and I use (and often lose) that take us to school, work, and movie theaters. The small card being witness to the laughter on the train and the anxiety that comes with getting home before curfew. In El Salvador, it's in the trees surrounding the exit of our only airport. The small airport being witness to cries of mothers seeing their kids off but also the cries of mothers seeing their kids come home.

My two little homes, both stained with orange. In New York, it's in the orange makeup bags my sisters and I share. These small bags cause many childish fights that turn into late-night bonding moments filled with jokes and love. In El Salvador, it's in the oranges and papayas grown and sold in markets. These small fruits turn into fresh drinks that cause dinners to extend longer, filled with joyous stories, folklore, and memories.

My two little homes, both stained with blue. In New York, it's in the Salvadoran flag my family owns—representing culture, determination, and joy. Shaken with vigor every time any of our people win a sports game, give a speech, or receive an award. In El Salvador, it's in the clear blue sky. Smiling with joy as it sees Salvadoran people grow, laugh, love, and **succeed**.

# LUCA SABINE BERNSTEIN

**GRADE:** Sophomore

**BORN:** New York, NY

**LIVES:** New York, NY

## MENTEE'S ANECDOTE:

Tuesday at 6:15 p.m. is always a time I look forward to; it's not the time itself, but it's the hour I have with my mentor, Sara. In our weekly meetings we respond to journal prompts, learn about different forms of writing, and work on finalizing work to submit. I am always inspired by Sara's responses and views on life, and I am so grateful to have her as my mentor because she gives me an amazing example of how to live real life while still doing what she loves.

---

# SARA FELSENSTEIN

**OCCUPATION:** Content Director

**BORN:** Ridgewood, NJ

**LIVES:** New York, NY

**PUBLICATIONS & RECOGNITIONS:** 2021 Women in Content Marketing Awards Judge, Notre Dame Young Alumni Essay Contest Honorable Mention

## MENTOR'S ANECDOTE:

Meeting with Luca is a joy. I am constantly impressed at the thoughtful, delicate way she weaves together poems in response to our weekly prompts. She is perceptive and creative, and has even inspired me to start a daily gratitude journal. I can't wait for more people to read her beautiful poetry!

# **Where**

## LUCA SABINE BERNSTEIN

*We all come from somewhere, but that doesn't mean we all belong somewhere. It took me a while to learn where I'm from, so now it's time to learn where I belong.*

I am from pleases and thank-yous, customs I've taken too far.

I am my anxious Mothers' greatest joy
and my Father's biggest mistake
      I'm from denial of who I am
And generations of pain.
I am from omens as truth
And moons that give me power,
From sunset to sunrise

I am from arrested stalkers.
4 charges to go
from freedom to fear.

      I'm from letting it be
           never giving up.

I am from unspoken perfumes

And divorced parents

Broken families
but powerful Women

I am from notes that my voice couldn't say
I am from wanting to run away.

But staying
        Staying stuck
in a mediator's office
holding it in.
I am from not crying,
from being what I thought strong was.
I'm grown, from growing up too fast.

And having been forced to give second chances, and thirds.
And from wanting to end on happiness,
when the end is nowhere near.

# CAMILA BONILLA

**GRADE:** Junior

**BORN:** Methuen, MA

**LIVES:** New York, NY

### MENTEE'S ANECDOTE:

Working with my mentor, Leslie, has been the best experience, especially when working on a piece like this. At first I thought my piece had no significance in my life. But once I started to explain the thought process within context to Leslie I realized that I had actually incorporated moments from my experiences. I am really glad that I had Leslie as my mentor because I was able to talk about everything behind the piece rather than only the writing itself.

---

# LESLIE HENDRICKSON

**OCCUPATION:** Reporter

**BORN:** Portland, ME

**LIVES:** New York, NY

**PUBLICATIONS & RECOGNITIONS:** *Mansion Global, The Wall Street Journal, The Hollywood Reporter*

### MENTOR'S ANECDOTE:

When Camila and I were thinking of a title for her submission, I suggested something using the song "Dos Gardenias" that Agustina and her grandfather talk about in the story. She laughed and said, "You literally read my mind." So that became the title of her piece, which captures the moment perfectly.

# Dos Gardenias del Campo

## CAMILA BONILLA

*Sitting in the Dominican countryside, known as El Campo, Agustina plays the guitar with her grandfather. She reflects on her time spent on the island and her anxiety surrounding her soon departure.*

In El Campo, the acoustics rang better than when played from the fire escape in a bustling city. The jungle behind croaked its own harmony in tune with the strings, while the cars below crashed into each note, leaving fragmented dissonance in its wake. Agustina felt at peace, here in El Campo, plucking metal twine for her grandfather, who sat across from her, a cigar in his yellow fingers, tobacco rolled tight in the factories miles away in Santo Domingo.

Agustina came to a stop, fingers resting on top of the frets instead of pressing into the board.

"*Maravilloso.*" Her grandfather smiled. "It only feels like yesterday when I was the one on that same guitar playing for El Campo. Even with *quipes* stuffed in their mouths, they slowed their chewing to listen closer to my playing. Breaths hitched, mine included. That was the only thing you could hear. The guitar and the cicadas buzzing in the palm trees."

Agustina waited before his next words how she always did, like carefully waiting for a coconut to fall from its tree on its own accord because you knew it would be ripe.

"How about 'Amada Mia'? Cheo Feliciano. Remember the one we learned last summer? Do you still remember that one? Or has it slipped from your brain? Everything seems to be slipping away, but what stays are songs. It's muscle memory, the dance of fingers over frets."

"I remember," said Agustina. "It goes like this." Her callused finger-tips pressed into the metal, taking obscure positions that shifted every few seconds, while her other hand gently picked over the gaping hole. Agustina closed her eyes and kept playing.

Everything was the same. The guitar, the same instrument her grandfather held sixty years ago. The palm trees rooted deep under the soil, gripping onto anything that would keep them tethered to a world in which time whipped everything away. El Campo, where the roosters cried every bleak morning, and rain showers drenched the steep hills and left behind a smell that you could smell only right here in El Campo. Only she had changed. Agustina was no longer the little girl who flounced in white skirts that became brown from the mud. Ever since then, the city hardened her, like the frost that came over oak trees and left them bare. Whenever she came back to El Campo, the snow melted off. It was in moments like these that she wished she could be a palm tree under the blazing Caribbean sun, where the cold never whispered in the winds except for those cool, damp nights spent talking with cousins in hushed voices. And when everyone went to sleep, you could hear the frogs croaking. Crickets chirping. Water rushing by in the river nearby. The soft acoustics of El Campo.

But eventually she would have to go back. Back to the city where she learned English. Where she bought her first apartment. Where the cold settled over her like a frosty blanket, and no matter how hard you blew on your hands while waiting for the bus, they never warmed up. Agustina found it hard to wake up on those days when the radiator was off. At dawn, she found comfort in burying herself under the blankets, imagining herself in El Campo. And if she listened hard enough, she swore a rooster cried outside her window.

"Agustina?"

Agustina slowly came to a stop, and took her eyes off the patch of green grass she had stared at while her mind had wandered. Her fingers still managed to play the song at least twice over before her grandfather snapped her out of it.

"I asked if you could play 'Dos Gardenias.' Are you feeling all right?"

"Yes. It's just so hot out here."

"What's on your mind? There's something bothering you, I know it. You and your father contort your eyebrows the same way, so they look even bushier."

"I don't want to go."

"You're sitting down right now. You're not going anywhere."

"I mean, I don't want to leave."

"You're not leaving for another two days."

"I know. It's just that when I do leave, I know I'm going to miss this place. I love the city, I do, but I don't know if I can bear another cold winter. I wish I had done more things. I wish I had taken you to the beach."

"It's hot right now."

"I know, *papá*. It's just that it won't be—"

"And it will be cold when you get back. You are sitting on this island with me right now. Enjoy it. You spend so much time thinking about what the cold will be like in New York, when you won't know for another two days. So why are you wallowing in your own sadness? You wanted to go to the beach? Good. We'll go to the beach tomorrow."

Agustina stared at her grandfather.

"What are you looking at me for? Now, 'Dos Gardenias.' Do you know it or not?"

The young woman smiled briefly before positioning the guitar over her thigh.

# BRISHTI

**GRADE:** Junior

**BORN:** Brooklyn, NY

**LIVES:** Brooklyn, NY

**PUBLICATIONS & RECOGNITIONS:**
*Taking Our Place in History: The*
*Girls Write Now 2020 Anthology;*
*The New York Times* Teen Life in
Quarantine; Scholastic Art &
Writing Awards: Silver Keys,
Gold Keys, Silver Medal

### MENTEE'S ANECDOTE:

Donelle is so cool. Every call we have on Zoom together is memorable and really fun! We laugh so much together and I always feel so high-spirited after our calls. I love talking about my week and my interests with her, and I love hearing about the things she's been up to recently, as well as hearing about her nephew! She's definitely been a huge driving factor in my writing productivity this year, as well as an awesome person to pitch my ideas to. She's a really lovely person and I'm glad she's been my mentor this year.

---

# DONELLE WEDDERBURN

**OCCUPATION:** Associate Producer

**BORN:** Maplewood, NJ

**LIVES:** Maplewood, NJ

### MENTOR'S ANECDOTE:

I was immediately struck by Brishti's wit, passion, and love for language. This love manifests through the written word and her creative experiments with design and fine arts. It's the process, not the end result, that they gravitate toward. I love listening to her muse about the expansiveness of their future. Their multidisciplinary approach has led to some amazing creative writing sessions! We've shared prompts that incorporate music, photographs, memory, and sensory experiences. My favorite part is after we put our pens down. When we read our work in our own voices, and share feedback on what we heard.

# cross stitch

## BRISHTI

**Content Warning:** body dysmorphia, body dysphoria

*there is something deeply wrong with the body.*

our skin feels too Tight. if we loosened the stitches in the back of our skull, would our skin sag in relief as the migraines fade into nothing. would it soften. if we knew how to embroider correctly, would we look more boy and less girl and more girl and less boy. would the darks under our eyes appear lighter. and if we unstitched our joints and the fat from muscle would the shooting pains stop. would the nausea stop. would the trembling stop. would the flaring stop. would—

i think every strand of hair is a frayed, loose end holding this body together.

i want to unravel our stomach and give it the ability to hold more. pull the stitches from our lungs. from around our rib cage. our liver. this body is too tight it feels too tight. our skin is too tight. our knuckles will turn white from pulling Threads. our knuckles will turn white from gripping Needles. our knuckles will turn white from gripping canes.

our knuckles—
*crack.*

for the first time, our skin feels loose. it is not the perfect fit i thought it
Would be. it is not the perfect fit i wanted it to be. we stitch them
tighter. we sew blanket stitches from cuticle to bone and it is still not
enough. i want to replace our blood. replace our bone marrow.
replace cartilage. our chromosomes. i want to replace—

*IT IS STILL NOT ENOUGH! WE MUST REBUILD THE BODY
FROM SCRATCH.*

# GABRIELLA CALABIA

**GRADE:** Senior

**LIVES:** New York, NY

**BORN:** Basel, Switzerland

### MENTEE'S ANECDOTE:

Kiki is truly a beacon of hope, inspiration, and joy in my life. I often find myself pulling out a notebook during our conversations to try and jot down all the wisdom she shares: on crafting powerful narratives, exploring through poetry, and, since we are two foodies, all the best bistros in New York City! Through unimaginable situations, Kiki's support is unwavering. I can't imagine a better mentor, and our second year together will only get better.

---

# KIKI T.

**OCCUPATION:** Author

**LIVES:** New York, NY

**BORN:** New York, NY

### MENTOR'S ANECDOTE:

The adventure continues with year two of mentoring Gabriella. Our mission: launching her further out into the stratosphere via all the opportunities that come with senior year. Filled with so many talents, I'm excited for her future and this world's, as she is already making her mark—which will be one among many. When they say, "The future is female," I trust Gabriella will be in the front line. Yes, I'm in constant awe of her!

# Bunk Bed Dreams

## GABRIELLA CALABIA

*Thoughts, consciousness, and imagination. A poem.*

The memory of my birth
town is twisted with cobblestone roads,

alpine cows descending the hills
of my mind. It's so golden and bright

when the moments swaddled beneath
the grassy valleys connect for an instant

and I am reminded of my flesh,
my heart, my lake-drenched clothes.

Under the late sun, my parents
share a cremeschnitte

licking custard off their fingers.
A thousand thousand-year-old flags

unfurl in my imagination,
and the song of a yodeler

drifts on the breeze. In the apple orchard,
Mama holds my sister. I sink

my teeth into the pink fruit
and sunlight, taste the sounds of joy,

the sweetness of these days
forever. My brother's laugh

rushes through a field of Christmas Rose
as he treks up the mountain

to touch the moon
next to the wolves that swallow stones.

How wonderful it is to dream.
To dream. To dream of home.

# CHRISTIANE CALIXTE

**GRADE:** Junior

**LIVES:** Brooklyn, NY

**BORN:** Brooklyn, NY

### MENTEE'S ANECDOTE:

The highlight of every Thursday is getting to meet with my mentor, Leah. I can remember our first meeting like it was yesterday. I was so impressed by her opinion article for The Duke *Chronicle*. Seeing that I was so deeply inspired by her work, Leah taught me op-ed writing strategies, and supported me in getting my article published in *The Washington Post*. Leah is someone you can rely on, whether it's for feedback on your Scholastic Art & Writing Awards submission or to share vegan birria taco recipes. She is an incredible mentor, a talented writer, and a caring friend. She is also a Gemini (like me!).

# LEAH ABRAMS

**OCCUPATION:** Director

**BORN:** Chapel Hill, NC

**LIVES:** Brooklyn, NY

**PUBLICATIONS & RECOGNITIONS:**
*The New Yorker, McSweeney's, Points in Case, The News & Observer*

### MENTOR'S ANECDOTE:

The Gemini symbol is a pair of twins, usually depicted back-to-back, gleaming through the night sky. Chrissy and I bonded almost immediately—through our love of opinion writing, our discomfort with poetry, our shared penchant for saying yes to everything. As some might say, our connection was written in the stars: We are both Geminis, two sides of the same coin, learning steadily from each other through our writing and weekly talks. Seeing Chrissy grow and chase her goals has been the highlight of my year—like meeting a long-lost twin and watching them shine.

# I Don't Listen to BTS

## CHRISTIANE CALIXTE

*This personal essay is a core memory of Summer 2019.*

"You're watching *Diary of a Mad Black Woman?*" the girl next to me asks, examining the DVD case I set between the two of us. (She's also looking at my hot chips. She's not getting any.)

Startled, I take off the headphones I have just put on. People aren't usually talkative in the library.

I turn and look her in the eye. If I were to use one word to describe her, I think I would say "bright." Her eyes have a certain sparkle to them. Maybe it's just the intense lights reflected off her dark eyes, but I still see it. She has those plump and wide lips, the ones you see celebrities paying for all the time, and they are made even wider by a foolish smile wiped across her face. Her most noticeable feature is her cyan headscarf, identical to the one I have at home but never feel like wearing.

She nods. "That movie is my favorite. Just wait until the salad scene. Watch what she does to her husband there. She's so evil, but he totally deserves it. It's so funny to watch her get her revenge."

After giving her a fake laugh, I quickly slip my headphones back on before this girl spoils the entire movie.

I haven't even gotten to the salad scene when I feel a hard tap on my shoulder.

"Do you like K-pop?" she asks.

"Yeah, I guess," I respond. (This is a lie.)

"Really?" (Why is she still smiling?) "Anyway, look at this!"

She points to her computer, where I see the BTS Instagram page. She clicks on a photo of one of the members and her smile grows even wider. I'm not sure how to react or what I'm supposed to say.

"He's so hot!" she squeals. (Okay?) "Why do I have to be fifteen years old? I wish I was as old as he is! Why couldn't Jimin have been born in my generation?"

Hearing a fifteen-year-old girl talk about a grown man like this makes me want to throw up. But she apparently *is* one of those die-hard BTS fans. It's not even close to the craziest thing they've said. I entertain her for a while, nodding my head in agreement until she runs out of things to say. When she's silent once again, I quickly put on my headphones before she can start talking. I am disturbed by the fact that while I was watching the movie, that crazy BTS fangirl spent the entire time *oohing* and *awing* at her precious K-pop stars. *Diary of a Mad Black Woman* is about two hours long. She spent *at least* two hours looking at random boys. (Heaven knows how long, since she was at the library long before I was.) And it's fine if she wants to gawk at those heavily Photoshopped Instagram photos. Heck, she could have even gotten on her knees and worshiped BTS and I wouldn't care (I wouldn't be surprised if she did).

I just wanted to watch a movie in peace without any fangirls interrupting me all the time. Little Miss I-Don't-Know-When-to-Shut-Up had a different plan for me, apparently. The girl just *had* to tell me how cute Jungkook looked sitting on that sofa or how she thinks blue is totally Jimin's color and not Suga's every single time she saw one of those wretched Instagram posts. So no, I did not enjoy watching *Diary of a Mad Black Woman*, nor was I having a good day in general. I didn't even get to finish eating my hot chips.

Perhaps I angered God by stealing my mom's DVDs. Perhaps he sent the cyan-scarf girl to punish me. When I go to the library to watch *Legally Blonde* the next day, she's there, smiling, waving, ready with her endless chatting. Over the next few weeks, I accept my fate. She wants to talk about her hair when I'm playing a video game. She wants to talk about a boy she likes when I'm curled into a beanbag, reading the latest volume of *Cursed Princess Club* (I literally waited a month for it to be released; I deserve some peace and quiet). She makes me stop listening to my music when I am breathing in the fresh air of the Botanical Gardens to tell me her birthday's coming up. (Please don't speak to me when I'm listening to music—I may become violent.)

The cyan-scarf girl talks, talks, and talks. I, not knowing how to push her away, have no choice but to listen, without any idea of how her shenanigans will come to an end.

I realize my wish for peace is granted at last when I see the spot she usually sits at is empty. Hallelujah. It's September and I figure she is probably busy with school. I have homework as well, so there goes my moviewatching and comic-reading. But at least I have peace and quiet once again.

I am picking up the cinnamon-swirl pancakes I ordered on Seamless when I see my former tormentor's cyan headscarf. I know it's her, even though she's wearing a mask. Who else could those eyes belong to? They wander as she studies every one of the old-fashioned tiles of Tom's Diner with the same childlike fascination she had when looking at Jimin or Jungkook.

Memories flood into my head as I see the girl from the library. The diner transforms into the computer lab as the smell of pancakes and coffee become the scent of the library café I had always longed to go to but never saved up for. The tiny stool I sit upon, waiting for my breakfast, is now one of the computer lab's small plastic chairs that I never found quite comfortable but tolerated anyway due to my love of the library.

I've never liked strangers. I still don't. They are mosquitoes during a summer vacation, gripping onto your skin when you want nothing more than peace and quiet, only to suck up every drop of joy and optimism in your blood with their *How are you?*s and *How was your day?*s. As much as you frantically swat them away, your attempts are only in vain. Ultimately, you will be left with no choice but to continue your vacation despite them.

It's funny how this stranger, this mosquito in the hot sun, has impacted my life without even trying. Her idle banter and gossip have become a staple of my Summer 2019 experience, yet I do not even know her name. When I am miles away from her, in the safety of my bedroom, tucked under a warm blanket, she continues to tap my shoulders with ice-cold fingers to tell me about her beloved K-pop group.

Her head darts up as she hears her order. She strides over to the cashier to pay, nodding her head and saying thank you to the old man as she reaches for her chicken and waffles.

She hurries out of the diner without acknowledging me (Rude!). I'm wearing a giant winter coat, so of course she wouldn't recognize me. But it is strange to see her pass me by without saying hello.

The diner's doors slam shut. As I scroll through my phone, waiting for my order, I realize that I too am wearing my cyan headscarf.

# ERIS CARSON

**GRADE:** Sophomore      **LIVES:** Brooklyn, NY
**BORN:** Brooklyn, NY

### MENTEE'S ANECDOTE:

I was definitely confused on how to work my way into journalism and creative writing. Then I met Mara, who I shared a lot of the same interests with. She taught me from her own experience, and talking to a person who has been in my situation really comforted me.

---

# MARA CAT DOLAN

**OCCUPATION:** Advocacy Associate      **BORN:** Columbia, MO
**LIVES:** Brooklyn, NY

### MENTOR'S ANECDOTE:

I remember in our very first meeting, Eris and I talked about our love of science fiction and journalism—and why certain genres speak to us at different times in our lives. I'm so grateful for Emely's thoughtfulness and creativity, which have been such a bright spot over the last year in my life!

# <8 year old>

## ERIS CARSON

*A poem about witnesses who have kept their mouths shut*

They dive into the ground,
yet they can't swim.
Dirt on my fingers,
spirits fly to the sky.

Heaven seems fairly close,
when arising with a bee,
cease with a bird.
Their wings resemble angels there.

Are they dying?
Possibly not.
Depriving them of the will to exist,
the more power running in my veins.

# AMINA CASTRONOVO

**GRADE:** Senior

**BORN:** New York, NY

**LIVES:** New York, NY

### MENTEE'S ANECDOTE:

Even though we are on different continents this year, our closeness has remained the same. Whether it be through the college process or relationships, Angelica has been an integral part of my life and I can't imagine next year without our mentor/mentee meetings! But I know that our Girls Write Now experience will live on and I can't wait to see how our careers and personal lives develop as we grow more into the perceptive, intelligent, and passionate women we already are!

---

# ANGELICA PUZIO

**OCCUPATION:** Doctoral Research Fellow

**BORN:** Charlottesville, VA

**LIVES:** Brooklyn, NY

### MENTOR'S ANECDOTE:

In our third year together, Amina and I have continued to build our relationship throughout change and geographical distance. I've watched Amina grow into a mature activist and leader this year, all while maintaining her spirit of wild resistance. I have always felt that our pairing was a bit star-destined, and I am honored to be a small star in her constellation of supporters and guides. As she takes the next steps toward college, I can't wait to watch Amina set her world ablaze with a groundedness and feminist fire that is all her own.

# Catharsis D'Être

## AMINA CASTRONOVO

**Content Warning:** difficult topics surrounding mental health

*This poem is dedicated to "re-becoming" during the healing process. It follows a narrator torn between acknowledging the truths of their past and growing through honoring honesty and dishonesty.*

*\*Note to reader: All bolded text from* The Woman Warrior *and "No Name Woman" by Maxine Hong Kingston*

**You knew from my birth that I would be taken.**

**I've looked for the bird,**
The "tiger place."
I remember the ache so clearly, but
When I get hungry enough, what do I see?
All I've found is the cenotaph of my past selves
Who couldn't re-become anymore,
Who disintegrated into sightless ghosts
Overcome with the haunting that is eternal knowing
Of the molting self—

I am the most sensitive person I know. I am the most dramatic. I am
the most caring. I am the most intuitive. I am the most loving.
I am the most passionate. I am the most. I am I am I am—

I can't rest.

sometimes i get a terrible feeling
like i died a while ago
and i'm only realizing it now.
perhaps i was just born,
but i—
i am exhausted from the
sound of my silence,
the constant
Rage, Terror, and Nothingness
that is existing between life and death.

it whispers:
*after you have ruined yourself,*
*what will you become?*
Please, **just make me good!**

**For a moment I considered rebellion:**
*I could never go back.*
***Those girls were from the bad old days.***
They gave me the knife and
They told me

**I died for a while** but it didn't work.
And that is why **women are so dangerous.**
That is why **we have to have our feet bound,**
That is why **they broke me with my own tongue,**
That is why they said not to commit suicide,
But to live hungry instead.

**When I get hungry enough, then killing and falling are**
    **dancing too—**

a masochism of hunger—
**When eating can't be a habit, then neither can seeing**;
The knife twists and punctures my chest—
A creeping, sour constriction snaking its way into my throat.
Like a cat with an overdue hairball,
I'm choking up everything—
the expectations of my father,
the pressure to be perfect,
and the reminders that my fire—the resistant ache within me—
is a self-imposed purgatory.

**"When you were little, all you had to say was 'I'm not a bad girl,'
and you could make yourself cry,"** well
Being bad will kill me, but so will being good.

After so long of hiding from the bird
I find myself trying to resurrect
Its remains—
*Who was I before I was taken?*
Very early in my life it was too late,
I tried so hard to be free
and that is why i am lost in the tiger place,
And that is why I am akin to no one.

At first, my body didn't know where I was.

i looked at my neck—
Red teeth crevices,
Bruises welting from mortality's climax—
and i wanted to cry.,
i stared at my body
and i was horrified by what it had done,
what it had consumed,

*who* it had consumed—
What has it become!,
and how can a place that feels like home push me further from myself?

Alas, one day **may my people understand the resemblance
so I can return to them.**
May my chest and throat return to me
So that I can scream at those who witnessed my creation,
Sitting back and watching the world unravel, revolving—
"Revolution!"—
Naming it makes it seem too small. It is infinite,
Like the first orgasm
a womb
blood on a newborn
a knife
.the end of The fucking World.

so we burn. it is unifying and catastrophic and the only real thing we've
ever felt.

Now that I've returned to the tiger place
**I am watching the centuries pass in a moment
because suddenly I understand time,**
I know what the ghosts were whispering all along.
**Perhaps I see two birds in their consecutive moments,**
Holding up the well I tried to drown myself in
So that a catharsis of my reflection stares back at me:

**"Which would you rather be? A ghost who is constantly wanting
to be fed? Or nothing?"**

Nothing!,
Always nothing.
Yet I am the most *everything* person I've ever met and I,

I'm tired of the tigers,
Of being the taken one.
I can never find the fucking bird
So I pretend that everything has wings
Because turns out,
I'm not as strong as you raised me to be.
I can lead everyone into battle

except myself and i will
drink myself into oblivion
before i learn anything from you.

But
I know how to sit in my vulnerability because it makes me stronger.
I know when I need to write like I know when I need to drink water.
I know how to make eye contact while being intimate, even if it lasts
    forever.
And I know when my soul is screeching for the tiger place,
It screams at me through an etching surfacing on my skin:

**just two black strokes—**
**The bird.**

# DOROTHY CHAN

**GRADE:** Senior

**BORN:** Brooklyn, NY

**LIVES:** Brooklyn, NY

### MENTEE'S ANECDOTE:

Each week, Marina and I start off our session by sharing how our week went. Whether talking about the latest shows that we watched or recalling a funny memory, our conversations go down many paths as we learn more about each other. We often have our sessions open-ended without a strict plan, but they still seem to fly by—especially during the times when we write and share stories of our own. Having worked with Marina for over a year now, I am happy to have grown as a writer with her and also to call her my friend.

---

# MARINA FANG

**OCCUPATION:** National Reporter

**BORN:** Albany, NY

**LIVES:** Brooklyn, NY

### MENTOR'S ANECDOTE:

Even though in our nearly two years of working together we've never met in person because of the pandemic, I feel really connected to Dorothy. Our sessions have been a balm through these difficult times and, no matter what, I've always looked forward to them each week. From the start, Dorothy was a really intelligent and observant writer, and I'm so proud of and inspired by everything she has accomplished (mostly without much help needed from me!), from her writing to her activism and so much more.

# Making American Holidays Our Own

## DOROTHY CHAN AND MARINA FANG

*Two essays about experiencing American holidays through the lens of immigrant families. Each of us has different stories of trying to figure out American holiday traditions, but we've also tried to build our own.*

### I. Thanksgiving

I can't remember the first time my parents decided to make turkey for Thanksgiving. Most holidays either we ate the Chinese food we were accustomed to eating or we'd go to a party at a family friend's house, where the spread of food would include a mix of various family-sized dishes guests had brought: Tupperware and aluminum trays filled with fried noodles, egg rolls, dumplings, and steamed buns. Sometimes there was some "American food" mixed in for the kids: plates of microwavable fish sticks or pizza bites, and plastic tubs of brownies and cookies from Costco.

But sometime during my adolescence, they decided they wanted to try "an American Thanksgiving." They bought a box of Stove Top stuffing. They googled how to make turkey, brussels sprouts, roasted sweet potatoes: the whole spread. Each year, I would ask them: "Why not just stick to roast duck?"—something with which they are far more familiar (and, frankly, tastes better). "We want to try something new," they would respond.

I think in trying these new things, they were trying to figure out how to be American. They were trying to figure out how to replicate what they saw in pop culture: that Norman Rockwell painting of a big family and the grandfather holding a giant platter of turkey, the festive scenes from holiday movies that play on a loop every December. I think they were wondering where *we* fit into all of that.

My parents often ask me questions like: "How do Americans *typically* celebrate Thanksgiving? What are we *supposed* to eat on Thanksgiving?" As if I know. I often remind them: Mainstream American culture isn't my culture either in many ways. I've had to learn it myself, cobble together what a life in America looks like.

In college and as an adult, I've often had Friendsgivings. Sometimes my friends and I eat the traditional Thanksgiving foods and, sometimes, we don't.

The COVID-19 pandemic has now upended multiple years of holidays for so many of us. This year, I spent Thanksgiving and Christmas alone. Sure, there were moments I wished I was with other people. But I also tried to make the most of it, making my own small meals and doing whatever I wanted.

Over time, I've figured out that a lot of it is an invention, a myth. There's no one way to celebrate a holiday, no one way to be American. We're all building our own culture and creating our own traditions.

## II. Christmas

Every year, without fail, my neighbors put up their Christmas lights outside their house on the first of December. Their astonishing arrays of reindeer and snowflake projections stand out in a row of seemingly lackluster homes. Even so, the view of their lights from my window across the street stays the same, a reminder of the traditional American holiday. The houses in the Nativity scenes that I browsed with my mom at Target depicted the same fairy-tale view, as if Christmas had the power to change a town through blankets of snow and strings of lights. For the longest time, I held that ideology, and relentlessly tried to convince my family to think the same way.

I convinced my mom one year to buy a Christmas tree. I spent a few hours meticulously planning the layout of each bulb based on size and color, making sure that there was space for silver tinsel spirals and lights to complement everything. When I finished, my tree shared a striking resemblance to the inspirations from my favorite holiday movies. It was the quintessential Christmas tree.

Since then, decorating the Christmas tree became my favorite holiday tradition, but one that I shared with myself. My family watched TV in the living room while I sorted our ornaments on the floor. When we lost our tree a few years later, my family was indifferent about it, while I was devastated.

My disappointment slowly dissolved as I realized the reason behind my family's lack of concern. The trees in the movies we watched were filled with ornaments passed on from generations, while ours came from the dollar store. Our tree didn't mean anything more than the quintessential example of American capitalism.

I overlooked my family's annual dim sum feasts and exchanges of li xi (red envelopes) to hang up red and green streamers and make cookies for Santa. They weren't much, but with the rest of our relatives in Macau, all my family had was one another, and we used these celebrations to cherish our time together.

I spent a large portion of my childhood trying to insert my family into an American mold, so much so that I ignored the fundamental meaning of Christmas—a time of thankfulness and celebration. My home didn't have extravagant decorations like the Nativity scenes I used to peruse or the elaborate generational traditions that holiday movies showcased. Even so, my Christmas celebrations shared the same Christmas magic, with or without a tree.

# SANDRA CHEAH

**GRADE:** Junior

**BORN:** New York, NY

**LIVES:** New York, NY

### MENTEE'S ANECDOTE:

This is my second year having Natalie as my mentor. I cannot thank her enough for all the support she has given me beyond my writing to all aspects of life. Every meeting felt like a FaceTime call with an old friend and an escape from the stresses and havoc high school has brought. With so much bundled inside me I know that, with Natalie, I am in a safe space to talk, learn, reflect, and release parts of myself. Thank you for everything!

---

# NATALIE DAHER

**OCCUPATION:** Social Publisher

**BORN:** Philadelphia, PA

**LIVES:** Washington, D.C.

### MENTOR'S ANECDOTE:

While Sandra and I no longer live in the same city (I'm in Washington D.C.!), we've gotten to explore writing, meditation, and our various apartment plants over Zoom for another year. I've enjoyed making space to journal and reflect during our pair sessions and to share and talk about current events and the news. Sandra brings endless curiosity, a sense of humor, and a wide range of interests to writing and brainstorming—and I'm glad we've been able to explore a mutual appreciation for politics, art, and, of course, food.

# Layers of Art & Me

## SANDRA CHEAH

*Family expectations. Fear. Uncertainty. Some of the many negative thoughts that flow in a teenager's mind. Cue art, a community, a tool, and a coping mechanism that changed a girl's life.*

Procreate is a tool used by artists worldwide to portray their ideas as digital pieces. Unlike traditional art, digital artists use different methods to formulate their pieces. Digital artists use layers; layers are essential, as they are the building blocks of your piece.

Growing up, my idea of "perfection" was living up to the skills and talents of my older, seemingly infallible sister. I watched on the sidelines as she would embark on competitive sports, from swimming and dancing to even baby crawling. These moments of my admiration and endeavorment would come frequently. Coming home each day, I would see the trophies that lined a shelf; they prompted acts of self-reflection that would torture me for a period of time.

But I wasn't a perfect child.

**Layer 1:** I spent years training to become a competitive swimmer. In my mind, I had sketched out a general outline of everything I wanted to be, everything my sister was. My body would stiffen at the sweeps of water that would flush at my skin with every stroke. Coming out of the pool, my body felt heavy and deflated. I hated the pool, the shivering, and I most certainly hated the competition.

**Layer 2:** After years of attempting to find a passion for swimming, I realized swimming was not my cup of tea. I learned that fulfilling someone else's passions didn't fulfill my own. The words of encouragement I longed for from my mother were never there because they were simply not my words to hear. It was at this moment when I began to map out a concrete sketch of my own life. I finally erased the remains of the sketch that I had drawn from my expectations. This was when I discovered the fascinating world of art. Art fostered a sense of community in me; through our unique artistic styles and creativity I found a space of growth and exploration. Amid the competitive pressure that runs through my family, art gave me a sense of fulfillment.

**Layer 3:** Art allowed me to express my emotions and solidarity in a new form. During the recent increase in hate crimes against the Asian American community, art became a coping mechanism after seeing my po pos and gong gongs fall under the hands of racist people. Seeing the work of Amanda Phingbodhipakkiya, a creator for the "I Still Believe in Our City" campaign commissioned by the New York City Commission on Human Rights, gave me hope for humanity. I visited the Museum of Chinese in America back in October. The wide range of exhibitions ranging from the immigration movements of the early industrial era to the modern day made me feel as though I was walking through the footsteps of the people who have come before me; I saw the work of those who have taken the risk, coming to an unfamiliar place despite the unwanted atmosphere.

**Merging layers:** Art became my version of the swimming pool. As my feet stepped closer to the tip of the diving board, my heart began to pound and my hands were suddenly drenched with sweat. I leaped, and my weight fell toward the water: arms first, then head, body, and finally my feet. For a while, I let my body sink into the deep waters in the swimming pool, feeling a moment of serenity. I lifted my head and looked for the scoreboard. To my surprise, there was none. There was no competition with art. It was a continuous journey to improve my skills and explore new realms. Relief flushed through my body.

# CHELSEA CHINEDO

**GRADE:** Senior

**BORN:** Bronx, NY

**LIVES:** Bronx, NY

### MENTEE'S ANECDOTE:

My mentor, Cherie, has been a huge support for me thus far in my senior year. She has helped me with my college list, college essay, supplements, mental health, etc. Even though we just met a few months ago over Zoom and haven't had the chance to meet in person yet, it feels like I've known her for a long time. She's been very considerate of my time and made sure that, first and foremost, I was always okay. She is warmhearted and I feel lucky to be paired with such a kind and loving mentor.

---

# CHERIE-ANN DARBY

**OCCUPATION:** Digital Platforms Manager

**BORN:** Kingston, Jamaica

**LIVES:** Mineola, NY

### MENTOR'S ANECDOTE:

Working with Chelsea has been such a joy! She has such a beautiful spirit and is talented in a variety of ways, including writing! She's managed her hectic schedule with grace and resilience over the past few months and that has inspired me as her mentor. I'm so proud of all she's done, including applying to twenty-six universities!

# The Sweet and Sour: Life as a Senior

## CHELSEA CHINEDO

*"The Sweet and Sour: Life as a Senior" is about the highs and lows I have faced thus far in my senior year that redefined my outlook of what senior year really is.*

**July 2021:** Senior year is approaching . . . Saying I'm excited does not give this feeling justice!

**August 2021:** I have the perfect idea for a college essay. I can't wait to write it!

**September 2021:** The volleyball coach (also my honors geometry teacher) really wants me to try out for the volleyball team and I don't want to let him down, but how am I going to balance maintaining valedictorian status, studying for the SAT, and applying for college while playing volleyball as well? It all seems to be so overwhelming!

**October 2021:** After being convinced by my coach, I tried out and made the volleyball team! I am feeling excited, but I know I have many tasks to complete before the end of the year.

My dad asked, "Are you sure that you'll have time for your studies? Sports are usually a big time commitment."

I responded confidently, "Yes, I definitely will!"

**November 2021:** "Practice is three days a week," says my volleyball coach.

Maybe this was a mistake. I don't have time for anything anymore. I'm just starting the college essay idea that I've been holding on to since August. What have I done? It's November and I haven't started anything regarding the college application process. I feel so behind!

**December 2021:** It's time to take my last SAT exam and I'm convinced my score will be above 1300. I have a little less than a month left to get most of my college applications in, I got this!

**January 2022:** So not only did I not get above 1300 on my SAT, but I'm also working on supplements hours before their deadline. How did this happen? How did I go from being so ahead to being so behind?

"Supplements are things you need time to edit over and over again. What you produce right now might not be your best work," my sister explained.

I can't believe I've allowed myself to get to this point. Doing well on my college applications was one of the most important things to me. Was taking on volleyball a mistake? Was I focusing too much on studying for the SAT? Where did I go wrong?

**February 2022:** I'm waiting to hear back from colleges. I'm excited but nervous at the same time.

I can't tell you how this chapter ends because it's not over yet, but I can tell you that even though things didn't go as planned, I'm proud of my work! I wouldn't have had it any other way.

Rather than looking back at all the times when I felt I went wrong, I chose to make peace with the fact that they were simply obstacles; obstacles that everyone goes through. I am proud of my perseverance and that I've made it this far!

I'm grateful for the challenges that I've faced. They are helping to pave my path to success. Sure, my senior year hasn't been what I expected so far, but that's what made it fun!

I don't regret joining the volleyball team; I've found a love for the sport. My only wish is that I'd started playing sooner.

As for college applications, I'm excited to see where I go. Will it be Johns Hopkins? Perhaps Yale? Who knows. I no longer feel stressed about which colleges will pick me. I've done my best through all of my high school years, and any college would be blessed to have me! My best is good enough. Why would I want to go to a college that doesn't want me anyway?

Now that all the heavy stuff is out of the way, I'm excited to make the best out of my senior year. Senior pictures, senior trips, prom, graduation, all of it. Although I'm excited to move on to the next chapter of my life, I also know that I'm going to miss high school. It's a bittersweet feeling.

Right now, I'm reminiscing about my journey and trying to embrace every second, every minute, and every hour of my senior year. I am counting down the days till I'm able to scream, "I graduated!"

Although I don't know exactly what the future holds, I am optimistic that it will hold many amazing experiences.

So, I'll leave you with one of my favorite quotes: "If something is meant to be, it will happen."

# KIANNA CHO

**GRADE:** Junior

**BORN:** Hoboken, NJ

**LIVES:** Palisades Park, NJ

### MENTEE'S ANECDOTE:

Immediately from first meeting my mentor, I was excited to work with her. Though I'm a reserved person, I quickly became comfortable with her and started to view her as more than my mentor. She's a friend and a support system, and I'm lucky to have met her.

---

# CRISTINA MIGLIACCIO

**OCCUPATION:** Assistant Professor of English

**BORN:** Brooklyn, NY

**LIVES:** Long Island, NY

**PUBLICATIONS & RECOGNITIONS:** *The Routledge Companion to Literature and Class, EDUCAUSE Review*

### MENTOR'S ANECDOTE:

Working with Kianna has been one of the highlights of my year! Kianna is a sensitive, intuitive human being with incredible determination. Through our weekly meetings, she has shared her creative and academic writing with me, which has been a pleasure to read and discuss. Kianna is also self-taught and gifted at illustration—a hobby that has been her respite through the difficult past two years. She is a master multitasker—juggling SAT test prep, an academic course load with multiple AP classes, a part-time job, and other commitments. Her peaceful demeanor despite all of these obligations is infectious!

# My Mind

## KIANNA CHO

*The mind is our greatest asset, one that is used every moment of our lives. Some, like myself, have found new purpose for our minds, as escapism from reality.*

If I could, I would live in my mind.

There, I imagine a memory bank. A bookshelf of everything I've experienced, categorized by years. Its dimensions too big for my comprehension, I'm unable to see its end.

I might first relive some older, important memories that I'm scared I'll forget.

Then, I'd again hear the voices and see the faces of my family that've passed from illness, in simpler times when I was unaware of their conditions.

I'd sit on the couch, across the one my grandma lay on, beside my uncle, the three of us watching television. My uncle would tell us of his dreams to buy a boat while I enthusiastically listened and chimed in. I'd promise to join him on one of his endeavors on the waters, though I'd know I can't keep it, as he never got his boat. I'd say it just for the sake of preserving the happiness in this memory.

I might also relive some memories I fondly reflect upon in times of needed comfort. Times in my early childhood that I recall to be perfect, void of any and all unhappiness.

Then, I'd again feel the New Jersey sun heat my skin as I ran underneath it, joining the kids I played with for those days that I was sure I would forever be friends with, who I've not seen since. I'd enjoy parties and field trips with classmates I've now grown apart from, in the years when I'd enjoyed going to school. I'd even just lie in bed and watch television, something I can still do in the present, but isn't the same with my worrisome mind making it impossible for myself to be at peace.

When I wish to venture somewhere else in my mind, I'd look beyond the bookshelf, where gateways to worlds from the depths of my imagination lie.

Many worlds come from books, games, movies, and shows already in existence, with myself as an addition.

There, I can be the things my child-self fantasized. A queen, a mythical being, or possessor of superhuman powers—the list is endless, my mind newly enriched with ideas with every day I spend online.

Other worlds come from my own, original thoughts. These worlds are nearly identical to my own, except I'm altered in them in ways that I think would make life easier.

There, I'm unafraid of how I'm perceived. I would change my appearance so that I'd outdo everyone's standards for myself, and my personality so that it would be impossible to come off as weird or unlikable to others.

Essentially, I'm all the things here that I'm not in reality. And like in my revisited memories, I'm disappointed once the illusion disappears and I'm again reminded of the way things actually are.

Though I try to refrain from living in the past or in my head for this reason, I find temporary happiness in escapism.

# FAIZA CHOWDHURY

**GRADE:** Senior

**BORN:** Sylhet, Bangladesh

**LIVES:** Bronx, NY

**PUBLICATIONS & RECOGNITIONS:**
Gotham Travel Caption Finalist,
MIST 2019 Regionals Short Film
First Place, MIST 2019 Nationals
and 2020 Regionals Short Fiction
Second Place

### MENTEE'S ANECDOTE:

I always look forward to getting to talk to Emily during my weekends. Since October, we have gotten to know a lot about each other and our creative spheres. We have crafted crazy writing ideas in our sessions, my favorite being coming up with a horror installment series, dedicating a horror trend to each decade. Example: one slasher installment taking place in the 1980s. From our silly writing prompt sessions, I have written short poems that mean a lot to me. Emily's mentorship has allowed me to explore my creativity through different writing styles and mediums.

---

# EMILY McCOMBS

**OCCUPATION:** Deputy Editor

**BORN:** Moore, OK

**LIVES:** Brooklyn, NY

### MENTOR'S ANECDOTE:

Faiza wants to grow up to be both a doctor and a successful novelist, and she's the only person I would believe can probably do it. She's just that whip-smart, focused, and creative. Aside from being my resource for all things Taylor Swift, she's taught me about fan-fiction apps, the Bangladesh Liberation War, and all things horror, and working with her has pushed me to stretch and try new things in the world of fiction writing. I am so excited to see what bright future she has in store.

# Good Riddance

## FAIZA CHOWDHURY

*Two kinds of beings rule this world: the human and the wiz. They have separate niches that should never overlap or exchange, because if the order is broken, all hell will break loose.*

Since the dawn of time, two powerful kinds have been put down on Earth to regulate order: mankind and wizkind. The man masters the tools, and the wiz masters magic. A wiz cannot master the tools, just as a man cannot master magic.

Procax specialized in using the ax. He rose and submerged with the sun, cutting away his hours. His carefree hours began to fog by the time winter arrived. It started in the neighboring houses; Procax could hear its drumming proximity. It was nature's punishment, banging at every door and demanding to be let in. He heard the bloodcurdling wails from the far distance, and soon enough, he heard nature's punishment linger outside his window, whispering to be let in. Sometimes Procax woke up in the night and saw villagers ring around a fire, chanting and attempting to harness the wizkind.

It didn't take long for nature's punishment to infiltrate every inch of the village. It drained the life of every living thing it touched, and Procax could smell the stench of death strengthen by the day. Procax was left deserted; he knew he was being preyed on, and though nature's punishment was taking its sweet time—prowling every acre of the empty village, observing and plotting—it would make its final pounce one day.

Procax was completely open to falling prey. Being consumed by it meant to be finally freed from his loneliness. Procax wanted it to be over with, for he couldn't fathom the endlessness of it all. Amid his anticipation, however, something dark and sinister began to plague him. He tried to resist it, but the dark wisp began to conquer with every passing day. The only thing that kept him grounded was his ax. He was a master of the tools, the only master of tools the village had left. His ax was his sole purpose now.

But one day, he found himself stopping amid his swings and raising his ax to eye level. He always studied the instrument with great respect, but this expression was unrecognizable, something void of respect.

*I'm the only survivor. Surely I am destined for greater things if I've survived this long. I may not have much time left before it finally strikes me, but if I've survived this long, I will survive through it all.*

Something as mundane as an ax would not help him survive through it all. Most mundanes couldn't even make it past a week, yet here Procax was, having dodged the punishment's exposure for a year now. He was no mundane. He tossed the ax away; tools were for the mundane.

*To survive through it all, I must master magic.*

There was a local legend about the woods; a mere mention sent immediate shudders among the villagers. For there was talk that a wicked witch inhabited the woods and constantly broke the world's order. They called her the portal between mankind and wizkind; she'd grant those who were worthy a taste of forbidden knowledge.

After surviving this long, how could Procax not be worthy? He left for the woods the next morning and spent days and nights searching. He would never dare to set foot in this territory a year ago, but he had seen the real, mythless horrors since then.

He stumbled upon a cave, and after hours spent circling the same steps taken, he was sure that if there was a witch at all, she had to be inside. It didn't take Procax long to find the witch inside; her grotesque features nearly illuminated the cave. She greeted him with a crooked smile.

"I've come to—"

Her hoarse snicker cut him off. "I know why you've come."

Procax stood stunned. "You do?"

She nodded. "Of course. I've been looking for a human who deserves to know the knowledge of magic. Amid this atrocious state the world is in, you've survived."

Procax grinned sheepishly. "I'm the only survivor in my village . . ."

"I know. You don't have to prove yourself to me. Do you want to master magic?" she asked.

"It's all I've wanted."

Her sly lips curved into a smirk as she held up a glass of sparkling substance. "Upon consumption, the divide between the two kinds will fall. Only then will you sense the magic." Before she could thrust the drink forward, Procax leaped to take the glass and gulped its contents all too quickly.

When he finished, he looked back up at the witch, blinking and looking around. "Am I supposed to sense anything yet?"

The witch smiled, and suddenly, Procax could hear the familiar, haunting whispers swallow the atmosphere. "Oh, you stupid, stupid boy. Don't you see? I've harbored a plague down on your people and you've fallen at last. I've been sent to eliminate those who dare to break order, and your village was corrupted with greedy disobeyers. Good riddance! And now you've proven that you're no different!"

Procax felt something sharp in his lungs, and his mouth began to foam in an instant.

"A human must never seek magic," the witch hissed, "or there will be consequences."

# FARIHA CHOWDHURY

**GRADE:** Sophomore        **LIVES:** New York, NY

**BORN:** New York, NY

### MENTEE'S ANECDOTE:

It was fun writing this poem as my mentor edited it along the way. Both my mentor and I are desi, so we could relate to the topic of this poem, and she can give me insight into her thoughts about the area I wrote about. We could relate to similar customs and cultures that I have included in this poem. I have grown to love the poem I wrote because I think it is unique and spreads awareness of a shy topic.

---

# SHANOOR SEERVAI

**OCCUPATION:** Researcher, Writer, and Lead Podcast Producer      **BORN:** Mumbai, India

**LIVES:** Brooklyn, NY

### MENTOR'S ANECDOTE:

I enjoyed working on this poem with Fariha. She worked really hard to find the right descriptive language to transport the reader to Bangladesh and give them a window into this world. Our shared experience of being South Asian made it easy to relate to the challenges and joys of sharing our culture with others in the United States.

# Where Reality Truly Resides?

## FARIHA CHOWDHURY

*As a Bengali woman, I wanted to voice my pain for the Bangladeshi fast-fashion workers who are thrown into terrible working conditions. My poem compares beautiful nature against the ugly poverty that drags Bangladesh down.*

Along vast, flat plains
And large rivers flowing from the Himalayas
Roam Bengal tigers

Their roars echoing across mountains

With crystal-clear water lakes
Surrounded by every green hill

Mothers carry their bald babies to the nearest nature tub
Gaunt, stray dogs scarfing leftover white rice

*

Hearing Bengali traders calling bargains
For everything under the sun

Smelling fresh kebabs and naan
Wafting through the busy streets
Being priced at the lowest, just to be able to make a guaranteed profit

Trading vivid pieces of clothing
Sarees, jewelry, blouses

And even bed covers, sheets, and lockets too

The beauty of the displayed colorful fruits
Juicy, plump full Mangos
Firm, yet ripe Papayas
Guava and Jackfruit, most loved

A fun street fair view to get your somber day by
You return to work for the bare minimum . . .

Little boys crying for their mothers
Working in the run-down factory next door

Falling asleep with wet tears rolling down their face
They knock their heads into each other
And doze off . . .

*

Men stand on noukas looking past the glass-like water
Peering for spots to drop their nets

Fish flee

Only little boys voicing their fun

Pure, large droplets of rain pat on the ground
Creating muddy slides of fun

*

Rickshaws nearly crashing into cars
Honking and cursing each other

Soft nature seeks to rid poverty

But how?

. . .

Garment factory workers' fingers cripple as their dreary eyes droop
With their only motive being to fill their rumbling bellies
They work endlessly

Killing themselves to earn the bare minimum
To get the bits and scraps
To piece together of what is
To simply survive—

Each stitch determines a fate
Each needle patches reality
Each loop repeats the cycle . . .

Clothes are piling up, closing in on our future
Suffocating us—

They are trapping us from change

They are trapping us from advancing

They are

Giving in to the larger consumers, the muscular trade networks
The hungry, ignorant clients

The supply chains
Feeding the system to grow bigger
And bigger
And bigger

And collapse—

But not on them, on us.

*2013 Dhaka garment factory collapse
Rana Plaza

# ALEXANDRA CRUZ

**GRADE:** Senior

**BORN:** Brooklyn, NY

**LIVES:** Brooklyn, NY

---

# PATRICIA ROSSI

**OCCUPATION:** Attorney

**BORN:** Brooklyn, NY

**LIVES:** Merrick, NY

### MENTOR'S ANECDOTE:

I'm looking forward to working with Alex. It's quite apparent that from the written work she has shared with me, she certainly is a talented writer and a very bright young lady.

# Beginning of a Lifetime

## ALEXANDRA CRUZ

*I wrote this while thinking about my experience with Girls Write Now and where my love of writing started.*

I hit the trackpad, hearing the loud plastic click once more—another failed recording. There I was, ten minutes into reading aloud the short story I had written for Girls Write Now, and I was nowhere near completion. I took a deep breath and reread the same words again. I knew exactly how I wanted my story to sound, but my mouth wouldn't cooperate. I felt ashamed recording myself in my bedroom at two in the morning, fearful my family, fast asleep, would wake up. When authors read their work, I admire the unique way they deliver their stories. They know which lines matter and which make the audience feel something. I read it one more time and correctly inflected the sentence that mattered.

I exhaled a breath I didn't even realize I was holding and stared at the last word. After fifty chapters, I finished my first full story. Beneath my initial joy were already thoughts about the prospect of starting another story. Although staring at a blank document isn't fun, I do relish typing out the last triumphant sentence. The feeling of elation outweighs the fear and keeps me writing. I never thought I could accomplish this as a teenager.

I remember in elementary school sitting on the multicolored rug listening to the teacher read. Some kids had far-off looks, imagining each scene in their heads. Others glued their eyes to the book: If they stared hard enough, maybe they could see what happened next. My mind would wander, accompanied by faint pictures. My fourth-grade teacher, Ms.

Pecoraro, was one of the best readers. She read *Because of Winn-Dixie* and *Sadako and the Thousand Paper Cranes*. Some left a warm feeling in my chest, while others left me blinking away tears. I loved listening to her read. The stories came alive akin to watching a movie.

One day Ms. Pecoraro asked the class to bring in a book and promised to give us a surprise. My options were limited, and I toiled over which book would be perfect. Finally, the day arrived, and I begged my sister to borrow her favorite book, *Dork Diaries*. As I walked into the room, I smelled something sweet. My teacher was mixing instant hot chocolate into paper cups—the chocolate aroma mixed with the smell of our books.

The class spent the day reading and sipping hot chocolate in the cozy, quiet classroom. Ms. Pecoraro taught me the special simplicity inherent in books. All you need is a quiet room and a good book (and some hot chocolate) to discover the adventure of a lifetime. I remember that day every time I crack open a new book.

One day Ms. Pecoraro handed me her copy of *Maniac Magee*. It still had her bookmark and a paperclip stuck on one of the pages, a prominent crinkle in the middle, and a textured gold medal on the lower right. The paperback was worn and warm in my hands—a gift for our shared love of reading.

A decade later, when I thought about writing my own stories, a little voice in my head told me I couldn't, but I remembered that book and the teacher who believed in me. I've never been a confident person; it was hard to compare my work to what I was reading. Sometimes I wanted to quit, but I remembered my joy in reading. Writing isn't a job. It's something I do for myself.

When I joined Girls Write Now, the world of literature opened up to me, and the confusing pieces of the writing puzzle felt attainable. I started writing stories I was proud of, and I showed them to anyone who cared because I couldn't get enough of the feeling. A feeling I can't wait to keep chasing.

# MAYA CRUZ

**GRADE:** Junior        **LIVES:** New York, NY

**BORN:** New York, NY

### MENTEE'S ANECDOTE:

My mentor, Meredith, and I always talk about how crazy it is that we were paired; we are extremely similar. I feel like there's little that shows more about the place a person is in than that person's writing, and having someone else read your work, back up your choices, and suggest new ones, generally feeling with you, is invaluable to an artist. I write what I write to be understood, and Meredith does that. She makes what I have to say feel valuable. And we have a great time getting it all done! She's an incredible mentor!

---

# MEREDITH WESTGATE

**OCCUPATION:** Author        **LIVES:** Brooklyn, NY

**BORN:** New York, NY

### MENTOR'S ANECDOTE:

Maya brings a tender artistic eye to her writing, informed by her skill as a visual artist and her curiosity and kindness. I feel so lucky to get to witness the magic of Maya's way with words, whether in a free-write or coming up with a revised line while editing. She'll read her new lines in the most humble, lovely way and practically knock me off my chair. It's been thrilling to see her begin this larger project that's so thoughtful and sharp—a perfect vehicle for her insightful observations and the effortless poetry of her words.

# Mental Whittling

## MAYA CRUZ

*Things you never had can be yours. Things you had for a time can be yours again. Carve your way, pay the price.*

Same walk, same route nearly every day. However, there are precious stones lodged in cracks among monotony, and anything can be a gem if you're paying attention.

"Mimi" was one of those things my mind's hands grazed every day, fingertips on every line and corner in the frame my eyes could see, placing it all in any open pocket like a Rite-Aid thief. Usually, my mind's hands would just brush over "Mimi" and her children and the way the sun caught on their teal-blue tent; maybe somewhere, my mind would exhale and think, *That's nice and soft.* That day my attention was grabbed with vigor, blade brought to my palms and moved in a manner that would surely scar. I don't know if I'll ever get to remember the frame as it was versus how it felt after spoiled and curdling attention, humanity, tainted it that day.

From what I'd seen, she was a gentle crier. The boy and the baby were too. They were in and out of being enveloped in embrace a lot, like falling in and out of sleep. Their three bodies seemed to join as one figure, exhaling when the kids were engulfed by the tenderness of her arms and her tumbling black hair. They all looked a mess, but they were settling to the eye like the satiating smell of basement.

This time when she brought them close to her ribs, she kissed them both on the forehead, and her cry was not so gentle. They cried too, a writing, ugly cry. "Mama has to go," she said through ugly inhales. "I'll be back, though. Please watch him, Juno. Please, don't leave this tent. I'll be right back . . . I'll . . . be right back."

And just like that, breast was torn from mouth; mouth left agape and wailing, Juno also left agape and wailing through his blank stare, holding tightly onto this baby his mother had just placed in his arms as she walked up the stairs. He was nameless to me until his mother's parting. The baby mumbled, "Mimi, Mimi," through blaring cries. And she walked off. She went above, ascending the stairs I hate so much, and that was all it took for me to understand exactly what was going on. She must've wanted to Trance.

It took me months to separate myself from the cotton that was that experience. Sticky cotton, dry and clinging to the hair on my arms, sticking in the crevices of my mind. I cried and dried my tears with the cotton to shrink it, let it dry, and pulled it apart to spin it. Notebook in hand, I collected myself to put together some stringy words:

*Sometimes tears of water can feel like acid. Other times, the sting ties in the center of your rib cage, and you tighten up; you can feel it extend downward, rooting at the earth, simultaneously ripping away into the atmosphere, leaving a wraithlike tension in the center. Sometimes that absence of everything, the fertilization, growth, buildup of antimatter inside, that vignette in your vision and hum in your ear, can gift you with true stillness. Still like a gargoyle is still, still like a photograph is still, still like a horrified person is still. I let it pass and kiss it goodbye, swallow hard and let my acid tears unfurl. I direct myself away, and the sheet of blankness settles over my shoulders and tickles my spine, brushing on the backs of my knees and resting atop my ears, covering my eyes. Moments like that make me a sheet ghost: eyes and not much else. I am still feeling to my fullest capacity, despite that.*

Many days passed, and many days the children remained, tightly enclosed by blankets and teal tent walls, patiently waiting for her return, like she'd left the nest to hunt. In reality, she'd left for herself, and they sat there, motherless. Their hunger was folded in the baby's rhythmic inhales and whines, followed by Juno's frantic hushing; they hungered for her in the sweat beading in the blanket and on their foreheads. I hoped their mother was a strong woman, the kind who could carry a lot in her hands and who loved like the mouth of a feline. Would lick their fur clean and still have fangs to bare, if need be.

# GRACE CUDDIHY

**GRADE:** Senior

**LIVES:** New York, NY

**BORN:** New York, NY

### MENTEE'S ANECDOTE:

My mentor, Caroline, has been an amazing presence in my life these past two years. She has helped me accept my disability, be a better advocate for myself, and push myself as a writer to places I never thought I would go. Her advice on how to "just write," time management, handling social situations, navigating my chronic illness, and successful editing is advice I will take with me for the rest of my life. I am incredibly grateful to have her as my mentor!

---

# CAROLINE SHIFKE

**OCCUPATION:** Freelance Writer

**LIVES:** New York, NY

**BORN:** New York, NY

### MENTOR'S ANECDOTE:

Grace is such a superstar! I'm blown away by their dedication to improving their writing craft, their exquisite Google Drive organizational skills, and of course their incredible creativity. Watching Grace push themselves to try new genres, from short stories to poetry, has been such a joy—and I'm awed by their talent across the new forms. While I'm sad not to work together next year after Grace graduates, I'm excited beyond words to see what comes next for them. With their activism, compassion, and drive, I have no doubt Grace will continue to make the world a better place.

# pretty vain

## GRACE CUDDIHY

*About loving your pretty*

it's somehow become necessary for men to like tell me that i'm vain
stop me when i'm taking selfies on the subway because my eyeliner
    looks, like, so good today
"how are you not embarrassed"—not a question, a statement
that pompous period framing his performative perplexity
*embarrassed?*
like, does he um even know, the effort that it took for me to like, look
    this pretty?
years of youtube tutorials and of like, steady, dedicated practice to get
    that flawless wing
and yet he tells me, with his pious attitude and paternalistic
    perspective, that, like, i cannot appreciate my own pretty
he calls me vain, conceited, like those are words that are going to, you
    know, hurt me
that those words will dampen my pretty, that i will, like, put my
    camera down, and like, wash my makeup off my face
but like, i won't, because um i love my pretty
i love my colorful makeup, and my cherry lip gloss
i love my lace, and my glitter, and my dress like, you know, pink candy
    floss
there is purpose in my vanity, power in my pretty,
and your pathetic passages don't hold like a candle to my poetry

and you have the audacity to like, tell me that no one will take me
    seriously?
when we both know it's my um, confidence that makes you like, scared
    of me
am i not tough or, you know, smart if i am making your dick hard?
my perky makes me, like, personable, my playful professional
i own my pretty and i am like, pretty exceptional
so you can fuck off with your patronizing pronouncements
because i love my pretty whether or whether not you allow it

# JILLIAN DANESHWAR

**GRADE:** Sophomore

**BORN:** Queens, NY

**LIVES:** Bellerose, NY

**PUBLICATIONS & RECOGNITIONS:**
Adelphi University's Poetry Day,
Citation in Poetry (Freshman)

### MENTEE'S ANECDOTE:

In all honesty, I waited until the last possible moment to apply to this program. I was anxious because I thought, *What if my mentor doesn't like who I am?* I took a leap of faith and submitted my application. When I met Marisa for the first time, all my doubts and fears, they ran to hide. She has been nothing but compassionate and sweet. So much that I look forward to the end of the week. I'm so grateful to have a mentor that I feel completely comfortable with. She is truly one of the best people to exist.

---

# MARISA SIEGEL

**OCCUPATION:** Senior Acquiring
Editor

**BORN:** Westchester, NY

**LIVES:** Mamaroneck, NY

**PUBLICATIONS:** "Inherited
Anger," *Burn It Down*, Seal Press,
2019; *Fixed Stars*, Burrow Press,
March 2022

### MENTOR'S ANECDOTE:

Jillian is a brilliant poet—even when we're working on a prose exercise, she crafts sentences packed with sonic resonances, seemingly without effort. I am always surprised by how quickly she can do this too. She has the sort of natural talent that can't be taught, and it's an honor to work with her.

# My Dear Friend, Writing

## JILLIAN DANESHWAR

*This piece is about my relationship with writing, and how my life has changed since I was first introduced to it.*

I once knew someone who would use a powerful weapon often. When it was pointed at me, I learned not only how it hurt, but how it healed. How I would feel when I wielded it, and I molded it into my shield. What was this material that killed and cured? Words. Once I realized that a pattern of curves and lines could help me free what was killing me inside, I was able to put together the shattered pieces of my life.

Over the past two years, I've been dedicated to my craft. I've joined clubs and programs; I even won an award. However, for me, writing isn't about the satisfaction of recognition. It's about how it makes me feel. When I'm alone in my room, with tears slipping down my cheeks, words will wipe them away. Whisper in my ear all the things I wish someone would say. Hold me in an embrace so gentle the pain will fade. I need no one else but this extension of me with a different face. I could be on fire, burning with rage. Then, no sooner am I doused by water once the ink flows across a page. It could be the sun evaporating the ocean which I produced and the boat keeping me above the deep blue. So variable, but a part of who I am. The transcendent part of being human.

Ingrained in the core of my identity is one day: August 11, 2019. A new document breathed to life on my computer screen. The cursor flashed inquisitively as it watched me attempt something I'd never done before. Deep in my mind, I approached a door. Littered in broken padlocks, and crudely zip-tied, all in order to keep the monster inside. With a decisive blow to my mind, it was let out from the prison in which it had been confined. It stung at my eyes, and went in my chest, and sped it up three times. I took all the energy that it did not eat, and forced the monster to reveal its identity. It told me to call it "emotions." Since it was what I was hoping, it was time to let go. Through the tips of my fingers, the monster flowed. The document came to hold and transform the emotions I had been fighting—into my dear friend, writing.

Finding writing is incomparable to any other discovery in my life. Nothing else makes me feel so alive. Feel myself. It's almost absurd to think that a side effect to the poison I was forced to ingest was the antidote. The answer. Solving all my problems and holding my hand firm. So, ask me: Who am I? *I am writing, and I am words,* I reply.

# YARALEE DE LA CRUZ

**GRADE:** Junior      **LIVES:** New York, NY

**BORN:** Bronx, NY

## MENTEE'S ANECDOTE:

I love Lisa as my mentor. I've really gotten to know her and relate to her. We are both Latinx women who love screenwriting. Before our meetings I knew so little about screenwriting, but now I know that there's more to it than just character names and dialogue. She's really helped me grow as a writer these past few months.

---

# LISA Y. GARIBAY

**OCCUPATION:** Public Relations/ Communications Manager, Division of Physical Sciences

**BORN:** El Paso, TX

**LIVES:** Los Angeles, CA

**PUBLICATIONS & RECOGNITIONS:** Film Independent Spirit Award Nominee, Sundance Institute Arts Writing Fellow, Think Write Publish Science & Religion Fellow

## MENTOR'S ANECDOTE:

Given her passion for film, writing, and exploring new ways of sharing her voice, being paired with Yaralee has been like looking into a mirror—that is, if seventeen-year-old me were as confident, expressive, and bold as Yaralee is. When I learned of her passion for screenwriting, I felt like the luckiest mentor in the world to help lead her on her journey toward bringing her passion to fruition. Each time I read something that she's written, I am left wanting more, more, more! Her imagination, voice, and stories are rich and real. The big screen sorely needs them.

# Excerpt from *El Barrio*

## YARALEE DE LA CRUZ

*During the hottest summer of their lives, two best friends, Manuel Polanco and Xiomara Vargas, slowly drift apart as they deal with gangs, drugs, and growing up in . . . El Barrio.*

Int. Mama's Living Room—Day

It's late June, a week after school ended. XIOMARA, 17, a brown-eyed, brown-haired Dominican American, sits on the plastic-wrapped floral couch watching telenovelas and eating los tres golpes with mashed potatoes. She wears a tourist T-shirt from the Dominican Republic. Beneath her bed head, her eyes are locked on the television where reruns of "Teresa" play.

We hear food frying faintly as the doorbell rings.

XIOMARA

(with her mouth full)

¡Mamá! ¡La puerta! ¡Es Manuel!

MAMA (O.S.)

(annoyed)

¡Ya, yo sé niña! ¡No soy sorda!

Xiomara's great-grandmother MAMA, in her
old-lady slippers and nightgown, shuffles
out of the kitchen to unlock the front
door. She opens the door to MANUEL, 18,
a clean-cut, light-skinned Puerto Rican
with an athletic build, brown hair and
eyes, and a pierced ear.

MAMA

(happy)

¡Hola, Manuel! Tu comida está en la mesa, mijo.

MANUEL

Gracias, Mama. Siempre es un placer.

He embraces Mama and limps over to
Xiomara.

MANUEL

Que tal, Virgin Maria. Ew! Why you look like that!

Manuel points like he's teasing someone
for pissing their pants. Xiomara swats
at him like he's a fly in front of the
TV.

XIOMARA

Move, conyo! I'm watching "Teresa"!

Manuel laughs and plops himself on the
couch, making it fart. Xiomara hits him
on his chest.

XIOMARA

Cuidado! You're gonna break the couch. Vete a comer,
cono. Your food is gonna get cold.

                              MANUEL

Yes, King Simba.

          Xiomara smacks him on the side of his
          head as he gets up and goes to the
          dinner table, where he now eats.


                              MANUEL

(mouth full)

I don't know how you Dominicano pero no comer mangu.
It's like a lion being vegan. No es natural. ¡No es!

          Xiomara rolls her eyes.


                             XIOMARA

Manuel, ¡no me jodas! Ok! You do this every time you
come over. Plus, you shouldn't be talking because
you're fucking Boricua y no comes mofongo. So why
don't you stop being so hypocritical and eat your
fucking food!

          They go back to eating their breakfast
          to the sounds of the TV and Mama running
          a shower. Their harmonized laughter cuts
          in as this is a regular routine for
          them.



                            Cut to:
                  Ext. Southern Boulevard—Day

     A cherry-red Tesla Model 3 cruises Southern
    Boulevard, music booming and the window open.

    CLOSE UP on a hand with cigarette smoking out the
      driver's window. The hand moves to the driver's
    mouth. Smoke brushes against the driver's mustache
                     and sunglasses.

Cut to:

Ext. Xiomara and Manuel's apartment building—Day

The Tesla stops in front.

Cut to:

Int. Xiomara and Manuel's building lobby—Day

Xiomara and Manuel exit the elevator, chatting
toward the door.

Cut to:

Ext. Xiomara and Manuel's apartment building—Day

PEPE, 20, a tanned Dominican with a chubby build,
curly brown hair and brown eyes, and earrings,
throws his cigarette out the Tesla window. He wears
basketball shorts, a wifebeater, a gold cross on a
chain, and Jordans.

He honks at Xiomara and Manuel, excited
with music blasting.

PEPE

¡Que lo que, manin! Check out your boy's new ride!

XIOMARA/MANUEL

What?

PEPE

What you said?

MANUEL

What he said?

                          XIOMARA

Pepe! Turn down the music!


                           PEPE

Huh?


                          MANUEL

She said——


                           PEPE

Hold on! Let me turn off the music!

          Xiomara and Manuel roll their eyes at
          Pepe's lack of common sense.


                           PEPE

You guys like my new ride?


                          XIOMARA

(suspicious)

Where'd you get it?


                           PEPE

Don't worry about it.

          Xiomara crosses her arms. Manuel tries
          to break the tension.


                          MANUEL

Well, I think it's nice, Pepe.


                          XIOMARA

Well, I'm not saying it's not nice. It's a great
car. I just wanna know how your broke ass got it.

                    PEPE

*(lots of hand gestures)*

Yeah and I got that. And I said don't worry about
it. Okay?

        Xiomara leaves it alone.


                  MANUEL

So y'all heard about the party Lenny's hosting
Saturday?


                    PEPE

First party of the summer, bitches!

        They all laugh.


                    PEPE

You know this gonna be our last first party of the
summer now that smartass is going to college.


                  MANUEL

*(elbowing Xiomara)*

So we better make it count. Right!

        Manuel and Pepe dab each other up,
        laughing as Xiomara's smile fades away.


                  XIOMARA

Actually . . . I can't go.


                MANUEL & PEPE

WHAT?

        Pepe stomps out of his car and slams the
        door.

                    PEPE

What you mean you not coming!


                   XIOMARA

I mean I can't come. I gotta start packing for
college.


                    PEPE

Pack for college! Manin! That shit ain't until
August.


                   XIOMARA

Yeah, but—


                   MANUEL

No buts. Live a little.

          Xiomara rolls her eyes. Pepe moves
          closer to the group.


                    PEPE

Yeah! Let's have fun!


                   MANUEL

Come on, what you say?


                   XIOMARA

I don't know, guys. Parties aren't really my thing.

Especially Lenny's. You know those shits get out of
hand.


                    PEPE

True. But who's gonna be our sober designated
driver?

                              MANUEL

Exactly! Our group doesn't work without you.


                           MANUEL & PEPE

(girly)

PLEASE!

          Xiomara, impressed by their dedication,
          smiles and nods. Pepe gleefully
          initiates a group hug as they jump,
          repeatedly chanting—


                               ALL

We're going to the party!

          Their chant fades as the scene . . .



                        FADES TO BLACK.

# AMIHAN DEL ROSARIO-TAPAN

**GRADE:** Sophomore                    **LIVES:** New York, NY

**BORN:** New York, NY

### MENTEE'S ANECDOTE:

Faran has a creative analogy for everything on the planet. From the paper towel test being like semicolons to colons being the \*ta-da\* sound, it's safe to say that she makes grammar and all things writing fun. We spend the first half of all of our meetings getting lost in conversation and almost always go over an hour each week. She has encouraged me to see and analyze the stories everywhere, deepening my storytelling skills. Her advice, prompts, and techniques have shaped me into a better writer and artist. She is truly a wonderful thinker and mentor.

---

# FARAN A. KRENTCIL

**OCCUPATION:** Editorial Director          **LIVES:** New York, NY

**BORN:** Boston, MA

### MENTOR'S ANECDOTE:

It's a little strange knowing someone twenty years younger than me will one day be my boss, and probably the boss of the world, but . . . well . . . meet Amihan. A scholar and an athlete, Amihan is also a gifted musician and writer with a knack for finding compelling stories everywhere, from the subway to the depths of the Seine. Amihan is wickedly smart but fiercely compassionate with her friends and family, and even a global pandemic couldn't stop her from writing deeply funny and compelling short stories.

# Paris: City of Love!

## AMIHAN DEL ROSARIO-TAPAN

*We have this funny little idea that romance completes things. I had this idea while studying abroad in Paris this summer. And when romance didn't magically appear I decided to look for it.*

I was fourteen and studying in Paris; I had settled in the new city and was looking for the final piece to complete the trip: boys. All of the students in our study-abroad group were in agreement. We wanted to meet French kids our age. This was most repeatedly expressed by Esteban, a senior, who respectfully said he wanted to meet French teenagers, when we all knew he really meant French *girls*. We looked subtly during our touristy excursions, before curfew, and on the streets. But after one week of being in Paris, they didn't magically present themselves. And so we decided to hunt for them ourselves.

My French pen pal told me most kids hung out at Invalides, a park in front of the old grand Hôtel. Esteban had done his research too, and confirmed this, which is why I ended up scanning the grass with my roommate, Cece. We got along fairly well, both experiencing very different New York cities: me being from *the* city, while hers was one I originally thought was a suburb.

The fields were arranged in a two-by-three grid in front of the palatial hotel, which was currently undergoing construction but managed to keep its glimmer. Directly in the middle, splitting the two sides of the fields, was a large road lined with old electric-powered lampposts. The road connected this part of Paris to the rest of it, meeting a car-trafficked bridge that reached across the Seine. The line between Paris and New York sometimes blurred; from the jaywalking and graffiti on the streets to the make-eye-contact-at-your-own-risk lectures from adults. But as we consciously searched for boys, surrounded by the elegance of the old Parisian architecture and French chatter, I was undoubtedly in another world.

We walked carefully, with the tourist effect of feeling like everyone's eyes were on us. The challenge we faced was age . . . That is, nobody there was *our* age. And although we knew the French started drinking before they could walk, with the full face of facial hair and the postpubescent maturity they carried themselves with, it was apparent that nobody there was under eighteen. Esteban had said that I could be "however old I wanted to be," even if it meant being sixteen or eighteen or twenty-five. He said it with good intentions, though looking back, I realize that I didn't need to say I was older than the fourteen I already was—men would choose to see me as however old they wanted to in order to justify their desires.

The longer we retraced our steps, the more it grew on us that the excursion was a failure. There would be no life-ruining summer fling, only gazes of creepy old men, and ignorance from hot college guys. We hadn't come prepared with drinks or a blanket, so Cece and I just lay there, side by side. She was two years older than me, but everyone knew NYC raised me quicker. We were laughing at ourselves, the ridiculousness of the whole idea, both swearing we would approach a boy if he presented himself. The sky was completely clear, save for the hints of nighttime coming, the shadow of a half-moon in our peripheral vision. I turned to look at her and she laughed, her jaw tipping up at the changing sky; the sole piece of jewelry she wore, detailed silver hoops, glinting. That night, she took the best pictures that exist of me. Even now.

The metro on the way back was crowded, and we found ourselves standing in the center of the car. Holding on to the pole in the middle, we suddenly realized our two hands shared the pole with two others: two boys who couldn't be any older than sixteen. One of them was tall, with brown curly hair, and from the mask above, exceptionally attractive. I stared. Well, we all stared, grabbing one another's eye contact, then breaking it and looking at our friend, smiling with awareness. We all seemed to be in acknowledgment of what was happening: two guys, two girls, all looking at one another. We opened Snapchat, letting small laughs escape. My attention was directed to the one diagonal from me. Aside from the Nike tracksuit he had on, he was perfect. (And since he was French—I saw a text message on his phone, definitely French—his style could be easily fixed.) I opened my phone, clicked "New Contact," and began to seriously consider handing it to him. Until the train stopped. And the boys got off.

# CAROLINE DER

**GRADE:** Senior        **LIVES:** New York, NY

**BORN:** New York, NY

### MENTEE'S ANECDOTE:

Girls Write Now brought us together in the midst of an unprecedented global pandemic. I'm so grateful for the time we have had together, be it creative or nurturing, or both, and I appreciate Girls Write Now's unwavering support.

---

# ORLA MURPHY

**OCCUPATION:** Chief Speechwriter      **LIVES:** New York, NY

**BORN:** Cork, Ireland

### MENTOR'S ANECDOTE:

Girls Write Now brought us together in the midst of an unprecedented global pandemic and we are so grateful for the creative time we have had together!

# Egg Washed

## CAROLINE DER

*The persistent presence of the past manifests in strange ways.*

Months after we moved out, the property continued to smell of eggs. I tried intensely to purge the house of such an incessant smell. I painted the walls, bought the most expensive air-freshener sprays, then potent incense sticks that left me dizzy. One day, I even left the windows open overnight, rushing there the morning after to check if the interior had been brutalized by a thief in the night. The house was perfectly intact, and with it, the smell. It was as if the very essence of eggs had fused with the house, had intimately embraced the fibers of the walls, and would forever cling to them. Like a lover's lingering perfume, the scent was stronger in some places and fainter in others, but always, always present.

Amid my fruitless efforts, my father called me from a payphone in Đà Lạt, and demanded I sell the house. "I'm running out of money here," he said.

"How?" I asked. Southeast Asia was supposed to be cheap; that reason had been why he chose to move there. That and to exploit women, I suspected. His wife had disappeared and, subsequently, his conscience.

"Never mind how. You know what, I'm starting to think you're purposely holding on to the house."

"For the good memories?" I replied, disgusted. There was a pause. This subject was the only one he would walk on eggshells for.

"Well, anyway. One of the guys I used to play golf with was a real estate agent. The only thing is, I've lost his number . . ."

"It's fine. I'll take care of it."

"All right. I've gotta go. Bye." The last word had a tinny, almost nostalgic quality to it, like a telegram. I was reminded of how far away he was.

So I headed to the Realtor's office. Mistaking my boredom for something more profound, the agent shot me comforting smiles as we finalized details.

"I just want it to sell fast," I told her. Her demeanor shifted a little bit, less matronly and more businesslike.

"Of course it will. It's nice your mother ran a bakery in the store downstairs. The industrial kitchen is an attractive factor."

I nodded absentmindedly, looking at the listing description she had written. I was thinking about the future family that would move in. In my head, the family had two children. The stench of eggs seeped into their clothes and they were badly ridiculed for it. In fact, they were friendless.

When I looked up, the agent was staring at me pityingly. Her eyes flitted to the paint-specked, tattered clothes I was wearing. It's my laundry day today, I wanted to say. "If you're worried, perhaps about the money, please don't be," she urged, staring at me meaningfully. "It will sell for a very high price."

After this, I began to have a recurring dream. My mother and I were in the old car, a secondhand Honda Civic with a badly dented bumper. She was driving down a highway and, every so often, she would glance at the back seat, where I was. I knew in the dream I was very young because of this, because I hadn't sat in the back seat in years. As the scene unfolded, I would feel increasingly uneasy. There was something wrong and, eventually, I remembered it was because my mother did not know how to drive. At this point, I would ask her where we were going. Which came first, the chicken or the egg? she'd say instead.

My voice would waver "chicken," and she'd shake her head. We'd start to accelerate. "Which one? What were you? What are you?"

"I don't know," I'd cry.

"Egg," she'd declare, grimly. "The most monstrous of all membranes."

Suddenly, I'd get the urge to scan my hands. Yolk would be oozing from my pores.

Two weeks passed like this. I strained my mind, dredging up murky memories to muster up explanations for the dream. I got a call from a pay phone again from Đà Lạt, in which the woman on the other side coolly informed me my father was seriously ill and that I should come see him. I booked a red-eye flight and was waiting in the airport when the Realtor called me.

"Hello?" I said. Everyone in my gate was asleep. A plane twinkled into existence from afar. I watched it glide onto the runway.

"I'm sorry to call at this hour, but did you ever smell eggs when you were at the property?" she asked nervously.

"Is there something wrong?" I was suddenly and irrationally afraid to check my hands.

"I'm so sorry. I don't know how it happened. There was an explosion. Apparently, gas was leaking for a while. The firefighter kept asking me, 'Did you ever smell anything?' and I couldn't think—" She let out a sob.

"Thank God," I said out loud, exhaling.

It was then that the loudspeaker announced the plane was boarding passengers. People began to stir around me. I rose from my seat, drifting toward my destination.

# LENA DiBIASIO

**GRADE:** Junior

**BORN:** New York, NY

**LIVES:** New York, NY

### MENTEE'S ANECDOTE:

My weekly meetings with Hayley are always something I look forward to, seeing as we always have a fun and productive time together. Many of our conversations help inspire me to write pieces that I enjoy, and it's wonderful to have a mentor like Hayley to talk through my ideas with.

---

# HAYLEY ALTMAN

**OCCUPATION:** Financial Data Analyst

**BORN:** Hoboken, NJ

**LIVES:** Hoboken, NJ

### MENTOR'S ANECDOTE:

Lena and I are now in our second year of Writing 360 as mentor/mentee. Our weekly pair sessions are always fun and thoughtful. I really enjoy writing together and sharing our ideas and perspectives on everything from the news of the day, to the impact of social media, to *Gilmore Girls*.

# happy birthday

## LENA DiBIASIO

*A poem written on the eve of my seventeenth birthday after realizing
what womanhood might mean for me*

i smoothed at my wrinkles this morning,
globbing moisturizer onto my fine lines
and rubbing in outward motions.
pulling the wrinkles away, pulling, pulling, pulling.
my father let out a belly laugh like he does on sunday mornings and
    told me
that i am too young to care about such things
leave that to your mother, he said with a smile.
i did not smile back.
i have a watch from my grandmother
*to mollie—you're finally a woman, happy seventeenth*
i wore that watch every day though it could not tell time
last week, i took it off and let it rest.
i turn seventeen next month. i am not ready, i am not a woman.
i needed to do so many things, be someone else, before i became a
    woman
my heart speeds up at the thought, and i know my time has run out
i complained about this to my father, who grinned with his crooked
    teeth like he does on a sunday evening
and proclaimed that i have so much life ahead of me
my mother sat silent.

i have no time left. i haven't fallen in love or found a passion or cleared up
    my skin or found real friends or decided what kind of a person i am
and i think knowing what kind of a person you are is mighty important
    if you are going to be a woman now, not a girl.
if i am a woman as of my seventeenth birthday, then i will no longer
    be me.
i'll have children and soon i'll forget that i like the beastie boys just like
    my mother did and i'll concede to adolescent whines and let them
    play their horrible pop music instead of what i really, truly like.
    because i won't really truly like anything anymore because i'll be a
    mother and mothers can only be mothers.
my father still likes the beastie boys.
i'm scared to be a woman, i can't be seventeen yet because i haven't
    grown up and yet already my time is gone.
i apply moisturizer before bed, and the small golden watch laughs from
    its drawer, mocking me.

# FREDA DONG

**GRADE:** Sophomore

**BORN:** New York, NY

**LIVES:** Brooklyn, NY

### MENTEE'S ANECDOTE:

This is the first short story that I have completed, and my mentor has been a really great help in making this work a success. She caught plot holes that I missed, helped me bring my ideas to life, and checked my grammar. I'm so grateful to have had so much help in writing this story. Thank you, Jen!

---

# JEN STRAUS

**OCCUPATION:** Development Coordinator

**BORN:** Washington, D.C.

**LIVES:** Brooklyn, NY

**PUBLICATIONS & RECOGNITIONS:** AWP Writer to Writer Mentee Spring 2020–2021

### MENTOR'S ANECDOTE:

I wasn't sure what it would be like to get to know a mentee entirely over Zoom, but to my surprise and delight, Freda has made it easier than I could have imagined. She is always open and friendly, eager to share her life and creativity with me. I've loved working on her anthology submission and really getting to see a piece through from the tiny seeds of an idea to a nuanced and polished piece of writing. I can't wait to see how her writing continues to develop as she hones her creative voice.

# i hope your life is filled with blessings

## FREDA DONG

*Based on the ending of a real friendship, this story is about what it means to let go of nostalgia.*

Five days ago, Rina began spamming us in our group chat, which had been inactive for months.

> **GUYS STOP BEING DED**
> **PLS TALK**
> **:D**

I was tired and didn't want to Deal with her antics. Nevertheless, I texted back.

> kinda busy rn

> **We should meet up at the library**
> **Or play roblox like before**
> **Just talk guys!**
> **I miss u:(**

> i dont miss u

I smiled a little, imagining Rina groaning Dramatically like she always does when I joke with her.

> but sure, we can do smth soon
> i really gotta go do hw though so ttyl

Through the whole exchange, Lucas remained silent.

Until now.

My phone buzzed with notifications. I read his incoming texts in a daze.

> Imma be honest
> We're not friends anymore
> I haven't seen you guys in five years
> I can't remember Isabel's face
> Katerina's voice

I felt like my heart was being stabbed.

> I don't know what u guys like
> I don't talk to u guys
> It's gotten to the point where
> If you guys weren't in my life
> Nothing will change

I began typing before stopping myself. What was I supposed to say? "Hey, Lucas, we could get to know each other again. We may not talk often, but I still want you in my life! You're still my friend!" But how would he react? He sent a final text:

> We're basically strangers

That sealed it. *Oh, Lucas,* I thought, *you have always been so stubborn. Once you make up your mind nothing can persuade you.*

Feeling numb, I left the cafeteria and headed up toward the sixth floor, where Rina was hanging out with her friends. I knelt and tapped Rina on the shoulder.

"Hey, Izzy," Rina greeted me before going back to her homework.

"Rina, can I talk to you?" I asked.

"Sure," Rina replied absentmindedly. "Hold on, do you know how to solve this cubic?"

I tugged on her sleeve. "Please, Katerina, it's important." Hearing her full name, Rina focused her attention on me. I gave her my phone with *the* conversation open, and waited for her reaction. I had never seen her so silent.

"So?" I prompted.

Rina looked at me with childish, passionate anger in the face of my tired emptiness. "How dare he!" she finally said in a soft yet indignant tone.

"He's right though, isn't he?" I asked with resignation.

"That does not mean he has the right to do this!" Rina exclaimed. Thankfully, Rina's friends, the popular kids, are loud, and their noise drowned out our conversation.

"It doesn't matter whether he has the right, Lucas decided to finally address our distance. He's not wrong. After we were separated in middle school, it was always just the two of us hanging out. Lucas was never a part of it."

"Stop picking this apart like you always do."

I responded as gently as I could. "Now that we're in the same high school but Lucas is somewhere else, it makes sense that he won't be close to us at all."

Rina said nothing.

I sighed. "Think about how you want to respond. This will probably be our final contact with him. Let's end things on a good note."

I stood up and patted Rina on the shoulder, but she grabbed my hand and said, "I don't believe this is the end for us."

"Then tell Lucas that. We can talk more later, but I need to get to class."

As I traveled up the escalator, my mind scrambled to find a response to this mess.

Even though I wanted a reconciliation between the three of us, I know it's impossible. I wished we could go back to the days of elementary school, playing and studying together, making fun of Rina and Lucas for liking Barbie. Sitting on a bench, I gathered all my sincerity, and opened up a direct message to Lucas.

> its true what you said in the gc which is why i wanted to reconnect with you for so long, but idk how

We can't

ik. Rina might think otherwise.
nevertheless I treasure the memories
we made in elementary school.
and I hope you'll be happy

I'll talk to Katerina about it
Same but it's time to just let it go
You too

best wishes to you! and i really hope you'll
remember us as I will you. maybe one day
we'll be friends again, but probably not.
i hope your life is filled with blessings.
goodbye

Same
Bye

Tears stung my eyes. Lucas doesn't give a shit about us anymore. Yet I couldn't help but be relieved everything's over. Lucas was the only one brave enough to speak the truth about our friendship. Rina had clung on to a past long gone and I was too cowardly to say anything.

I wiped my eyes, took a deep breath, and composed myself. This was for the best. For all of us. No matter how I felt. As the bell rang and students poured into the hallway, I put a smile on my face and walked into class.

# NYELA DOUKOURÉ

**GRADE:** Freshman

**BORN:** New York, NY

**LIVES:** New York, NY

### MENTEE'S ANECDOTE:

Meeting once a week has increased my writing habits. Whenever anyone asks me how Girls Write Now is going, I say, "Well, I'm writing a lot more!"

---

# JENNY BROWN

**OCCUPATION:** Copy and Research Chief

**BORN:** West Orange, NJ

**LIVES:** West Orange, NJ

### MENTOR'S ANECDOTE:

I had the privilege of watching Nyela write in real time, and see beautiful phrases come out naturally and spontaneously. It was wonderful to witness!

# The Inheritance of Hate

## NYELA DOUKOURÉ

*A short poem from the thoughts of a Black girl*

*"If there is no enemy within, the enemy outside can do no harm."*

If there is no hate within, no hate can escape
But how can one rid oneself of hate when one is born with it?
Hate passed down through generations
Built up over centuries, getting stronger and stronger
My anger is not mine.

I inherited it from those before me, a fire they constantly add wood to
Hatred of those who swim in gold
Envy of those who bathe in milk while others are famished
Scorn for those who lay in their mansions and scoff at those who beg
Loathing for their ignorance, their unawareness and unwillingness to
   understand
Resentment of those who live in the body of my dreams, which I will
   never achieve.

That bitterness runs deep through my blood
I cry from pain that is not mine,
I scream in agony from the open wounds from centuries ago that
   should have been closed.

From a young age I knew I was not wanted
I didn't belong

I envy those with smooth silk that runs from their head
Their long shiny hair that moves like wind, overshadowing the cotton
    that is sprung from my head
Their eyes come out in rainbow colors that reflect the world and its
    elements
While mine is comparable to manure.

There is nothing beautiful about the color brown
It is often associated with dirt, worthless and repulsive
The color brown is not lovable, it's not beautiful.

Is my life worth less than your feelings?
Always told to be proud of my color but never taught
Use your "black power" but not against your master
Why can't I raise my fist to fight and protest?
How can I say I love to be black when that very thing puts me in
    danger?
Everything I was taught was to ensure the comfort and safety of other
    people
Bending over backwards and taking every negative comment
God forbid you ever fight back
Raising your voice makes you angry and an animal who needs to be
    muzzled and contained.

Like a snake I wish to shed the blood of the past
To let go of everything to stop the lingering pain
I wish to get rid of the enemy within.

# MIA DOWDELL

**GRADE:** Junior

**BORN:** Redondo Beach, CA

**LIVES:** Redondo Beach, CA

### MENTEE'S ANECDOTE:

I learn so much from T.D. each week. She is able to make such wide, unexpected connections between words in a way that has changed the way I look at things in my day-to-day life. It's like she can find meaning in anything, and can transform even the most mundane details into a story. T.D. is insightful, well-spoken, and very dedicated to helping me with my goals. Even though she leads a busy life, she still makes time to talk to me and sort out the nitty-gritty in my writing.

---

# T. D. MITCHELL

**OCCUPATION:** Playwright, Screenwriter, Speechwriter

**BORN:** Brooklyn, NY

**LIVES:** Brooklyn, NY

### MENTOR'S ANECDOTE:

When Mia and I began this program, she was already a practiced journalist, actively writing. We're now having fun exploring various other forms, genres, and styles to free up our imaginations to employ imagery and symbolism, fictions and poetry, dialogue and wordplay. Her reporter's keen sense of observation coupled with her fierce curiosity make for a dynamic combination, and always stimulating conversation during our meetings. Her questions keep me on my toes! We're outliers—on the left coast most of this school year—and ambassadors of a sort as Girls Write Now expands its scope. Mia leads us bravely onward!

# oysters & ceviche

## MIA DOWDELL

*i am suffocated in it.*

my throat inflates, a starchy desperate
life vest at the sound of sharp
linen slacks flicking political
venom off their tongues. cellar Burgundy
sends mildewed arrows through the cartilage of
my blunt nose. i guess the cup of Tide and my
bathroom sink weren't Enough to
wash the grisliness from my hollowed-out
pocket. it was never
this difficult to swallow. just two
days ago, i laid in an ocean. i let the
shy babbling of the living room heater
cradle my shoulders, let it inhale
peripheral noise. now, i am newborn
sea kelp tugged in every direction and
nailed to hardwood floor. cyclical fading, tarring
of the sky does little to dim the sour of
these chandelier lights. circling of
shadowed sharks; raw red donor dollars their
highlighted entrée. and there they are,
my parents, making their twentieth act
as their circus seals.

# JADE DUFFUS

**GRADE:** Junior

**BORN:** Tampa, FL

**LIVES:** New York, NY

**PUBLICATIONS & RECOGNITIONS:** Winner of the OCA-NY Hate Crime Prevention Art Contest 2021; Winner of the Arts Connection: The Unsounded Path (Writing and Art)

### MENTEE'S ANECDOTE:

Being with my mentor, Donica, has been such a wonderful experience. I have never really had a mentor in my life before, but Donica has become such an inspiration; she is more than just my mentor. I have learned so much from her and her experiences in the "Down Under." I love how open-minded and courageous she is, especially in terms of writing. Her creativity truly inspires me and pushes me to have that same authenticity in my writing. Even though we may have completely different cultural backgrounds and her accent is way cooler than mine, I am so proud to call her my mentor.

---

# DONICA BETTANIN

**OCCUPATION:** Graduate Student

**BORN:** Benalla, Australia

**LIVES:** New York, NY

### MENTOR'S ANECDOTE:

Meeting up with Jade is always a highlight of my week! We both find inspiration in writing and art, and always have fun comparing notes on the talks and workshops we attend together. We come from opposite sides of the world (and grew up pronouncing "Adidas" totally differently!), but we both love learning about other cultures, whether that is from each other or through reading and exploring. Jade is brilliant, kind, curious, and full of purpose. She amazes me with her capacity for critical thinking and creative expression, and I can't wait for the whole world to hear her voice.

# Eat My Brain, I Dare You

## JADE DUFFUS AND DONICA BETTANIN

*A cocky girl in the midst of a zombie apocalypse. Will she survive?*

"Tick, tick, tick." That old dusty clock hanging on the old dusty white wall keeps making that weird scratching sound as the hands tick.

It moves so eloquently but makes the most annoying noise as it barely touches 11:26 a.m. I can't even focus on this stupid test. I can feel the beads of sweat drip from my forehead and slowly, ever so slowly, creep to the tip of my chin. My ADHD gets the best of me, and I tip my head to the sound of Shirley McLogan tapping her pen on the hard wooden desk, swirling it around and around as she does so: "Tap, tap, tap."

I can feel Smelly Sammy's hot, shaky breath on the back of my neck as he sighs in desperation for some answer. As if his brain could regurgitate a math equation. Everything around me starts to slow and my senses quicken. I finally acknowledge our proctor. She is an old, raggedy woman with a deep scowl on her face; I've never seen the woman smile once. For someone of such an old age, she can hear the slightest movement of a pen dropping. She slowly raises her head from her big book and searches the classroom for her next victim. With slight tension, I focus my attention back to the question before I become Ms. Cadwell's next meal.

*

*In the building next door, Assistant Principal Reggie Tang leans back in his chair. With the students' bags and cell phones secured in lockers outside his office and the SATs under way, he finally has a moment to himself. Reggie refreshes the* New York Times *website, curious about the human outbreak of the "zombie deer" virus that's been traced to Hudson Heights Hospital. He opens another tab to check Google Maps. The hospital is just a couple blocks away. The name of the virus has to be an exaggeration . . . doesn't it?*

＊

I've been stuck on this stupid question for a while now. I should've studied Linear Equations instead of kissing Bryan Barlowe under the bleachers after his amazing, death-defying football game.

The classroom is completely white: no posters, no wallpapers, no signs that scream "VOTE FOR BRIE LOCKWOOD FOR SENIOR PRESIDENT" or bright blue stickers that say "GO WILDCATS." It's empty and bare, a reflection of what the education system is like in America, a system that keeps pushing exams and tests to separate the dummies from the Einsteins, the future 7-Eleven workers from the MIT graduates.

In this hot, smelly, anxious, depressing, bare white room I can't focus on anything but the end of this day. There aren't any windows, just large gray shutters to shield us from the outside world. The sounds of honking cars, wheels smashing against the wet, slick roads, and the rushing of the rain falling from its gray counterparts engulf the space.

＊

*At nearby Hudson Heights Hospital, Nurse Selma Kale unwraps the bandage on her arm. She's running a fever, and the skin where Patient X—the "zombie virus" patient—scratched her is pulsing. Nurse Kale signs out early and swipes a tube of Neosporin from the supply cupboard for the scratch. She wants to pick her son up from school then go home to get some sleep.*

＊

I turn my attention back to question number five. The lines showing a linear graph mark my paper, pushing me to write at least a number down, but absolutely nothing comes into my mind.

"Noah! Noah the Know-It-All," I scream in my head. He could probably give me the answer, if I could get his attention. Out of hope, I slightly angle my head in his direction and tap my sneakers on the hard concrete floor: nothing. I do it again but louder and closer: nothing. Sighing in defeat because Noah is obviously blind. My attention goes back to number five, which is my lucky number, but today this number is not on my side.

*

*Reggie Tang looks up in surprise as his office door swings open.*

*"Mrs. Kale—" he begins, noticing that she looks a little, well, a little green. When she opens her mouth the sound that comes out is low and coarse.*

*"My son," she growls.*

*"He's in the SATs," Reggie says. He tries not to stare at the thin line of drool extending from the side of her mouth.*

*"My son," she insists. Selma Kale lurches forward and climbs over the desk, sending papers sliding to the floor. Reggie realizes too late that she is strong—supernaturally strong. In his last human moments he thrusts his hand under the desk and slams the red emergency button labeled LOCK-DOWN.*

*

"BRRRINGGG." The bell for dismissal rings and I look at the old, dusty clock, on the old dusty white wall again. It's 11:55 a.m., but I thought we had about an hour and forty-five minutes left. That stupid old clock is broken and I'm definitely failing!

As the proctor comes around to pick up our exams, the croaky, brittle voice of Principal Ahmed descends over the small classroom, but he doesn't sound cocky and miserable like usual, with his thick Russian accent. He sounds desperate. And . . . terrified?

# SALMA ELHANDAOUI

**GRADE:** Junior

**BORN:** Brooklyn, NY

**LIVES:** Brooklyn, NY

**PUBLICATIONS & RECOGNITIONS:**
Moth All-City StorySLAM
Participant; Founder and Writer for
PARAEDU; Social Media
Ambassador and Activist for Girls Inc.

## MENTEE'S ANECDOTE:

Ashley is an amazing person. While meeting for various months, I noticed that we shared interests in particular genres (horror and mystery), and we had deep-rooted conversations about current events, historical events, and interesting concepts of transcendentalism. These conversations lightened our meetings significantly, and helped me understand her perspective and belief systems. She has been productive, helpful, and friendly as she guided me throughout the writing process and advised me to brainstorm my story ideas extensively so that we could make the best out of our submission.

---

# ASHLEY ALBERT

**OCCUPATION:** Freelance
Proofreader and Copyeditor

**BORN:** Brooklyn, NY

**LIVES:** Brooklyn, NY

**PUBLICATIONS & RECOGNITIONS:**
Coeditor of *Drawing Power: True
Stories of Sexual Assault,*
*Harassment, and Survival* (winner of the Eisner Award for Best Anthology, 2020); Editor of *The X-Files: The Official Archives: Cryptids, Biological Anomalies, and Parapsychic Phenomena* by Paul Terry and *The Illustrated Feminist* by Aura Lewis

## MENTOR'S ANECDOTE:

Salma and I have so much in common, it's spooky. Not only do we both love horror, mystery, and true crime, but we are also both insatiably curious about the inner workings of society and human nature. Our conversations feel like they could go on for hours—we never run out of things to dissect and analyze. I can always count on her to be up for a wide-ranging discussion about fascinating subjects—and to swap film, TV, and book recommendations with me. Salma's perceptiveness, curiosity, and appetite for art and wisdom are what make her such a creative and inventive writer.

# The Artificial Universe of Imminent Destruction: Diary Entry One

## SALMA ELHANDAOUI

*A human female refugee records her perceptions of a universe controlled by unethical robots while anticipating an attack from bloodthirsty vampires that want to destroy humankind and AI beings alike.*

### DIARY ENTRY ONE

**Date:** Ludimina 24th, 3007 Anno Domini (A.D.)
**Day:** Tuesday
**Time:** 6:30 Post Meridiem

Dear Diary,

Last night, I had nightmares unlike any that I have had before. My human structure was consumed by bloodthirsty snakes who robbed my soul completely and shattered my human form into empty space.

Yesterday, I remember the school day finally ending while depressed clouds darkened and compressed. Amid feeling relief to arrive soon at our mansion, I saw my father, his shocked face, boiled with fear as he drove me in his Dominacol Valdo car. Amid watching the one-thousandth episode of *Trakasi Racamali* on the electronic screen attached to my pale skin. Amid the atrocious laughter tingling through my soul. Amid the screeching noise coming from the speedy vehicles, I saw a galvanized billboard spanning thousands of feet across the Town of Lamlo, depicting a "Battle of Impending Doom," and depicting that my life might end soon, perhaps that very day!

That's all I can remember, a clear memory among millions of shattered and unimportant scenes. I still can't forget the president's face, smiling from thousands of miles away. I still can't forget the fact that vampires will be raging into this universe to destroy humans yet again and drink their blood. I can't forget this particular day, which I thought would be my end. Nevertheless, I can't wait to bring you with me on this hazardous journey that might be like heaven or like hell.

Today, I woke up to the domineering noises blazing outside of my bedroom windows. Threatening alarms overflow my ears. Electromagnetic airplanes fly in the dreadful sky. The extravagant cars drive above ground level with glamorous sounds. Again I can see with my passionate eyes hundreds of billboards of Gelfling Ureu, the president of the Universe of Belinda, on an infinite loop. I can see him telling humans and robots to prepare for the worst . . . throwing propaganda through electronic screens without endeavoring to prevent war. I know we're doomed and it's crystal obvious. Vampires from the Universe of Nosferatu always defeated us in previous wars.

How are humans even alive anymore? We should be extinct by now. We are controlled by machines and robots as they become more powerful than the human race. We lost our original home, the Universe of Virgo Supercluster of Galaxies (UVSG), to robots that destroyed our universe using advanced computational algorithms. We have been living under the control of computers for eight years. Now that I'm in my twenties, I've begun to realize that I, and ALL other human beings, have no clue how this destructive domination came into play. Gelfling Ureu hid everything from us to promote censorship and to eradicate free speech, but I won't let that happen any longer. I will prevent the "War of Impending Doom" and those vicious vampires from gulping human blood and flesh yet again, but stopping this event comes with uncertain consequences.

As I stand up from my comfortable bed to recharge my energy, I use a lifelong Rybome Reflex device to acquire vigor for the rest of the week without the necessity of sleep so that my liveliness can escalate tremendously. Eventually, I position my radiological detector in my brain to present my Intelligence Quotient identification visibly on my head as regulated by the government and analytics. Entering the family dressing room, I see my parents as they exit from their transmogrifying dressing machines, which automatically place robotic shields on their bodies. My father, Ambose Lucinda, dresses himself in his bespoke white coat with black denim pants, preparing to commence his driving journey to Invincible Scientific, the most prestigious science company in Madagascarophis Castaway, the largest city in the Universe of Belinda. Simultaneously, my mother, Aurora Manich Lucinda, wears a shiny dress with a brown coat layered on top before driving her vehicle to the Electrical Engineering Facility where she works.

I feel like my heart might burst any second as I realize humans are conforming to the emotionless creatures who run our universe, and that I'm one of those people who is obliged to obey such powerful yet pitiful machines. My heart is telling me to go to Konoha Onegai Island. Seeing Gelfling Ureu's mendacious face fueled my desire to discover the history of these three universes. To know if the UVSG still exists. To know if humans can escape from any more suffering inflicted by these selfish creatures. To know if I'm capable of entering this island to expose Gelfling Ureu's lies. To know if I can awaken people from their blind adherence to strange policies. To know if what the witch, Dramali, said to me were lies. Now, I must go to Konoha Onegai to find the TRUTH.

—CHARMAINE LUCINDA—
*From the Universe of Belinda*

# ALLISON ELLIOTT

**GRADE:** Senior

**BORN:** Brooklyn, NY

**LIVES:** Brooklyn, NY

### MENTEE'S ANECDOTE:

To me, Crystal is one of the friends I never knew I needed in life. She has always been more than willing to not only absorb and appreciate my work, but critique it in a way that makes me learn and grow as a writer. Whether it's a shared love for Marvel or an understanding of my general thought process, we can relate on topics and ideas, making two heads much better than one in every meeting that we have had. Crystal truly is a lifeline, and I look forward to keeping her in my life for years to come.

---

# CRYSTAL CAIN

**OCCUPATION:** Literacy Tutor

**BORN:** Baltimore, MD

**LIVES:** Baltimore, MD

**PUBLICATIONS & RECOGNITIONS:** The Morgan State University Adele V. Holden Creative Writing Prize

### MENTOR'S ANECDOTE:

Allison is a girl that is always full of life and new ideas that take us on a new adventure every meeting. She has always been receptive to new ideas, and I have watched her grow as a writer over our time spent together. All of her ideas bring something new and inventive to the table so we can spend hours discussing them. I truly enjoy working with her and being able to guide her on her creative journey, and I cannot wait to see what comes next.

# Always There

## ALLISON ELLIOTT

*Bed-Stuy had always been home for Jordan, but what will he do when something seems to be coming for him? Sometimes the real monsters are closer than you think.*

The ache of his muscles weighed him down as he landed onto the long bench that made up the subway car seats. Jordan spread out in the car, his belongings melting off of his body as he melted into the seat. As the train began to move, he shut his eyes, oblivious to the judgment-filled glares directed his way from other commuters. Taking solace in the rest space he purchased for $2.75 through his ocher-yellow MetroCard, he allowed the movement of the car to relax his body.

Jordan quickly shot up as he felt something stare at him. As he glanced around the nearly empty car and the previously judgmental passengers averted their gaze, he still felt the piercing stare of dark eyes. At each stop, the feeling grew, and he felt it as he caught the movement of something not inside the train . . . but outside. He noticed it out of the side of his eye, moving just out of sight before he could truly take a look. His legs bounced as his eyes followed everyone who got on or off the train, counting down the stops.

As his stop came, Jordan gathered his things, dashing out of the train car, unaware of the woman who unclutched her handbag once he left. He fought against his fatigue as he ran up the stairs and out of the station. Something lurked in the shadows, moving at the same pace that Jordan did. Something so menacing, daring him to look back. Soon, he felt his spirits lift as the bus stop came into view, having a few other people already waiting.

Stopping just before he ran into the other people, he strolled under its cover, ignoring the hammering of his lungs and heart. He shut his eyes once more while he smoothed the waves of his hair. Once the bus rolled up the street, Jordan opened his eyes. He was the first in the line to board, unaware of the massive gap between him and other passengers. He dropped his MetroCard into the card slot, satisfied by the high-pitched beeping sound of his free transfer taking effect.

By then, the film of sweat that covered his forehead was only one of the many signs of anxiousness his body was producing. It was a battle between his mind and his nerves to see which would win control of his muscles. His legs wouldn't stop bouncing while his bottom was glued to the seat, trying to stop himself from running off the moving bus. He watched the streets go by, the multiple buildings blurring while the vehicle gained speed. His heart sank. There it was again, the dark figure, moving fluidly alongside the bus, as if it was preparing to board at the next stop.

"Damn it!" Jordan cursed out loud, dropping his backpack to the ground. He was shocked by the hurried movement of people to the back of the bus that followed directly after, bringing their things with them as they shuffled past. In disbelief, he looked around, as he was the only one left in the front. Before he could say anything, he caught the movement of the figure out of the corner of his eye once more.

His breathing began to steady as he recognized the buildings that surrounded his stop. The old house that was turned into a set of new apartments, all decked out in the same bland "modern" exterior with the highest prices in the area. The well-known thrift store that was still overrun with teenage girls who had deep pockets and reseller accounts tucked away on their phones. Taking this as a sign, he got up from his seat, tuning out the people who backed away despite being bunched up into the corner of the bus. Jordan bounced with anticipation as he watched the dark shadow trail behind, waiting to see the green lights over the exit door come on. As soon as they did, he pushed out of the bus and began running in the direction of his house.

The recently altered businesses soon grew apart in frequency as his feet hit the sidewalk. He felt the shadow draw closer and closer as he pushed himself to run faster, quickly making the turn at the Jamaican restaurant that had managed to stay open since he was a child. His hands reached into the pocket of his pants to find his keys as he skipped up the stairs leading to his front door. Fumbling as his heart raced, he opened the front door, not daring to check where the figure was. He immediately turned to lock the door, not wanting to invite the figure, or its menacing presence, inside. As the locks clicked, he breathed a sigh of relief, his shoulders visibly sinking as the anxiety slid off of his body.

Putting down his backpack on the ground, Jordan looked up to the ceiling in thankfulness, oblivious to the odd darkness and silence that hung over the house. As he turned around, he saw it, waiting to come for him.

# ANAÍS FERNÁNDEZ

**GRADE:** Senior

**BORN:** San Francisco, CA

**LIVES:** Astoria, NY

**PUBLICATIONS & RECOGNITIONS:**
Scholastic Art & Writing Awards: Honorable Mention

## MENTEE'S ANECDOTE:

My second year working with Kayla has been amazing. Although we live on opposite sides of the country, for an hour every week it feels like we're in the same room. Kayla has been extraordinarily helpful in my college process, as well as continuing to develop my writing as we prepare portfolio pieces. Kayla is an incredibly important mentor and supporter in my writing and my life, and I know we will continue to stay in touch past my graduation from Writing 360.

---

# KAYLA THURBER

**OCCUPATION:** Student

**BORN:** Boca Raton, FL

**LIVES:** Tempe, AZ

## MENTOR'S ANECDOTE:

Anaís and I are working together for our second year now, and what a wonderful second year it has been! Although there's now a reasonable distance between us—2,444 miles from Queens, NY, to Tempe, AZ (to be exact)—our relationship continues to grow closer. As a senior, Anaís is spending most of this year applying to colleges. Through completing applications, I have been able to support her as she creates a polished portfolio, allowing me to read all of the fantastic work she has written. I am extremely proud of her and cannot wait to see what she achieves!

# i'm worried about her

## ANAÍS FERNÁNDEZ

**Content Warning:** transphobia

*An ode to hers everywhere*

she worries enough already
worries enough to worry at her years
her worry watches the time
with quaking knees and scared eyes

her,
who stares out the window like
some unsmiling Mona Lisa
counting her heartbeats like a countdown
believing the world turns too fast

have you heard her?
she cries for help and refuses it in one breath
a nasty cycle, passing tidal
waves in her pillow, caught by cotton
her mouth tired of holding itself up

her,
who cries
her,
who lies

her,
whose eyes
see nothing but the hers left behind

her,
who cradles her child, who freefalls,
spine spinning to the concrete
who tries to be an octopus mother even when
the sharks won't eat

her,
who holds her hands up
palms up
psalms up
looking for help from a man who hurts her
with a Bible in his belt

her,
voice loud even with her mouth closed
who stands up and whose eyes glow
fists clenched even with her heart open
skin bare even with herself roped in

her,
who loves her,
her,
who everyone still calls "him,"
him,
who is trying, trying to understand,
what it means to be
her.

her,
who isn't here yet

her,
who left too early
her,
who's right on time

her,
who gives herself without losing herself
her,
who doesn't yet know how it feels to be prey
her,
who has known since puberty
her,
who feels unwanted fingerprints like dried paint
who has nightmares that taste like copper.

her,
who's waiting for someone
to worry about her

i'm worried about her.

# JAZMINE FLORENCIO

**GRADE:** Senior

**BORN:** Queens, NY

**LIVES:** Ridgewood, NY

### MENTEE'S ANECDOTE:

My mentor has inspired me to write more deeply about my feelings and experiences. In addition, she motivates me to be more descriptive in my writing. There isn't a moment when I don't think of what she might suggest when I am writing on my own time.

---

# MARY DARBY

**OCCUPATION:** Public Relations Writer/Editor

**BORN:** Peekskill, NY

**LIVES:** New York, NY

### MENTOR'S ANECDOTE:

Jazmine is so insightful. It's one of the reasons I love working with her. She is observant and compassionate, which makes for lovely writing. This particular piece was a real process of exploration for her, and I love how it came out.

# Pan Dulce in My Veins

## JAZMINE FLORENCIO

*This piece is about my life in a family of bakers.*

Everyone's family has a thing—a trait that is particular to their family. They might have a long line of science lovers. Or maybe excellent cooks. In some cases, singers.

My family's "thing" is baking. We have four competing bakeries in the Florencio family. My father opened the first one in 2001, before my sister and I were even born. Soon after that, many of my aunts and uncles were inspired by my father's success and decided to open their businesses, all of them less than a mile from one another. In 2013, after my father passed away, my mother took over the business with the help of my step-father.

While many families argue about politics and money over holiday dinners, my family argued over eggs. Who took eggs from whom? Who stole whose recipe? Even after my dad passed away, the bickering continued. Customers often come to our bakery and complain about prices or even poor customer service at the other bakeries. The drama never stops. But at the end of the day, my relatives compete with one another because they want what's best for their own families.

Most of my childhood took place in my parents' bakery, which specializes in tres leches cakes and pan dulce, also known as sweet bread. I always loved the sweet bread, often topped with sugar and accompanied by coffee in the mornings. My favorite smell of all smells is the pan dulce baking in the ovens. The aroma has also captivated people walking by, many of whom come in to ask about that delicious smell.

My dad tried to pass down his passion for baking to me. But the brown sticky dough in between my fingers always made me feel uneasy. I was never too fond of the dough and how hard it was to work with. I knew that baking wasn't my strongest suit, even at the age of five. The form of my pastry demonstrated that. Mine stood out—the only rectangle in a tray of eleven flat brown balls.

After my dad passed away, my stepdad always welcomed me to the bakery's kitchen, where the magic happened. I would sit on a closed bucket of strawberry icing while watching the way his hands delicately placed rectangular-shaped bread into a container of tres leches, letting the bread soak in the milk for a couple of seconds before carefully placing it on a plate for the fruit and icing.

I watched in awe, taking everything in. The smell of the pan dulce baking in the giant out-of-date ovens that my mom had been trying to get rid of for years. My brother working at the cash register, catching up with a regular customer on neighborhood gossip. Beside him, my mom eavesdropping while looking over the cake orders for the next day. My twin sister decorating the cakes that my stepdad had finished baking. It was always her favorite thing to do.

I noticed over the years the impact that the bakeries had on my family. My aunts and uncles worked so hard to open the businesses. But they never wanted their own children to take over their jobs. Instead, they wanted them to move up in life.

Just like my father. Even though he founded the first Florencio bakery, he encouraged me not to work there. He didn't want me to work at the family business. Instead, he wanted me to study hard to one day become a doctor or a lawyer. He always told me I was destined to do better.

Of course, at seven years old, I didn't know what he meant. But, to be fair, I also thought that having a family of bakers was normal. Didn't everyone's families argue over eggs and milk?

But deep inside, even at seven years old, I knew that I was destined to become a lawyer. Although I didn't have delicate hands to make pastries, I did have a strong and firm voice that I could use for good. I could use that voice to help underprivileged communities.

Although my dad was proud to be the first business owner in the family, he knew that he had sacrificed a lot. He didn't want that for me. He wanted me to have a job that didn't require a lot of physical labor. He often spoke of how I should have an office job, where I could sit at a desk in front of a computer instead of standing all day and getting swollen hands or feet.

Pan dulce continues to be a significant part of my life. It grounds me and reminds me of where I come from. Where my parents came from. But regardless of what I accomplish or where I am destined to be, my family's bakery will always be my first home, where I learned to walk, where I learned to climb the Bimbo bread cart, where my aspirations developed. Pan dulce is a part of my family, a part of me, and in my veins.

# ALYSSA FOWLER

**GRADE:** Junior

**BORN:** Queens, NY

**LIVES:** New York, NY

### MENTEE'S ANECDOTE:

Every Thursday we meet, and for sixty minutes, I am finally able to breathe. In our first meeting, Sherrill told me that she would always challenge me, but I did not realize how much I'd look forward to this challenge. She's taught me to tell a story through the rise and fall of the voice and has been a mentor not only in writing but in life. Being able to work one-on-one with her has been amazing and I look forward to more learning in the future.

---

# SHERRILL COLLINS-RICHARDSON

**OCCUPATION:** Program Administrator

**BORN:** New York, NY

**LIVES:** New York, NY

# Alyssa

## SHERRILL COLLINS-RICHARDSON

*This poem is for my mentee.*

Our first meet
Well, what did you think?
Professional apparel with book in hand?
No, that wouldn't work
Because I wanted more!
I wanted her imagination
Her thoughts
Her creative juices
I wanted her to Déverse son âme
Pour out her soul!
We sat on Zoom
She sipping OJ and I warm tea
In our cozy space
With our thoughts
Our imaginations
Our creative juices pouring from our souls
Silently we played with words
Juste nous, Just us
Juste moi, Just me
Juste toi, Just you
Just Alyssa

# Thoughts of an Insecure Man

## ALYSSA FOWLER

**Content Warning:** domestic abuse

*This piece takes a deep dive into societal expectations while empha-sizing the importance of asking for help. Everyone, even someone who doesn't look like it, needs support.*

Lingering eyes • Anger • Agitated cries • Sadness • Embarrassment • Shame

### Thoughts of an Insecure Man

He wore this dark cloak to protect himself
Thick and pigmented, it should have been impregnable
So why did he still feel their eyes on him?
Why did the heat of their prodding stares still poke through?
Could he be seen underneath this mask?
And would they?—

"Julius" a voice calls distantly

Could they?—

"Julius" he hears

The voice softens, "Jules" they say

"Yes" he responds

Finally facing her, she's allowed to gaze into his eyes where the suppressed flood is threatening to take over

Her arm tries to stabilize the tremors, a promise of safety stands in the embrace

Julius almost wants to lean into her touch, but "a man never leans on a woman" he remembers

So he stays still

"What happened?"

She asks carefully, studying the motion in his eyes

Julius can't quite bear the heat of her gaze, so he lets his eyes fall

He hears her breaths getting deeper and feels his heart shatter because he shouldn't be the one to need help

Look at how much distress it's bringing his friend

Julius doesn't know if he could handle the sound of her cry, which was so profound that with one crash, it'd break his fortress down and the bricks would dissolve into concrete, mixing with the water, and leaving no hope for repair

So, he relocks his eyes with hers, and without words, she knows

Her mouth parts slightly, as a concentrated look takes over her face

It is as if she is recalling all the scars that she'd dismissed as personal injury

A tired sigh leaves Julius's mouth

The armor that he had spent so long carefully crafting was brought down within an instant

Protection, up in the air

With the buzzing hospital lights edging him on, he pulls back the gown to look at his body in the light for the first time

His skin was black and blue

Cuts raked up his body, stopping at the neck, where his dad knew he'd be facing life if he cut any further

All of his knuckles were red for every single time he tried to leave and his legs were covered in welts as punishment

They were far up enough so that a nosy neighbor wouldn't see, but
     close enough that Julius was reminded of his deviance every time he
     tried to pee
His forearms were completely spotless, but his upper arms had been
     sliced long ago
His body struggled to heal wounds from somebody who they did not
     recognize as an enemy
When he touched his stomach, he could almost hear the words of his
     father as he rammed into him
The cigarette ash once again overwhelmed him and the game show he
     used to watch with his mother was playing in the distance

"Worthless"
Wheel
"Useless"
Of
"Piece of crap"
Fortune

Out of pure reflex, he'd tried blocking a hit
And he felt his father's heavy brown boots slam back into him so
     forcefully, that his eyes threatened to close
His father told him to stay awake, that he needed to remember what
     he'd done, that he'd deserved this
And the memory is enough to make his breath shake fiercely as he
     draws in
Exhaling, tears rack his body, his shoulders shake and reduce his voice
     to an unrecognizable blubber
Soon the flood overwhelmed all vision
With these tears, the boy lost so long ago was being called upon
He cried for all the tears that could never fall because "a man wasn't
     supposed to cry"
He cried for all the days gone by that he could not sleep because he'd
     wake up to his nightmare

He cried for all the people he'd shut out because the truth would be too
    much
He cried for his mother who was probably in Heaven, feeling torn apart
He cried for the person he could have been if only his destiny had not
    been intertwined with a monster's
He cried for all those times he could not bear the sight of himself
Julius cried because he was afraid to prove his father right
He was afraid to be a burden
He was afraid to be unwanted
He was afraid to be anything like people's expectations of him
But he feels a hand wipe his tears away
He feels her hold him and say "it's okay"
"It will be okay" he could hear his mother say
So he held on tighter to the girl and held on tight to the words
It will be okay
Somehow

# KAMARA FRASER

**GRADE:** Sophomore

**BORN:** Brooklyn, NY

**LIVES:** Brooklyn, NY

### MENTEE'S ANECDOTE:

Meeting with my mentor, Katy, has been a refreshing experience for me and has really helped me improve the quality and caliber of my writing. She has really helped me with planning and formatting my work to make sure it reads nicely. One way we practiced this is by doing the "Stream of Consciousness" exercise, which helps me to get all of my thoughts out, from which she would help us pull out pieces and build on them. She's very understanding and flexible, and I've enjoyed getting to know her!

---

# KATY SACKS

**OCCUPATION:** Executive Assistant to Senior Vice President of Integrated Marketing (CBS News and Sports)

**BORN:** London, England

**LIVES:** New York, NY

### MENTOR'S ANECDOTE:

Kamara is a bright and curious person. It was no surprise to me when she decided to write about a career in medicine for her anthology submission. Her eagerness to learn and develop her writing made my role as her mentor incredibly easy. I have no doubt that she will achieve whatever she sets out to do. I have loved every moment and hope that we will write together again in the future!

# My Saving Grace

## KAMARA FRASER

*"My Saving Grace" is about my dream of becoming a doctor as a high-schooler during the COVID-19 pandemic.*

I once found pleasure in a place most children dread
The home to checkups and surgeries
And emergency room visits
Where I would observe my heroes helping and healing

Using Walmart stethoscopes and toys from Target
I used to diagnose my best friend and stuffed animals
A game I enjoyed
Playing the part of the hero

On career day, my white coat was buttoned
I wandered the school halls with my tools in hand
Proud of my make-believe profession
Then the world changed

The pandemic spread quickly
With it, loneliness became all too familiar a feeling
Locked-down, locked-in, and lock-ing people out
Together, my family watched the news

Could we be next? The fear splintered me like a puzzle
Death rates rose, my sanity declined

Agonizing news lingered and my helplessness grew
But always, the end-of-shift applause would piece me back together

Essential workers up at the brink of dawn
Dressed in hazmat suits and superhero capes
Making sacrifices that nobody can see
Scrubs on, saving lives and gifting breath

I dream of becoming a hero
Of protecting a life with my bare hands
I will bring color to a world in black-and-white for I am the light in
    the dark
Remember me

# CLAIRE GIANNOSA

**GRADE:** Senior

**BORN:** New York, NY

**LIVES:** New York, NY

### MENTEE'S ANECDOTE:

I am so grateful I have gotten to know my mentor, Anna, over the past three years. Her strength, kindness, and intelligence continually inspire me. Although our relationship has mainly been virtual, she has been a constant support, one that has completely changed me for the better. We've bonded over Taylor Swift, Jane Austen, and our March birthdays, and we've also written about our similar experiences turning sixteen and have turned visual paintings into poetry—Anna's writing is beautiful. Because of her, I am proud of my writing evolution, and have the confidence to take the next step in my life.

---

# ANNA HUMPHREY

**OCCUPATION:** Consultant

**BORN:** Lexington, KY

**LIVES:** New York, NY

### MENTOR'S ANECDOTE:

The first time I met Claire, she was so quiet I wasn't sure it was going to work. How could I get her to open up, help her find her voice? The first time I read her work, I realized I'd worried for nothing. Her voice was so crisp, so clear, so strong it practically leapt off the page. No matter what genres she tried or edits I suggested, it kept on shining through. It's been a joy to watch her grow in confidence, both as a writer and a young woman. I'll miss her greatly next year.

# Lost Child

## CLAIRE GIANNOSA

*In this short story excerpt, immediately after her (supposed) imagi-
nary friend saves her from a terrible fall into a ravine, a young girl
is whisked away from her lonely days into a world of adventure.*

"Ellie?" the voice asked.

Eloisa knew that voice; she would know that voice anywhere.

She opened her eyes. "Wren?"

Wren exhaled and collapsed over her. "Oh, Ellie, I thought you were
dead!"

"I'm not dead," Eloisa croaked, wondering if she actually might be.
"You saved me? How?"

"I just pulled you from the water," Wren replied.

"But . . ." Eloisa growled in frustration and sat up slowly. "*How?
You aren't—you're not—*" She paused, then started again. "Wren. You
aren't *real.*"

Wren simply laughed. "Come on, I have to show you something."

He started moving purposefully through the woods, and Eloisa had
no choice but to follow.

"Where are we going?"

"You'll see," Wren replied, slipping through a dense brush and dis-
appearing.

Eloisa followed, peering out at what lay beyond. They were in a large
clearing: A circle of elm trees acted as a border, and Eloisa could hear the
faint roar of the ravine close by. A firepit sat in the center, a dull orange

flame flickering off dozens of stones surrounding it. On the stones sat children—all of them staring at her.

One of the kids, who appeared to be the eldest of the group, turned to Wren. "Who've you got there?" she asked, twirling her long braid.

"This is Eloisa," Wren replied. When Eloisa continued to stand there, frozen, Wren spoke again. "These are the Lost Children."

The Lost Children waved.

They introduced themselves and then turned back to conversing with one another. Eloisa veered over to Wren. "Why did you bring me here?"

Wren smiled softly. It was the first time he made an expression that Eloisa couldn't name. He looked so different from the playful, dramatic, outgoing Wren she knew. He looked old. He looked *human*.

"We're lost, aren't we? Just treat this like another adventure. The Lost Children love adventures."

Almost as if on cue, one of the boys jumped up from his seat and yelled, "To the water!"

Eloisa was swept up with the other children, carted back toward the ravine, where a long rope was attached to a tree, a small loop tied at the bottom.

"We should let Eloisa go first," a girl said, gesturing for Eloisa to get on the rope.

Eloisa suddenly understood she was supposed to swing over the ravine. Cold fear shot through her spine.

"What! No . . . I—Wren!" She turned to him, eyes wide. "I just *fell in!*"

Wren's eyes crinkled. "It's okay, Ellie. You can do it. Here, I'll help you get in."

He dragged her over to the rope and instructed her to loop her feet through the hole, and push off the trunk of the tree when she was ready. Her heart was pounding so loudly she could hear it even over the cheers of the rest of the children.

"All right . . ." Wren said, and pushed her off.

"Wait!" But Eloisa's screams of protest were cut off as the rope swung down. She arched over the water, the rushing rapids looming closer to her bare toes. She shivered, clutching the rope for dear life as she watched the monster ravine rush past her in a blur. The rope arched up, up, up, and she took in a deep breath as the blue sky stretched out before her. And then she was rushing back down to solid ground, the wind blocking out her squeals of delight.

And that was all it took. Eloisa got off the rope, breathless and grinning, watching as the rest of the Lost Children took their turns.

After the ravine, the children raced up a hill, breaking off branches of trees and using them as makeshift swords in an epic battle. A small boy immediately picked Eloisa to be on his team, and the two of them sprang out of the bushes and knocked their branches against the other children's ankles.

When the twigs snapped from overuse, the children stuck their feet in the mud and tried to see who could stay in it longest without giggling. A girl named Ruby with fierce dark eyes won that one.

The eldest girl taught Eloisa how to keep her balance cartwheeling on a line of rocks and asked Elosia to decorate her hair with wildflowers. Soon all of the Lost Children were following suit, picking daisies, buttercups, and clovers. Eloisa placed a crown of bellflowers in her hair, earning a winning grin from Wren.

When the sun came down, the children made finger puppets in the shadow of the fire, telling stories of pirates and lost ships, of crumbling monarchies and trapped princesses. Eloisa watched in awe as shadows of the flames danced across her face.

"You look like a warrior," Wren whispered in her ear.

Eloisa felt her cheeks warm. "Thanks."

She hadn't had a chance to ask him more about the Lost Children, about himself, about what it all meant. But at that moment, she didn't care. She was finally surrounded by kids her age, kids who wanted to daydream and get messy in the dirt, kids who seemed to have no care in the world. She never wanted this night to end.

# LILIANA GREYF

**GRADE:** Senior

**BORN:** New York, NY

**LIVES:** New York, NY

### MENTEE'S ANECDOTE:

Annie and I spend most Monday evenings discussing a healthy mix of grandiose philosophy, absurd pop culture phenomena, and foundational childhood events. Then, as should seem quite logical, we write. When the Google Meet feed glitches, we both get snacks; when it's back, we return to searching for literary inspiration, which really means sending each other links to Poetry Foundation and free-writing lists of our favorite things. We read each other our sentences, which are sometimes coherent. We laugh. When we hang up, I have always done something I am proud of.

---

# ANNIE BRYAN

**OCCUPATION:** Digital Editor

**BORN:** Philadelphia, PA

**LIVES:** New York, NY

**PUBLICATIONS & RECOGNITIONS:** *Politico, The Philadelphia Inquirer, Time,* CBS News, and more

### MENTOR'S ANECDOTE:

Liliana is a step ahead of me in everything. Because of her insatiable hunger for knowledge, she's always faster than me to pick up a new book, or hear about a fresh writer, or find a new line of poetry to fall in love with, or go on a deep dive of some interesting thread within the history of gender and sexuality. She both inspires and challenges me every time we meet and I am so lucky to call her my friend.

# Learning to Linger

## LILIANA GREYF

*That moment when you have to go but want to stay—so you decide
you really don't have to go at all*

When the waiter asks, eyebrows raised, if you'd like the check
say *no*.
It's true, you've eaten so many pastries
and the bit below your bellybutton has begun to droop
but it's in a girl-like sort of way, you think,
so today you deserve a treat.
You deserve to buy yourself a bunch of yellow roses,
like the ones Tanya bought for your birthday
because she couldn't remember the English word for sunflowers.
But because the flower shop is far, and because it is warm here,
say *no* and order a coffee with cinnamon and milk.
Or cinnamon milk with no coffee.
Back home they don't pour foam into
swans or hearts, and the mugs certainly aren't as clean.
Plus the barista's face is getting familiar enough that
it's become appropriate for you to think
about what your theoretical kids would look like. Or maybe
a dachshund will lumber in
with a beautiful person on its leash

and who could miss that?
Perhaps you should move into this café,
because there is enough room on this bench for you to stretch your legs.
You can always undo the top button of your jeans
and breathe.

# LENA HABTU

**GRADE:** Senior

**LIVES:** New York, NY

**BORN:** Addis Ababa, Ethiopia

### MENTEE'S ANECDOTE:

I'm endlessly grateful for my last four years with Sammi. She has met me with nothing but grace, love, and understanding, pushing me as a writer and moving through life with me as a friend. Her endless supply of prompts are so thought-provoking and conducive to our never-ending tangents. Here's to our perpetual search for New York's best hot chocolate!

---

# SAMMI LaBUE

**OCCUPATION:** Founder and Leader

**BORN:** Moorpark, CA

**LIVES:** Brooklyn, NY

### MENTOR'S ANECDOTE:

I have been lucky to work with Lena during all four of her high school years. We have both grown so much, forced to in some ways by the pandemic, but we create a little light for the other to grow into during our writing sessions. Lena has taught me how to write and to love truer, and I know she will be a source of inspiration for me and many others throughout her life.

# spacetimecontinuum

## LENA HABTU

*This poem was originally rooted in the pandemic and quarantine but
evolved into a piece on introspection, rumination, and growth.*

i've grown weary of my lavender universe,
each wall its own galaxy
each artwork its own divine star
i've spent the last fifteen months
flitting between solar systems,
but it's been too long,
and i'm homesick

i curl my graying corporeal form
into a cocoon of my own making
my lips kissing my knees as my arms hug my chest

and what does a butterfly do during metamorphosis?
in her cocoon, she sits, she meditates,
she jots down her musings on the world
and herself, on unlined pages
she memorizes her interior
and yearns for more

i emerge, slowly, assuredly,
a whole new woman, if you will.

in my rebirth, things have shifted
i no longer seek a great cosmic alignment,
i find solace in my placement, in my here and now
in my rebirth, i am
birthing with every droplet of water i pour
each sprout is a new lifeline

the water that pours from my fingertips,
like the first rains after a season-long drought
laying among my creations, i arch
my back and tilt my head towards
the sun, throw my arms
up in unabashed embrace

# AMELIA HARRINGTON

**GRADE:** Senior

**BORN:** Queens, NY

**LIVES:** New York, NY

**PUBLICATIONS & RECOGNITIONS:**
Scholastic Art & Writing Awards: Gold Keys (2); Honorable Mention in Short Story at the Brooklyn Public Library Teen Writing Contest

## MENTEE'S ANECDOTE:

I've really enjoyed working with Emily these past months. She is incredibly supportive and kind, engaging with me in in-depth discussions about the very personal themes in my writing. Her critiques have helped me build my confidence in writing about sensitive subject matter. She also aided me in practicing for my college interview for my dream school, for which I am incredibly grateful.

# EMILY HEIN

**OCCUPATION:** Senior Story Producer

**BORN:** Mineola, NY

**LIVES:** New York, NY

**PUBLICATIONS & RECOGNITIONS:**
Senior Story Producer at *Insider*; Master of Social Work Candidate at NYU

## MENTOR'S ANECDOTE:

Working with Amelia has been an absolute joy. Amelia has shown huge growth, vulnerability, and commitment in her writing, which has spanned across several different genres and story types. What I love most about working with Amelia is watching her tackle topics that are meaningful to us both, like mental health or LGBTQIA+ representation, with such thoughtfulness and creativity. Her interests in music and magical realism often appear in her writing as well, and while many stories share these common threads, each contain dynamic and unique characters who you find yourself rooting for. I'm eager to see what's next!

# Excerpt from
# *Intangible Things*

## AMELIA HARRINGTON

*Sybil was waiting on the train platform absentmindedly during her morning commute. Then she fell onto the tracks. When she awakens alone in the hospital, she finds her injured body and soul split apart. This is an excerpt from a larger novel manuscript currently in progress.*

The roar of the train collapsed into stillness, the cool blackness of her mind without sight. Gradually, sound began to emerge. A persistent, agitating beeping sound, quite close to her ears. It was infuriatingly constant. She thought it was a metronome at first, with its electronic tone. With the lingering fog over her mind, she hardly considered why she had left a metronome on her bedside. She was lying down, after all—she could feel that much—and nestled into soft bedding. As the metronome went on, she wondered how dumb with sleep she had been to not turn the thing off before she stopped her practice the night before.

But hadn't she already woken up and walked to the train station? She had probably just been dreaming. She tried to flail her arm out from the blanket and blindly search for the metronome and the coveted off button. She did so, but as soon as she moved her joints, there was a strange hollowing sensation. Not pain or muscle soreness, just a strange feeling of lightness. Taking it as the product of an unfortunate sleeping position, she continued to search around with her open hand, clawing for that obnoxious metronome.

Her fingers kept brushing something, but it wasn't her metronome, the soft mahogany of her nightstand, or the neck of her reclining guitar. It seemed, rather, to be a thick bundle of cords that hummed with their own internal life, as if hooked up to some larger rumbling machine. That deep mechanical growling triggered something in her mind.

The train. The last thing she had seen had been its screeching metal wheels and its dark underbelly, approaching to consume her. She had been carrying her guitar on her back, headphones in her ears. She was late for school, but her mother was working, as she always was, and so wouldn't care or know either way. The thick silence here was characteristic of her home.

Her eyes forced themselves open. The blaring light of a ceiling lamp was there to meet her, embedded in an unfamiliar gray ceiling. Her bedroom at home was painted light blue.

Her breath beginning to quicken, she forced herself up, glancing frantically around the room. There was no metronome. Only the calmly rising and falling line of the heart monitor, letting out a soft beep every other second. The cords she had touched were indeed hooked up to monstrous machines she did not recognize, all of them whirring busily to themselves. The sterile light reflected off of the polished tiled floors of a hospital and two empty visiting chairs.

Trying to stop herself from total panic, she quickly looked down at her own arms. She was relieved to see that she was still in the clothes she remembered putting on, and that there were no IV tubes or plugs in her skin. She touched her head and found no bandages. She was even still wearing her shoes. There *was* a white laminated hospital band around her wrist, but what truly scared her was that there was no black guitar case left beside her bed.

After standing up and searching around, she discovered it wasn't anywhere else in the room either. She felt inclined to open the door and call out, but she was scared of what she would find. She was finding it hard to breathe at all now, her heart accelerating till she heard it in her ears and felt it in her veins. No. No, this wasn't right. That train, the fall, the whole thing was so sudden and random. How could she have even fallen? She hadn't felt anyone push her, she hadn't even seen what had happened. All she knew was that there had been a slight ripple in the crowd and some cries, and then she was off the edge and on the tracks.

She touched her head again on the exact spot she remembered, but her hands came away with no blood. Yet even as she did, she finally had the clarity to realize that something had changed in the room. The heart monitor, the only noise to be heard in the eeriness, had quickened its rhythm. The sounds became more erratic and uneven, following what she felt in her own body.

But how could that be?

She wasn't connected to the machine. She turned to watch the monitor and nearly let out a scream. On the bed, her bed, was another body. A girl, clothed in a hospital gown and smothered with medical contraptions, was lying in her place. Completely limp, she lay asleep with a peaceful, blank expression. Her hands, lying flat beside her, were covered with scrapes and bits of grime, and remaining stains of blood showed through the gauze on her face. Her frizzed, deep brown hair was sectioned off awkwardly to make way for a large bandage around the side of her head.

She was staring down at herself.

# RUBY FAITH HENTOFF

**GRADE:** Junior

**LIVES:** New York, NY

**BORN:** New York, NY

### MENTEE'S ANECDOTE:

When my mentor and I met last October, I mentioned my passion for musical theater. She said that she was also a Broadway fan, and I was surprised by the number of shows we both loved. She even knew *The Last Five Years*, a musical written two decades ago that none of my friends have heard of. Few people in my life love theater and writing the way I do, so it was amazing to connect with someone else who shared my enthusiasm for those art forms. My piece for the spring anthology is an original musical.

---

# BRIE SCHWARTZ

**OCCUPATION:** Deputy Editor, *Oprah Daily*

**BORN:** Long Island, NY

**LIVES:** New York, NY

### MENTOR'S ANECDOTE:

From the moment I met Ruby and learned that we shared a mutual love of obscure musical theater, I knew Girls Write Now had made a perfect match. I feel like I'm being transported back in time during our pair sessions, staring at a (more prolific) version of my younger self. There are few folks who can swiftly switch from talking about William Finn to writing about epilepsy awareness and creating fantasy worlds where constellations take on deeply relatable personas. I often forget that I'm talking to someone who is, err, way less than half my age.

# The Boy West

## RUBY FAITH HENTOFF

*Kym finds herself at a mysterious beach in her dreams. There's a boy there too—one she's certain that she's seen before . . .*

During her third attempt, Kym nearly got massacred by a wave. She was standing by the shore, eyes shut tight in concentration. It wasn't until she felt the drizzle of fresh salt water on her cheek when her eyes flew open, and she noticed the fifteen-footer approaching. She scurried back, foam and sand spraying her face and clouding her hazy vision.

Kym growled and brushed off her loose-hanging T-shirt. She stood and scanned the beach. She was still East; she could tell by the commotion on her right. Vacationers swarmed around tents and tour shops, holding tiki drinks in neon cups, laughing with one another.

She considered her options. She could do more exploring East, but that might get her lost. It might even wake her up. But no. She was still dead set on finding the boy West.

Night after night, Kym tried to control her dreams. Her habits were unpredictable, and she'd often end up in different places. But this beach was distinctive. She'd been here enough times to know it was important. Something connected to reality.

While East had a lot of activity, West was the polar opposite. Not a single person played in the sand. The shell-dotted area was more elevated and closer to the dunes than East. However, this was the most precarious part of the beach—whenever Kym started to cross West, she could feel her consciousness arising. From there, she had no idea how many days it would take to reappear.

Kym had seen the boy West once. Last week, she had spotted a figure by the dunes while roaming. He was slender and tall, with flaxen blond hair and a pale complexion. He wore a flannel top and jeans torn at the knee. Although he remained completely silent, his hands were in continuous motion. As Kym looked closer, she noticed what he was doing—crafting paper origami stars at the speed of sound.

No one on the beach dared to go near him. The first time Kym advanced, remaining twenty yards away, he scowled at her with his icy cobalt eyes, flashing a handful of paper stars menacingly.

Kym quickly retreated.

Most mornings, every moment of last night's dream would drain out of her mind the minute she woke. She forced her eyes closed, trying to hold on to every remnant possible, but by the time sunlight lined her curtain, her thoughts morphed into liquid slipping from her grasp.

Every now and then, however, Kym would remember a specific person or two. She could still envision his shaggy blond hair, red and blue paper stars in hand. She knew that she had something in common with him. She only had to figure out what.

She had to find him again.

Tonight, she appeared East, which wasn't much of an advantage. After nearly getting drenched by a wave, Kym knew she had to try harder to control her space. She had to go West and search for the boy. But she could only see the other side. One wrong turn and she might step into oblivion for the rest of the night.

After several minutes of searching, Kym found a small, isolated spot by the beach. She split her mind in two—half of her focus directed on the horizon, the line far out where the current was smooth and touched the sky. She then envisioned herself West, West, West.

There was no sound whatsoever except for foam gently licking the tide. When she turned around, the boy West was hunched over in the dunes, his mop of shaggy hair shielding his eyes, hands in vigorous motion as usual.

To stabilize her position, she knelt down and picked up a shiny, almost translucent coin-sized oyster shell, like the ones she used to make jewelry from as a kid. When the boy West finally spotted her, he was glaring intensely. She jumped, and he flashed three paper stars in his left hand. She had the feeling that if he threw them like Frisbees, three of her fingers would go missing. Her mind instantly screamed, *RUN!*

But it was too late to make a decision. She clutched the oyster desperately, its sharp edges digging into her palm. Kym could feel her consciousness dissolving into reality. She stared at the boy West, trying not to wake up, but the blue and gray of the beach was soon painted bright gold and her eyes fluttered open.

Now awake, Kym cussed to herself and sat up groggily, running her hand through her tangled obsidian hair. She opened her palm, wishing that the oyster was there, but all that remained were memories.

*Memories!*

A smile tingled on her lips. *She'd done it! She'd made it West!* For the first time, her strategy didn't slip away.

Kym didn't know when she would next see the boy West. But she was positive that she would find him again.

# LILIANA HOPKINS

**GRADE:** Senior

**BORN:** New York, NY

**LIVES:** Secaucus, NJ

**PUBLICATIONS & RECOGNITIONS:**
Scholastic Art & Writing Awards: Gold Keys; Runner-up for National Vans Custom Culture Contest; Semifinalist for Penn State's Lake Effect National High School Poetry Contest

### MENTEE'S ANECDOTE:

Kathryn is both a guide and a friend. She's given me so much career guidance and the confidence to pursue a degree that combines my passions for science and writing. Our weekly meetings inspire and restore me. They are a time in which we have intellectual discussions, including analyzing Western society's switch from religious to scientific fanaticism, and lighter topics, like recaps of our weekends. I'm excited to spend the second half of this academic year working with her.

---

# KATHRYN CAVES

**OCCUPATION:** Senior Medical Writer

**BORN:** Normal, IL

**LIVES:** Astoria, NY

**PUBLICATIONS & RECOGNITIONS:**
*Past Ten, The Daily Drunk, Weekly Humorist*

### MENTOR'S ANECDOTE:

Liliana has been a joy to work with! I feel so lucky that I get to read her creative and engaging work. As a fellow writer who also has an interest in science, I have enjoyed how her writing uniquely weaves science into compelling stories. I'm excited to see where her talents for writing and scientific insights take her next!

# Lotus Flower

## LILIANA HOPKINS

*This is the first chapter of a longer science-fiction work titled "Lotus Flower." In the excerpt, the reader is introduced to a scientist and his life's work.*

Mel pulls his coat tight around his waist. A mean cold rattles the spines of the few surviving trees. The chill remains, long after he enters the lab and thaws his tired, old bones.

The lab is an ant to any hawk that roams over the rolling plains, but to Mel, it's his entire world. The facility is flat, one story, and wide: a snowy sandbar in the winter. He spends most of his isolation either wasting time in the kitchen or absorbed in his project, shuffling back and forth between the machine and operation rooms.

He prepares a pot of coffee while waiting for the neuroimaging machines to shudder back to life. A small photo of him and his daughter rests in a gilded frame near the sink. Whenever he does the dishes, he indulges himself with a conversation.

"How's calculus going? Never was very good at math myself."

"Remember that waterpark I took you to the summer before you started middle school? What was it called? Crocodile Cove, Alligator Cove, I don't know. You had the best time. The whole ride home you cried and cried and kicked my seat, telling me you wished I left you there."

"I bought your favorite coffee beans today. Want a cup? No sugar, lots of milk, right?"

There are never enough dishes to wash for this long, but Mel is sure to drink three cups of coffee in the morning, each time in a different mug.

After his first coffee, he checks on the MRI scanner. It's an older model; it takes half of the morning to power on. He writes to his supervisors every month, requesting technological upgrades and giving updates on his advancements. They go unanswered. The longest he's worked without instruction is five years.

Mel shuffles to the operation room, which is adjacent to the machine room. The doors swing open. Covered with a tarp, the body lies still on the surgery table in the center of the room. He moves around the edges to collect his tools and jars of organs. Mel prepares his workstation at the surgeon's table in the center of the room, near the body's head. Gray, gelatinous chunks bob up and down in a glass container filled to the brim with yellow liquid. Years before, he spent most of his days looking through a microscope. Then there were only threads of neurons, tangled nerves with sparse neural networks, and now, the mucousy beginnings of a cerebellum.

Mel leans into his chair, his back groaning from decades of hunching over desks. The scalpel sneers at him, silver-toothed and quick-witted. It knows Mel is no surgeon.

# STELLA Z. HU (AKA TWIG)

**GRADE:** Senior

**BORN:** New York, NY

**LIVES:** New York, NY

### MENTEE'S ANECDOTE:

This doesn't feel as much like being mentored/taught/whatever, as it just feels like having a good writing friend to talk to and do writing stuff with. It's always fun, definitely a highlight of my week. One time, we even just spent a session making memes. I made a galaxy-brain meme that was like, "shooting for the heart in an 18th-century duel"; "aiming your pistol at the sky"; "aiming for an arm or a leg, dominant side if you're angry enough"; "aiming for the groin." Credit for that last one goes to my imaginary friend.

---

# EMMA WINTERS

**OCCUPATION:** Communications Manager

**BORN:** New York, NY

**LIVES:** New York, NY

**PUBLICATIONS & RECOGNITIONS:** *CMSOnAir, America: The Jesuit Review*

### MENTOR'S ANECDOTE:

One of my favorite memories with Stella is cowriting a dialogue exercise about a family gathering gone awry. We laughed so much, as a few folks got tossed into an ocean full of sharks. Both Stella and I like poetry writing, and she has inspired me to get back into my own poetry practice.

# Behind doors are secrets (to discover or not)

## STELLA Z. HU (AKA TWIG)

**Content Warning:** blood, possible death

*A liminal space I found in my school, and what I left there*

There's an odd, twisted kind of whimsy to be found on an empty
hidden stairwell
In the wings of an auditorium stage
When your teacher is absent and your classmates are all on their
phones.
The corners have dust and cobwebs.
The walls are yellow, cracked, warped, and peeling, with a few
fluorescent lights
Illuminating red stains on them.
They're probably watercolor paints,
but I can't help but think of some innocent fellow child's blood.
The thought makes me both shiver and giggle.
There's no telling where it goes.
I pulled a little on the two doors on either side of the landing at the top,
but I couldn't open them.
Might be for the best.
I don't try to pull harder. I'm not quite brave enough for that.
For all I know some nightmarish creature could be sealed behind one
of them.

Probably not. But the thought won't leave my mind.

I can't tell if it makes me feel more terror or glee.

I might give it another shot sometime.

Once or twice I think I hear voices from above,

and I wonder if I should run before I'm caught.

I don't. I freeze and wait until they're gone.

I sit on the landing in the middle, and I read a book.

I feel the need to add something to the atmosphere,

make it raise just a few more questions and few more neck-hairs for the
next person.

I take out my pencil and scrawl a message on the wall:

*Don't ask.*

*Don't listen.*

*Don't forget.*

# CELINA HUYNH

**GRADE:** Senior

**BORN:** Queens, NY

**LIVES:** Maspeth, NY

### MENTEE'S ANECDOTE:

I am so grateful to Girls Write Now for allowing me to meet Liz. She's the best mentor I could ever ask for: fun, caring, open-minded, and not to mention a great writer. We have so much in common that I think we are secretly the same person. It's so cool that I can have such a meaningful relationship with someone much older than me. Not only is she a great friend and writing mentor, but she is also a great adult role model. We learn from each other, and I'm grateful for the impact she has had on my life.

---

# LIZ VON KLEMPERER

**OCCUPATION:** Essay Specialist Supervisor

**BORN:** Darien, CT

**LIVES:** New York, NY

### MENTOR'S ANECDOTE:

Last year Celina and I delved into heavy topics, from mental health to sexual assault. I was proud of the bravery and candor with which Celina spoke her truth. This year, when Celina suggested we focus on positive prompts, I found myself excited to explore a different side of my own writing and to learn more about Celina and her goals. We wrote about the lives, relationships, and communities we want to cultivate going forward, and I left each meeting rejuvenated and hopeful. There's power in positivity, and I'm thankful to Celina for pushing us in a new creative direction!

# Nesting Doll

## CELINA HUYNH

*Imagine being in a room with your younger self. What would you tell them?*

If I were in a room with my ten-year-old self . . . for some reason, the first image that pops into my mind is of us in the room where I used to have therapy in person. Maybe it's because the dynamic between us would be similar to that between me and my therapist.

I imagine it would feel weird for me to see myself from an outside perspective, in 3D, the full 360, because I've only ever been able to see myself from within, in the mirror, and in pictures. I forgot how tall I was at age ten, but I imagine both of us are standing, and I squat down to match her height, as good adults do when they want to make a kid feel welcome and connect with them, unlike the condescending adults in my family who always made me feel small.

I imagine she'd be shy at first. *Why is this person squatting down at me . . . ?*

I'd say, "Hi, what's your name?"

"Celina," she'd say.

"That's my name too."

"Really? How do you spell it?"

Would my ten-year-old self recognize me? Would she wonder if that's her, from the future? Or would I seem like a totally different person to her? How would she feel about me? I hope she would think I'm cool, that I'm kind and pretty and loving, and that I have my shit together, even if I really don't.

I'd notice her slick straight hair, not yet frizzy and damaged. I'd notice her nerdy rectangular glasses that don't fit her face at all.

"Look at these circular ones," I'd tell her as I show her mine. "I think they might suit your face better."

I'd notice her chapped lips, the eczema rashes on her arms, neck. We are not so different from each other now. We're the same people, but different versions, neither one the better one.

I'd give her a hug, a long one; I'm not sure when she last got one of those—an *I love you* one, a *There's nothing else I want to do today but hold you* one, an *Everything's gonna be okay and I'm here for you* one.

Maybe I imagine this scene in the clinic because if I imagined it at home, it would be too hard to separate the two of us. I still live in the same home as her. It's both of our homes. If I imagine us at Grandma's house, where we spent most of our time, well, that would get me too emotional, and I wouldn't be able to focus on her. So I guess the therapy room is a nice objective middle ground, sterile and empty, so we can just focus on each other.

I'd give her some eczema care, some ChapStick, some lotion to put on her rashes. "You should apply these products twice a day." I'd show her how to better take care of herself, how to tie her shoes, the seemingly small things her parents neglected to teach her, small things that are actually really big things.

I notice I'm focusing on the practical things right now. Let me try to cut to the bigger emotional things I'm avoiding.

I would tell her that she's enough and that she has a place in this world, and not to be afraid to take up space and be herself. I'd tell her to ignore the adults, that although they say hurtful things to her and make her feel bad, they are just mean, and wrong, and one day, she won't have to deal with them anymore; she'll find better adults who are nicer to her and treat her the way adults should treat children.

I wish I could be there for her, like a mom, or an older sister. We could be friends. I could be what she longs for deep down: someone to take care of her, to keep her company and make her feel loved.

I want to tell her that she's capable, that she's pretty just the way she is, and that her hair, her body, her face, are all beautiful and worthy of love. Even though it's hard for me to believe those things of myself now. I would advise her to brush her teeth better, though I still have a hard time doing so now at age seventeen. I realize that although I'm seven years older, I don't have much on her. I still can't love myself the way I want her to love herself.

In some ways, I'm still her, deep down. She's inside me, a part of me. Her insecurities are mine, her pain is mine. I guess all I can do is focus on caring for myself now, but I'm not exactly sure how. Maybe I can empathize with myself by telling myself the things I wish I could say to her: *Life is hard and it's not your fault. It's okay to not know what you're doing, but I'm here for you, babe. I care about you, and we'll get through this together, yeah?*

# NICOLE ITKIN

**GRADE:** Senior

**BORN:** Brooklyn, NY

**LIVES:** Brooklyn, NY

### MENTEE'S ANECDOTE:

A highlight of working with Holli was experimenting with different voices and creating a variety of characters. When working with dialogue, as one example, we would go back and forth for hours. I found that work so incredibly important to my writing!

---

# HOLLI HARMS

**OCCUPATION:** Guest Lecturer/ Screenwriter

**BORN:** Frankfurt, Germany

**LIVES:** New York, NY

### MENTOR'S ANECDOTE:

Nicole has beautiful enviable curls and a quiet wit that will have you howling with laughter. She has a depth of understanding of human beings and all our idiosyncrasies that is way beyond her years. Her writing is funny, honest, and thought-provoking. What has been so extraordinary for me are our online meetings where we have together worked on a new idea and literally in that hour created a new piece. It is exhilarating and incredible to watch how Nicole's mind is slamming together ideas and thoughts and then shaping them on the page, like a sculptor would shape clay.

# Where To?

## NICOLE ITKIN

*Desire. Loss. And then what? The poem weaves those ideas together.*

My heart bounds up, up, Up, contrary to ballet shoes that make their
start simply (*simply!* ha!) by flitting across a stage. No. No. Here, the
girl leaps across the stage, the boy a half-step behind, the two in a
dance they'll never meet in, a dance they could have met in.

They step back, tie silks around their legs, and, with a tug, soar up into
the air. She spins, arms crowning her back. He spins, arms crowning
the audience. Watching. She yanks. (Did she mean to?) He unspools
downward, legs almost bare. He grabs. (Did he mean to?) We're left.
With bare legs. And dangling silk. (Timing, after all, keeps us up.
*Simple.* How simple, then, is it to fall?)

No. They never made it into the air. Never, at least, for more than a
leap or two. There they are: on the ground grounded. Their steps
are soft, furiously so, on the moonlight-dusted stage. Up. Above.

Above their heads, the roof has slid away with a groan, the night sky in
with a sigh. On its side, newly toppled, the roof leaks rain like
perfume, blending into the charcoal backdrop Behind it. The
backdrop takes it in with heavy resignation. Happy? no.
Determined? to stay still despite whatever goes on before it.

I look at it all, the stage, the sky, the rain, and the rain and my heart
pumping there in the night in the sky, in the midst of its flight.

With the sudden certainty of a (previously crouching) breeze leaping
up and setting off an alarm in the night, I know. Opportunities don't
last long, never too long, my heart knows that, knows it *well*. And so,

my heart, making patterns and swirls, climbs softly and then
outside.

My heart is Brave (they—the ambiguous—tell me). But. What? My
heart? my heart? it's just running! Where from? Where to? Hell if I
knew. I wonder, often, who I would be if I had the strength to not lie,
at least to myself, to me.

And then, just then: one wrist. Then another. Mine. Moving without
me, pulling my feet forward. And I know. I *know* I'm not in control
anymore. I push, I pull, I scream, and shout, trying to reel, reel, reel
my limbs back to me.

Quiet.

I quiet.

There's a hand. On my shoulder. Keeping me here. Under the rain.
Soaked, fidgeting, here.

   I

      still

         want

         to

   run.

but.

I don't.

I stand still.

And watch.

# ISABELLA JIA

**GRADE:** Junior

**BORN:** Queens, NY

**LIVES:** Flushing, NY

**PUBLICATIONS & RECOGNITIONS:**
*The Stuyvesant Spectator*

### MENTEE'S ANECDOTE:

I used to never believe there was such a thing as a match made in heaven. But Girls Write Now made this possible by matching me with Jen. Our vibes and energies complement each other so well and our weekly calls on Sundays make my day. Not only is Jen my mentor, she is my best friend, and I am comfortable telling her about anything. From hearing updates about her cute dog, Charlie, to her new role as a fitness instructor, I can't wait to learn more and watch our relationship grow! :)

---

# JENNIFER PRANDATO

**OCCUPATION:** Associate Art Director

**BORN:** Sandpoint, ID

**LIVES:** New York, NY

**PUBLICATIONS & RECOGNITIONS:**
*Time, The Boston Globe, Chicago Tribune*

### MENTOR'S ANECDOTE:

I loved watching Izzy grow not only as a writer, but as an individual. There was a moment working on this piece when everything just clicked and it was incredible seeing her face at the exact moment she realized how it was going to come together. Izzy reminds me so much of myself when I was her age, and I've been delighted and honored to be her mentor. I'm proud of her work, in both this program and her outside experiences. I look forward to our weekly chats and know she's going to continue to astound me in the future.

# The Karate Girl

## ISABELLA JIA

**Content Warning:** assault

*A harrowing experience during a late-night commute in New York City teaches a teenage girl more about finding her inner strength.*

Clutching the brass-coated key in her hands, the girl felt the ridged crevices, positioning the blunt tip precisely between her index and middle finger. The incongruous edges poked her skin. Lifting a finger up slightly, thin, fragile scraps of brass parachuted, falling to the ground.

Though her house key was only a small alloy, it was compressed and shaved deliberately with purpose. It wasn't meant to just fit into the doorknob of her main entrance; it was her katana. Her ancestors, the samurai, used their sacred katanas to defend their nation and she too carried the key for protection, ready to strike if anyone attacked.

Throughout her childhood, Obachan always told her to find her inner katana as a way of building a defense and protecting herself. Taking these words from her grandmother to heart, she registered for Shotokan classes, earning a black belt in the span of eight years. Though her moves were adept and powerful, she was prudent and unleashed her power only when necessary.

When the frigid wind sliced through the air, the strands of her hair fluttered aimlessly, blocking her vision momentarily. Even the fleece-lined jacket Obachan knitted for her wasn't enough to keep her warm as she clutched the unzipped ends together.

The girl walked hesitantly into Penn Station with its dilapidated interior, streaks of graffiti littered on the cobblestoned walls, plastic bags strewn all over the ground. Sensing it was past rush hour, she noticed the usual clamor of Wall Street businessmen and firm executives muttering impatiently was muted.

Nearby, a blanket shuddered and wobbled under the impending thumps of her footsteps.

The girl swiped her flimsy MetroCard, only to halt as the turnstile didn't budge. Realizing her card had $2.40, she groaned, heading toward the card refill machine. She pressed refill, not noticing the disgruntled man who suddenly awoke from his slumber. While she fed the crumpled twenty-dollar bill, the man loomed closer and closer, the wad of cash captivating him.

Having not eaten in two days, he was craving something to sustain himself. Looking at the girl and her puny size, he knew he could easily overpower her. The money opened up unlimited options for him: a nice hot meal at the nearby halal cart, two slices of dollar pizza, or even a McChicken from McDonald's. These thoughts excited him and he couldn't care less about anything else.

The man approached her, asking if she could lend a five-dollar bill. The girl was used to this and had been told from an early age not to talk to strangers. She always handled the situation the same way.

Keep your head down. Don't talk back. Walk away as fast as you can. Steer clear of danger.

So, after retrieving her newly refilled MetroCard, she turned to walk away.

The man was used to this. Ignored by others. Shamed by the public. Pushed and kicked by the police. Feeling undeserving of a single glance by others. The anger toward society bubbled inside him and this was the last straw.

The girl felt the two hands on her back, forcefully propelling her forward until she lost her balance, clashing with the debris on the ground. Bruises already started bursting on her knees, but her backpack shielded her head from the impact. She realized at that moment this was real life and not just a karate competition.

"Give me your goddamn money RIGHT NOW!" the hungry man screamed, revealing his yellow, rotted teeth. Alarmed by his tone, she froze, but eventually picked out her wallet from her side pocket, threw it onto the ground, and ran.

The wallet lay lifelessly on the floor, its leather edges peeling and dollar bills peeking out just a teeny bit. The man picked it up, cheekbones rising with his first smile of the day.

The girl ran and ran and ran, no destination in mind, her head clouded with regret now that the feelings of danger had fleeted away. Why did I succumb to him? Why did I freeze? Why did I give up?

She should've fought back. She should've pushed him, beat him up, kicked him until he bled, so he wouldn't dare to do the same thing to any other girls her age. She should've unleashed her inner katana, knocking some sense into him.

But she didn't. Instead, she chose to run away like a coward. The countless hours sparring, the gold medals hanging on her wall, the black belt wrapped around her waist: Everything felt useless.

Slowing down, a tear slid down her glass skin, staining her jacket. Reminded of Obachan, she remembered her words: Her inner katana was supposed to protect her at all times. Though she didn't fight back physically or defend herself, she was unharmed in the end.

All these years, she had tried to sharpen and whet her inner katana, through grueling karate practices and carrying her key everywhere she went. But all along, her instincts and conscience were the most powerful tools she carried.

Looking down, she noticed her house key in her hand and realized she'd made the right choice.

# ZIYING JIAN

**GRADE:** Junior          **LIVES:** Staten Island, NY

**BORN:** Jiangmen, China

### MENTEE'S ANECDOTE:

My mentor and cheerleader, Sunny, has been a big part of my writing journey. I've learned about new genres, read short stories that have blown my mind completely, gained insight into jobs or industries that involve writing, and redefined what it means for me to be a creative and influential writer. We've supported each other emotionally as well, recently starting off our meetings with an exercise that makes us reflect and share how we've been feeling to each other.

---

# SUNNY LEE

**OCCUPATION:** Copywriter/Editor      **LIVES:** Brooklyn, NY

**BORN:** Ulsan, South Korea

### MENTOR'S ANECDOTE:

I had so much fun editing this piece with Ziying! After she had written many single-spaced pages, we sat down together to look at where the heat of the story was. We had a lot of fun maintaining the personalities of the ghost parents. The challenge came from maintaining the personalities of them, in addition to the other characters', in an excerpt of the story that could still stand alone. We worked hard to cut all the empty modifiers and accomplish just that!

# Death Follows

## ZIYING JIAN

*Bex Foster has a secret: She can hear the voices of her dead parents.*
*How will her friendships and relationships be altered by this secret?*

"Pssst . . . Brad! Do you think our little girl will be okay? Going to Manhattan all on her own?" said Rachel.

"Bex will be fine, honey," said Brad. "The first rule we taught her growing up is to avoid strangers! She's very smart. I'm sure she'll find her way home."

"I'm just worried. We can't actually protect her . . . What if she does get into trouble, then what?" Rachel replied, her voice becoming increasingly thin.

"True . . . She might fall down the subway tracks! Or worse, get pushed off!"

"OUR POOR SWEET CHILD! DON'T GOOOOOOOOooo . . ." Rachel and Brad screamed in unison.

Bex snapped the curtains of the windows open in annoyance. She wiped the condensation and saw snow falling in wisps outside as she tried to ignore the incessant voices of her dead parents.

"Oh, what a beautiful morning to go to Manhattan," she declared loudly. "I'm going to see Kate!"

You thought the voices would stop after the first week of their passing. You thought their presence was all a figment of your imagination. *It'll end,* you said to yourself. You're just stressed out. But the voices persisted in your consciousness. Dialogue that could belong only to your overprotective parents. Or, rather, your former overprotective parents.

It's been almost a month. You are parentless now, but it feels like they never left you.

Were. Are. English tenses were not meant to deal with spirits.

You turn on your heel and head toward the bathroom to take a hot shower. Mornings like these clear your mind. The state of water acts as the only barrier between you and your parents, their airy existences unable to penetrate its liquid nature.

The smell of sweet nutmeg hits you once you enter the kitchen. On the table, you see your favorite homestyle omelet in all its eggy glory. A small drawing made with tomato sauce tops the omelet, stick figures of you and your grandma in Santa hats holding hands, just like how your mom used to do it. Your eyes well up with memories.

"Grannie, you shouldn't have." You dig in and find comfort in the sweetness of the tomato balanced with the saltiness of the eggs.

Grannie is sitting on the other side of the table, a bowl of oatmeal in front of her. "Merry Christmas, sweetheart," she says. "Let's focus on the present today. I'm blessed to have you, little pumpkin, in my life."

"Love you too, Gran," you say. There's a lump in your throat. "Gran, I'm going to Manhattan later today."

Gran's eyebrows raise up. "Oh? What's the occasion?"

"I'm meeting up with Kate," you say, hesitating to meet her eyes. "It's been a long time. We have a lot to catch up on."

"Ah, Kate!" Gran exclaims. Her eyes cloud with worry. "You haven't seen her since the funeral, right? She needs you."

"I promise I will make sure she's all right," you say.

You feel a small vibration in the back of your head. Something drives you to ask: "How do you deal with the pain, Gran? Of losing your daughter and son-in-law?"

Grannie sets down her spoon and looks up. "Bex, when you're pushing eighty-five, you'll find that a lot of things die. I lost your grandfather when your mom was just in college. He was a helicopter pilot, and—" Grannie's voice cracks. "One day, he disappeared while flying from Brooklyn to Chicago alone. His body was never found."

You stop chewing.

Grannie continues. "It was really hard to care for the two of us without him. But we managed. Your mom was juggling two different jobs and her studies, all to keep us going," Gran says. "She said, 'Dad wouldn't have wanted us to go down without a fight.'

"And for some reason, that stayed with me." Grannie laughs, leaning back in her chair, closing her eyes. "You never go on without them. You go on with them. Who knew she had so much wisdom."

You gulp down your food. This is the first Christmas you're spending without your parents. As you eat and watch the snow fall, your mind wanders back to them.

Grannie calls you over to the shrine after you're done. You grab a handful of incense sticks from a drawer before using a match to light the top. A few seconds later, your grandma blows out the spark and wafts of lavender, marigold, and peppermint fill up the room. You tilt your chin and close your eyes to breathe in the scents and pay your deepest respects.

Now your parents are the most mysterious beings in your life. Their presence waxes and wanes, like the phases of the moon. Rather than voices, you hear echoes, but you know echoes eventually fade out forever. Your parents' reality—the reality of them still alive—will disappear entirely once their voices dissipate. You find it difficult to pray, but you try your best anyway, for their safe journey to the other side.

# MEGUMI JINDO

**GRADE:** Sophomore

**LIVES:** Bronx, NY

**BORN:** Bronx, NY

### MENTEE'S ANECDOTE:

First off, I would like to say that I LOVE LOVE my mentor! Maddie is such a kind and easygoing person and I just love how we're so alike! We have talked and argued together about the *Court of Thorns and Roses* series—how the author/editor should have done this or that and made the action of the plot speed faster. I love the deep talks that we have and how she inspires and encourages me to really make my writing my own, and helps me edit my writing while always insisting on doing what I think is best.

---

# MADELINE WALLACE

**OCCUPATION:** Junior Literary Assistant

**BORN:** New Castle, IN

**LIVES:** New York, NY

### MENTOR'S ANECDOTE:

Megumi and I clicked almost instantaneously from our first meeting, and it's so hard to get us to stop talking. Sometimes, we're so in sync that it's scary! During one of our many chats, we got on the subject of birthdays—and discovered we both have our golden birthdays this year, which seemed like a very niche commonality. I've loved making these sorts of discoveries about where our lives overlap, but more than that, I've loved learning about who Megumi is as a person—someone with energy, drive, and tenacity that never seem to diminish!

# the stars in disarray

## MEGUMI JINDO

*When you meet someone over a writing platform and fate encourages you to share your socials to get closer, the relationship does not become as fruitful as you want it to be.*

*i don't know anymore—*

was the fact that we both knew who we were
in vain, or was it for the better?

did it harm "us" or
did it cleanse us?

nowadays,
when i talk to you—

you seem different

or maybe it's just me
and that we were just different from the beginning—
not meant to be—

*you know?*

i thought finding and sharing the reality of our lives
would help us bond or something but

*i think it made us worse.*

i think we've drifted apart from the ship
that should have set sail but never did.

i think God or fate or the stars,
just led us astray.

*and i know*

if i was different,
if life was different,
if we were Different,

we could have been the stars.
we could have been the infinite.
we could have been the forever without the end.

*but we're not.*

and all i'm left with is the ticking of sand—

as i know,
somewhere in there,
we could have been *we are.*

so the glass shatters,
as i touch it—
ever so innocently and quietly with the brush of my
pale, delicate forefinger—

and the *us,* becomes *the end.*

# ALYSSA JOHNSON

**GRADE:** Sophomore

**BORN:** Bronx, NY

**LIVES:** Bronx, NY

**PUBLICATIONS & RECOGNITIONS:**
Top 100 of *The New York Times*'s Short Story Student Writing Contest

### MENTEE'S ANECDOTE:

A lovely and kind soul. She is a hero to my writing, willing to do everything she can to improve it. She has built up my confidence, complimenting my ideas even when I don't think they are the best. Every piece of feedback that I have gotten from her has strengthened my writing to the point where I never second-guess myself. She has introduced me to different writing exercises that have helped with my writer's block and have elevated my creative ideas and thinking. My mentor, Kayla, has been a savior to my writing. I am thankful for her.

# KAYLA RUTH LEVY

**OCCUPATION:** Field Editor/ Reporter

**BORN:** Brooklyn, NY

**LIVES:** Brooklyn, NY

### MENTOR'S ANECDOTE:

Alyssa and I have never met in person (because of the pandemic), but even through the Zoom screen she radiates positivity and optimism. This became particularly apparent while working on a piece about her Crohn's diagnosis: a scary medical journey that she has turned into a personal lesson in self-care. Alyssa naturally sees the silver lining in challenges and assumes the best in others. She also commits wholeheartedly to what she cares about (whether that's writing, dance, or her friends) and sticks by her values. I'm impressed by her fortitude and sense of self.

# A Manageable Change

## ALYSSA JOHNSON

*This is a short personal story about my journey navigating a major change that happened to me recently. It is a great description of the ups and downs of adjusting to a permanent, everlasting change.*

In the beginning of August, the pain started to get so intense that I was comfortable only when crouched on my stomach with my legs tucked under me. I was frustrated with the discomfort every night and not knowing the reason for it. I told my mom, thinking that something would happen right away. But since she seemed relaxed I decided to calm down and pray that the pain would go away. Every time I prayed, though, things just got worse.

The first day of in-person high school was two weeks away and I was nowhere near ready. I wasn't nervous about meeting new people or getting lost, I was scared that I was going to be too sick for school. One day I was coughing so much that I had to go to the hospital. Another day I woke up with a mysterious pink eye, which sent me to the hospital again. Every time I went to the hospital I felt deep down something bigger was wrong. That was the first time I felt somewhat depressed. I wasn't motivated to do anything and I looked and felt horrible.

The first week of school was rough. I tried to hold in every cough because I didn't want to seem like I had COVID-19 (many tests proved that I didn't). During the end of the school week I went to my school clinic and told the doctor about my coughing attacks, which she thought could've been COVID. She was correct in some ways, but it was annoying that she didn't hear me. *What about the other symptoms I've told you, Doctor? Did you listen to those?* I thought.

I ended the first week of school in the emergency room. I was pale, shivering, and cold to the touch. I had to be wrapped up in hospital blankets like a burrito. That weekend turned into a week. Every day blood was taken from me multiple times for testing, which made me feel abnormal. I had bruises on both my forearms from having so many needles poked into me for bloodwork. I never really got great sleep because nurses would come in the middle of the night to check my blood pressure and vitals. The whole time I was stuck in a miserable hospital room, lying in a bed that wasn't mine. I didn't even feel sad or happy. All I could think was, *When am I getting out of here?* After being in the hospital for a week I was able to leave and, surprisingly, it didn't take long to get right back in the game. I caught up with work and I was able to make friends quickly. Going back to school made me feel normal again. But then I got diagnosed: "Crohn's disease," my doctor said.

I found it very weird that right when I found out my actual diagnosis, I started to feel new symptoms that weren't there before. When I danced, my legs shook, since I'd lost muscle. I felt dizzy in the gym and could barely stand up straight. It was annoying having to wake up at the crack of dawn to take one of my three pills of the day. I would even forget sometimes, which angered my mom. I would say sorry to her face but then tear up when going to bed because it was so stressful to deal with. I felt useless and weak. I didn't feel like my normal self. Things got even worse when I started to shed a lot of hair. Before, my hair was beautiful and thick, but in a few weeks it had become thin and flat, which made me feel insecure.

It's been a few months since my diagnosis and I've started to adjust to my new habits and the differences in my body. I've realized that I can still be myself, I just have to find new ways to live a normal, happy life. Things like my appetite and my weight have improved, and I have the energy and strength to dance like I did before my diagnosis. I started taking a multivitamin that's helping me get the fullness of my hair back. I'm starting to feel pretty and confident again.

Being hospitalized and going through a slow recovery reminded me how strong I am, and that I am capable of overcoming obstacles that come my way. In fact, I've learned that some obstacles can even be a path to growth. When I was first hospitalized I thought Crohn's was a curse, but now I'm starting to think of it almost as a blessing: I can now live a healthier and happier life knowing the truth about my body.

# YAAMINI JOIS

**GRADE:** Junior

**LIVES:** Coppell, TX

**BORN:** Tokyo, Japan

### MENTEE'S ANECDOTE:

This year, I've been able to work with my mentor, Sasha, to improve my creative writing. Though I write in a lot of other genres, I was able to work on a skill I haven't actively worked! Sasha has really helped me with my edits and helped take my work to the next level.

---

# SASHA BROWN-WORSHAM

**OCCUPATION:** Editor

**BORN:** Dayton, OH

**LIVES:** Acton, MA

**PUBLICATIONS & RECOGNITIONS:** *Namaste the Hard Way: A Daughter's Journey to Find Her Mother on the Yoga Mat; The New York Times, The Boston Globe*

### MENTOR'S ANECDOTE:

Whenever we chat, we talk about books, writing, and journalism. Yaamini is a driven and incredibly smart person who is going to rock the world!

# Excerpt from
# *Her Confession*

## YAAMINI JOIS

*Just when you think you've caught the criminal of the biggest case in your town, a meddlesome young police officer is there to foil your plans. Maybe he's right, but what are you to do?*

It was my thirteenth day on the job as a police officer. I had spent almost a year in training, and I was a well-respected man. I was in peak physical condition and trained for all kinds of situations. There should have been nothing that I couldn't handle.

And there wasn't—not until the day I was assigned an interrogation. My very first interrogation.

A young girl stood in the dark room. It was quite peculiar: She contrasted with the background. She had light blond hair and piercing blue eyes. She was quite tall. She couldn't have been older than twenty, though her wrinkles and tired demeanor made me think otherwise. She hung her head.

I stood outside the door, watching her from the window to my right. I didn't dare walk in, though I didn't know what stopped me.

"Who're you waiting for?"

I snapped out of my daze and turned around to face the deputy sheriff. He stood on the other end of the dimly lit hallway, his hands crossed over his chest, leaning on the doorframe.

"Waiting for someone to tell you how to do your job, kid?" He chuckled. "Get in there and do what I asked you to."

"Sorry, sir," I replied, "I was about to go in."

I grasped the door handle and walked in. At the sound of my entrance, the girl jumped sharply and stared at me, suddenly aware of her surroundings.

"I—I'm sorry," I said, "I didn't mean to startle you . . . Could you please take a seat?" I gestured at the chair closest to her.

I felt pathetic. I was a police officer, not an amateur detective. I'd been training to face worse criminals and now I was saying "please" and "sorry" to a girl who wasn't even speaking to me.

The girl still stood. I drew the chair in front of me and sat down.

The girl stood perfectly still, her eyes now focused on me. Her lips were a thin line, her expression unreadable. I hadn't understood the phrase *pin-drop silence* until this moment. I sat, transfixed, as my mind went blank. None of my training had prepared me for the state I had gone into.

A moment later, she drew the chair out and sat down in one motion. I instantly snapped back out of my transfixion.

I noticed a delicate ring on her right hand. It was intricate, unique, and . . . I had surely seen it somewhere.

Before I could think, she broke the deafening silence that had settled in the room.

"What do you want from me?" she asked as she leaned in, her voice a faint whisper.

"I—I'm sorry?" I said, my mouth dry, my voice a bare croak. "I just wanted to talk to you, that's all."

"That's not true," she said coldly. "You want my confession, don't you?"

Her voice was clear. She scared me. In all of my bravado, I couldn't bring myself until this moment to realize just how scared I was of this frail girl.

"It's nothing like that," I said, shocked. "See, I don't even know—"

"I did it," she cut me off. "It was me. I admit it."

"What?" I said. "No, you don't have to do that, what are you even confessing to?"

"What I was brought in for," she said. "My husband's murder. It was me."

I stared at the girl, my mouth gaping. I knew what I was told to do, I knew why she was there, and I knew that I didn't want to be sitting in this cold, dark room talking to this strange girl. But I didn't expect her to confess. It didn't feel right. It didn't feel like the truth. I had only just registered what she had said when I heard the door open. I couldn't stop remembering the ring on the girl's right hand. She wasn't guilty, and I knew it instinctively.

The deputy sheriff stood in front of us, grinning widely.

"Nicely done, kid."

"No—wait, I haven't gotten to talk to her yet," I started, but he held a finger up.

"No need, kid!" he said, shifting his focus on the girl. "She," he said, now pointing at the girl, "just gave me the confession I needed."

I stood up, facing him.

"Surely you can't be serious? That was no confession."

"It's all I needed," he said. "I don't need the details. What I need is to finish my job, but she's already done that for me!"

I looked at the girl next to me. She wore the same expression she had since I entered the room.

"The girl spoke, the girl spoke!" the sheriff said, chuckling. "Isn't that all that matters? She fessed up to the crime. Guilt got to her faster than we did. Don't worry, boy, you've done your job!"

He ushered me out of the room without giving me a chance to say goodbye to the girl. The girl did not look at me as I left.

# FARIYA KABIR

**GRADE:** Junior

**LIVES:** Jamaica, NY

**BORN:** Dhaka, Bangladesh

### MENTEE'S ANECDOTE:

Spending time with my mentor is always a joy. She has a very unique style of making me practice writing and learn new writing techniques, but through stress-free and enjoyable ways. We check in with each other each week and every meeting I get with her is worth the time. My sudden emergency trip to Bangladesh caused a huge conflict with my schedule and learning time, but she was always there to help and was really flexible with the time. I really love her and feel grateful for getting her as my mentor.

---

# CAILEY RIZZO

**OCCUPATION:** Writer

**LIVES:** Brooklyn, NY

**BORN:** Buffalo, NY

### MENTOR'S ANECDOTE:

Meeting with Fariya always puts a smile on my face and reminds me of the powers of writing and reading. She is always full of energy and eager to learn new ways of improving her storytelling. Fariya teaches me so much about her culture and also what it's like to be a kid these days—and, thanks to her, I am even improving my own English grammar. Our meetings together have been a source of sunshine throughout the pandemic.

# Bye Bye, My Home Country

## FARIYA KABIR

*This winter, I returned to Bangladesh for the first time in years after living in the United States.*

From the sky, my town looks different. It looks so small, calm, and able to melt my heart. A question that I am often asked is: "Which do you like more: Bangladesh or the USA?" I have never been really able to answer that question. There can't be any comparison between the two for me. I can't compare Bangladesh with any other country since it's not just a "country" for me. It's way more than that. It's my motherland, the land where I was born, brought up, nurtured, loved, cared for, pampered. That land has witnessed my childhood: my preschool life, my growth, my tears, and my smiles. I feel proud while thinking that I am from a place where you don't have stunning buildings, you have nature and its beauty. I am from a place where you don't have five-star restaurants, you have food from your mom's hand. I am from a place where you don't have advanced technology, but you do have the chance to live together. There aren't great vacation resorts, but there are marvelous hills and sea beaches. There may not be the best educational opportunities, but there you'll learn how to be a good human instead of just successful. Bangladesh may not have the best of everything, but there you have love, care, and hospitality. The U.S. has, without a doubt, played a huge role in making me who I am today, but indeed Bangladesh holds a totally different place in my heart. It's the country that has shaped me as a person and prepared me for my future.

Human lives are often so weird. We don't always get what we want, nor can we always predict what will happen. In 2018, when I was thirteen, I had to shift with my parents to America because of educational purposes and family reasons. It has been almost four years for me living in the U.S., very far from my motherland. In four years, I have had two trips to visit my home country, Bangladesh. The last was in 2019. This time, we came in November 2021. Today, it's January 19, 2022. I am going back to the USA.

A safety announcement suddenly took me out of my thoughts. It was time for dinner. I finished dinner, plugged in my headphones to play my favorite song on my phone, laid my head on the shoulder pillow my boyfriend gave me, and tried to sleep. But I couldn't. Something took me back to my trip. The trip went by in a flash as I was engaged with so many responsibilities, but it was great.

The main reason for the trip was the birth of my baby niece, Zayra. She was born October 31, 2021, and is the first baby of her generation in our family. Meeting her was one of the very best moments of my life. I can clearly remember holding her in my arms for the first time. She was so small, lightweight, cute, and warm. All the days I stayed, I couldn't go without playing with her, talking to her, and having her in my arms for at least an hour. Some days, my favorite cousin came over. We are close from our childhood. Her arrival added to my joy. We had so much fun together.

Also, my elder sister got married. I was really happy for her and her family, but at the same time, her leaving our house and going to a new place did make me really sad. To comfort me, I reminded myself that she is just leaving the house, not the family. That made me feel a bit lighter, but it didn't bring me complete consolation. Her marriage ceremony was really fun, though. In Bengali culture, our marriage ceremonies go on for four to five days. My sister's wedding lasted five days. We all got to dress up, click pictures, and enjoy all the moments together. Ceremonies like those are the only ways to bring loved ones together now that the world is so busy.

Something that also added a great meaning to my trip was my new relationship. After my last heartbreak two years ago, I spent some time away from love and relationship things. But my new boyfriend has something different.

We met through mutual friends and started talking while I was in the USA, but we didn't get together until after I went to Bangladesh. I wasn't really in love at first, but couldn't deny that the boy has something special that I haven't found in anyone else in the past years.

He always makes me feel better in my bad moments. He is not one of those really sweet or cheesy boyfriends, but he is the perfect definition of a partner for me. I love him so much and am really grateful to have him.

I took a deep breath after remembering the last moments I had in my home country. I adjusted my pillow, paused the song, and fell asleep with a smile.

A new announcement played in the background and woke me up from sleep, saying, "Hi, New York!"

# JASMINE KAPADIA

**GRADE:** Senior

**BORN:** Palo Alto, CA

**LIVES:** Palo Alto, CA

**PUBLICATIONS & RECOGNITIONS:** *Good Morning America*'s AAPI Inspiration List (nominated by Malala Yousafzai), 2022 Best of the Net Anthology Nomination; *Kissing Dynamite*

### MENTEE'S ANECDOTE:

I'm so grateful to have met Lucy. Our weekly meetings are a safe space for me to share my writing, and she always has such incredible insight. I've learned so much about myself and my writing through her interpretations, and I treasure the conversations we've had surrounding trauma, healing, and writing as catharsis. Previously, my editing process was nonexistent, but with Lucy's guidance, I've been able to implement one. Lucy has also introduced me to amazing authors like Toni Morrison, something I'll always treasure. Writing and developing our work together has been incredible.

---

# LUCY TWIMASI

**OCCUPATION:** Associate Attorney

**BORN:** Springfield, VA

**LIVES:** Springfield, VA

### MENTOR'S ANECDOTE:

Jasmine is not aware of this, but I have joked around with a friend that Jasmine is rather my mentor, and I her mentee. I am honored to be part of her journey and unique writing process. A writer's creative process is a personal, often protected activity. However, Jasmine has been vulnerable in permitting me a front-row seat, for which I am appreciative. She is a fierce talent, but importantly, Jasmine is an amazing human being. I only foresee great things for her future, and I am assured that we will soon hear about her on a larger scale.

# mama, they asked for an artist's statement

## JASMINE KAPADIA

**Content Warning:** suicidal ideation

*Why do I write? / Why do I do this to myself? / How do I Stop? / How can I stop?*

i guess i am afraid that to be a poet is to suffer.

mama, after we talked about qiu miaojin's suicide in paris at twenty-six, after i told you about how sylvia plath stuck her head in the oven at thirty, i know you said you tried to steer me away from this path. tried to make me less sensitive.

i think about how ocean vuong writes in *on earth we're briefly gorgeous* about violence. the way he doesn't defend it, but also treats it, almost, like a gift. how he recalls his mother's hand against his cheek, white-hot, a storm, and then writes, "i looked at you hard, the way i had learned, by then, To look into the eyes of my bullies." how i scribbled in the margin afterwards. *the way ocean teeters between calling it a lesson and something else. violence as an heirloom, to calcify & harden, to ensure survival.* violence as the Lifeblood of a culture.

mama, are you afraid that i Am too sensitive to survive? do you wish you had helped me harden a little more? a few pages later, ocean writes, "perhaps to lay hands on your child is to prepare him for war." do you wish you had prepared me for war?

sometimes i wonder if i am writing myself into trauma. if every word I put down to revisit the past is getting me closer and closer, a dizzying cyclone. if one day i'll wake up and i'll be stuck there. like how with time travel, they always say, don't Touch anything. leave before you get trapped. don't ever let yourself see yourself.

maybe to be a poet is to forever see yourself. is to look yourself in the eyes for a million lives, a million times over. is that a blessing or a curse?

ocean writes, "only the future revisits the past." where do the lines blur?

only the future revisits the past. but what if to be a poet is to be the past? is to resin your body, to become something for others to study?

mama, i'm afraid that to be a poet is to forever circle my own tail. to be half-headed Like a june-rot peach. you know that some people blame poetry for sylvia's suicide? they say her poems, her words, drove her to death. is that why you think to be a poet is to self-destruct Into an early grave?

i told you that for some reason i can never stop looking back. my brain keeps retracing; i can't seem to move on the way that everyone else can.

i guess i'm Scared i might believe that to be a poet is to teach others what it means to be human. does this mean that i am never fully human, then? or am i more? i worry that my urge to transcend myself is something deeper. sticky. i worry that that my urge to transcend myself will only hurt those around me. that when i say to be a poet is to suffer, i mean i am worried that i will cause those around me to suffer.

i mean i am terrified of my hands, and my body. i mean i don't know what to do with all of it. i'm worried i won't live past thirty. not because i'm suicidal but because sometimes it seems like a prophecy. i worry to be a poet is to write oneself into a never-ending cycle of turmoil, is to write oneself into a legacy of death, is to write oneself into knowing too much and living too little. i guess i'm scared of waking up one day and realizing that i have been trapped within myself all this time. to wake up gasping for air that never comes.

mama, i know you're scared that my grandparents fished themselves out of death only for me to wade into it again with every Touch of a pen to paper.

there's that tumblr post that goes, *every poet writes from a central emotion.* what is mine? dread? restlessness? look, i know you said you've realized it's no use. that it's just the way i am. i was born with my brain working like this.

and i read the other day about this poet who used to be a painter. said all he wanted to do was paint, but those damn poems just kept coming. so mama, i hope you understand. i don't think anyone becomes a poet. i think a poet is a state of being, and these damn poems just keep coming. i'm scared that they're a finite resource. i'm so scared that i'll write poem number eight thousand eighty-eight or something, and then i'll have no need to be here anymore.

ocean writes, "how so much of the word passes through the pupil and yet it holds nothing." calls it god's loneliest creation. what is a poet but a pupil?

mama, i'm scared too. i am, you know?

# SUHA KHAN

**GRADE:** Senior

**LIVES:** New York, NY

**BORN:** New York, NY

## MENTEE'S ANECDOTE:

I am so grateful to be embarking on another year with Vanida's mentorship. The beginning of this academic school year was chaotic with college applications, but having Vanida by my side has helped me find my personal voice and hone my creative self. I look forward to every one of our mentor sessions, and I could not have asked for a more understanding and amazing mentor.

---

# VANIDA NARRAINEN

**OCCUPATION:** Corporate Attorney

**BORN:** Quatre Bornes, Mauritius

**LIVES:** New York, NY

## MENTOR'S ANECDOTE:

My favorite moments with Suha this year have definitely been the time we spent working on her college applications and her personal essays. It gave me an opportunity to really get to know her better and to witness the way she has grown into a confident and talented writer over the past two years. This is such an exciting time for her. I cannot wait to see what she will accomplish as she embarks on a new chapter of her life. I feel lucky to have accompanied her on part of her journey as a writer.

# Tongue-Tied

## SUHA KHAN

*The feeling of having an ocean of ideas at the tip of your tongue,
watching each one disappear once you open your mouth*

Like an ice cube in palm,
On a summer's day
Gone before my eyes,
But I saw it
You missed it
I know.

Speech
Like fog on the window when it's wiped clean;
It amounts to nothing
Like a shy kitten,
It disappeared around the corner
Is it a roadblock or a car crash?
I wonder all the time.

Like water cupped in my hands
I had it,
Like clockwork,
It slipped right through
It's all bubbling underneath though,
It was.

The greatest gems you'd ever witness,
I promise.

But when the time comes,
Watch the weight of my words
Hardly make a ripple.

# LUCIA KIM

**GRADE:** Junior          **LIVES:** Douglaston, NY

**BORN:** Queens, NY

### MENTEE'S ANECDOTE:

Every time Kat and I are editing, we sound like Lorelai and Rory ordering food at Luke's: "Ooo, let's get pie and doughnuts . . . and cheeseburgers." We're always building on each other's thoughts and finding ways to add more personality to a piece until we're happy with the result. After working with Kat for the past two years, I can say that she is the most generous and supportive mentor I could ever ask for. She has taught me the beauty of slapping things on paper, taking a break, then revising later, and I've become a better author because of it.

---

# KATRIN VAN DAM

**OCCUPATION:** VP, Editorial          **LIVES:** New York, NY

**BORN:** Boston, MA

### MENTOR'S ANECDOTE:

Lucia and I got matched up after each of us had been ghosted by our original pairing. I'm so grateful to those other two people for dropping out! Every session with Lucia is a reminder of the power of saying "yes" to things. She is so enthusiastic about trying new things that I find myself opening up to possibilities I wouldn't otherwise even consider. Thanks to Lucia, I'm learning to be less rigid about everything needing to be perfect. Look, I'll show you: I'm not even going to bother coming up with the perfect closing sentence for this anecdote!

# Polished

## LUCIA KIM

*At 11:32 on a typical Saturday night, a mom and daughter chat while doing their nails.*

"Did you choose your color yet?" my mom asks. She rips off a paper towel and places it on the kitchen table to avoid any permanent stains on the first thing guests see at dinner parties.

"Should I do this one or this one?" I hold up two nail polish bottles next to each other. "I feel like the pink matches my skin tone better, but I always do pink."

"Then do the blue one."

"Actually, I like the pink one more."

"Then why did you ask?"

She picks up my finger and begins to file my nails, then pauses to look up at me. "Oh, wait, I can't see. Can you find my glasses? I think they're over there." She waves her hands, not pointing in any specific direction whatsoever.

"Ugh, fine." I sluggishly push my palms against my knee, forcing my weight off of the chair. "Where are they, Mom?" I ask, even though I don't expect much of a helpful response. I look through a tiny basket we keep on the edge of our kitchen table that holds random envelopes and bills.

"Yeah, they're probably in there," she says, watching me shuffle through the layers of old receipts.

When I finally find the glasses, I hand them to her as I sit back down and she resumes filing my short nails into shape.

"Ow! Don't do it too fast," I snap at her, my fingertips burning from the friction.

"Beauty is pain. If you want pretty nails, you have to be patient," she tells me, her eyes glued to my hands.

I sit back on the chair and look around. "Mom, what kind of life did you imagine for yourself when you were growing up?"

"When I was younger, I thought I would live in a mansion with a huge backyard, have a personal chef, and drive a different car each day of the week."

She pauses and slides the glasses back up her nose. "I was too naïve. I thought everyone owned a house and a car after they got married. I never knew that people actually had to work to afford these things."

"How could you think that?" I ask, handing her the pink polish.

"You see, when I was a kid, my mom bought me everything, as long as it wasn't too big. Sometimes I wonder if it was because my dad passed away and she was trying to fill what I was missing with money. So, whenever I wanted something, I could expect it to be in my room the next day."

"Wow, that must have been really nice."

"Yeah, very nice. But it doesn't quite prepare you for when you're married and your friends aren't bragging about their pens anymore, but their new cars and houses."

I lift my hands to inspect her work. "Mooooooooooom."

"Okay, okay I'll fix it," she says, using her thumb to wipe off the polish that got on my skin.

I put my hand back down, signaling for her to resume. "Well, if you weren't concerned about the money, what did you want to be when you grew up?" I ask.

"I think I wanted to be an elementary school teacher or a doctor."

My mom lays down polish on my pinkie with one swipe, smoothing out all of the imperfections. As she places the topcoat between her palms and picks up my thumb to put on the last layer, I ask her, "Then why didn't you?"

She pauses and looks up to the side like she's trying to remember. "When I first moved to America, I took English classes with this woman who also moved from Korea. She told me she wanted to make money to give her son as many opportunities as possible. So she worked hard, opened a couple of nail salons, and made a lot of money. But she said if she could do it over again, she would spend more time with her son instead of working until late at night trying to make extra cash."

"Oh, so is that why you chose to stay home with us?"

She opens the cap and wipes the excess polish on the bottle's rim three times, ensuring that she has the perfect amount on the brush. "Yeah, I think the best thing a mom could do is to put her kids before everything else. Your kid's success is more gratifying than your own."

"But what about your goals?"

"I want your sister to be safe in San Francisco, I want you to be able to do everything you want, and I want your dad to get more orders for his business."

"No, I mean what are you looking forward to? What do you want to do?"

"When you're older, just buy me a house next to the church. I want to go to morning Mass every day and pray for you and your sister. That's all I need."

I look down at my nails and let out a gasp. "IT'S PERFECT!"

"I know. I did a good job, right?"

"Yeah, Mom, you did a good job."

# LIANA KOMENG

**GRADE:** Junior        **LIVES:** Uniondale, NY

**BORN:** New York, NY

### MENTEE'S ANECDOTE:

I enjoy working with my mentor, Jillian. She always provides me with writing prompts that help me explore varying genres of writing and assist me through writing styles that I am unfamiliar with. Jillian consistently supplies me with beneficial feedback in my writing that gradually helps me to improve as a writer. She is positive and never ceases to remind me that every improvement is another step closer to excelling as a writer. It is a pleasure working with Jillian and I have had a remarkable experience with her mentorship.

---

# JILLIAN EUGENIOS

**OCCUPATION:** Reporter        **LIVES:** New York, NY

**BORN:** Mountain View, CA

### MENTOR'S ANECDOTE:

Liana is a focused and ambitious writer who creates beautiful, nuanced work from the very first draft. We started our pair sessions with poetry, but more recently we've been reading and writing flash fiction, which has been a fun space to play in. We're going to start working on short stories next and I can't wait to read the worlds she's going to imagine. I'll also note Liana is an impressive student with an intimidating GPA and I'm looking forward to working for her one day!

# Broken Masterpiece

## LIANA KOMENG

*"Broken Masterpiece" is a poetic piece revolving around the mis-construed perceptions of what it truly means to be an African American living in modern-day society.*

I feel it, the dark, smooth, cocoa outer shell that covers my blood,
The blood of those who came before me,
The blood of those who fought for my right to be this exquisite and
    rare work of art.
But they don't want to see me
They want to brush off my existence, shred my work,
Because history tells me I am broken.

I hear it, the softly spoken tongues and expanding cultures that
    surround a family of beige, connected roofs,
The place where music and friendly faces greet you at every corner,
The place that my God gave me the opportunity to reside in.
But they want to tear it down
They want to dismantle my home, destroy what we have built,
Because maliciousness tells me I am broken.

I see it, the vibrant, luscious, varying shades of black and brown
    meshing together to form one beautiful and diversified picture,
A picture that has long been ready to be valued,
A picture that longs to be desired and placed among those that so freely
    earn a spot in the gallery.

But they despise our paintings,
They want to water it down, flush our stories,
Because privilege tells me I am broken.

They judge and disassociate themselves from us,
They don't want to live in a world where our existence is inevitable,
They believe that we are ruined,
A mistake, just an accident that continued to spread like a plague.
Ignorance tells me I am broken.
And maybe I am. But this is
MY
BRO-
KEN
MASTERPIECE

# SIA KORTEQUEE

**GRADE:** Sophomore

**LIVES:** New York, NY

**BORN:** Brooklyn, NY

### MENTEE'S ANECDOTE:

I enjoy talking about movies with my mentor and learning new things from each other.

---

# JAIME BROCKWAY

**OCCUPATION:** Copy Editor

**BORN:** Springfield, MA

**LIVES:** Somers, CT

**PUBLICATIONS & RECOGNITIONS:**
*Time Out, Well+Good, Food52*

### MENTOR'S ANECDOTE:

It has been a pleasure to chat with Sia every week. She reminds me that being a high-schooler and a teenager is really hard, and I'm amazed at how well she handles her intense workload. And I'm glad that during our sessions, we've been able to talk about movies, music, writing, and life in general. I hope she's enjoyed the time as much as I have.

# Racing Mind

## SIA KORTEQUEE

*I have been running track since the age of nine. I am now on my high school's track team, and these were my thoughts at my last meet.*

I wake up on a freezing Saturday morning.

It's the day of the meet. I can feel every bone in my body chill. The thoughts cloud my mind.

*How can I pull a win?*

*How can the girls beat our biggest competitor, North Rockland?*

*Am I going to be late to the bus?*

The thoughts are interrupted by my mom, sparking the start of the knots forming in my stomach. "How are you gonna run like that?" She points to my large legs, my stretch marks, my everything. The thoughts flood my mind again.

*What am I going to do?*

*Is my body holding me back?*

*Will my lack of muscle hinder my performance?*

*Does my body fat percentage determine if I am a good runner?*

My mom was right: I'm not committed enough for this. The feeling of inferiority floods my brain and crushes my heart, my stomach churning and my body shaking. The memories of past meets—of when I failed, and how I can fix it this time—go in and out of my mind as I wait out my remaining time at home, before I have to meet with the team and get on the bus.

I quickly hop into the car, and my mom speeds through neighborhood after neighborhood until we arrive at the school. I look out my car window and see the big yellow school buses. The thought of the cold leather seats and metal makes me break out into a cold sweat.

As I step onto the bus and take my seat, the bus is too loud, filled with other people talking and thinking about their own events. Each conversation is a blur. All I can think about is my first event. The fifty-five-meter dash. The dreaded dash. I am all by myself; no one else is entered from my team. No one to fix my mistakes. No one to walk with me to the infield.

The bus halts, causing me to break my focus about the fifty-five. I step off the bus. I pull my phone out and show the security guard my vaccination information. Hand shaking, I open the doors to the armory.

I start to warm up. The hallway is crowded and sticky. I try to run back and forth in this hallway. Then I hear it.

ALL DASHES, CHECK IN.

That is my call. I rush up to the track, run across the infield, and ask the angry old man for my heat and lane.

HEAT 2, LANE 5.

I reply thank you and am dismissed right away. I wait and wait and wait. I can't help but shake and sweat. I feel fear. I step on the line, do a few jumps, then start thinking of my shoes. I look down, think, think, think.

*Are they tied? They are too tight.*
*Are my spikes in correctly?*
*Do I have all of the spikes in my shoes? No, they are too loose.*
*Am I going to lose because of these shoes? I should've worn my other ones.*
    *Should I change? I can't. I'm literally on the line.*

ON YOUR MARKS.

Oh, God, focus, focus. Think about accelerations. The first step is the most important step. Get out and go, get out, get out, get out.

SET.

*Oh, okay, okay, raise my legs, take my time. Am I starting on the right foot? Okay, open your eyes. I just want to scream. I can't breathe. This needs to be over.*

GO.

It all goes black until I finish. I need to see my time, my place. I see the screen and my heart sinks. Tears won't form. I feel rage, anger.
*I wasn't good enough.*
*I'm never good enough.*
How am I going to look anyone in the eye? That's eight points I could have scored. We are going to lose.
*It's all my fault.*

# ALICE KRESBERG

**GRADE:** Senior

**BORN:** Seoul, South Korea

**LIVES:** Long Island City, NY

### MENTEE'S ANECDOTE:

Amelia and I have been working together for the past three years. We share a love for cats, and her writing suggestions are always just what my piece needs. I really enjoy meeting up each week to catch up on cat drama, shows we've been watching, and more. Also, it's fun to try new writing activities and tactics since one thing I like to do is explore types of writing. I feel like my writing has evolved a lot with Amelia by my side, because she has pushed me to produce works that have now become my favorites.

---

# AMELIA POSSANZA

**OCCUPATION:** Assistant Director of Publicity

**BORN:** Bryn Mawr, PA

**LIVES:** Brooklyn, NY

### MENTOR'S ANECDOTE:

It's hard to believe that Alice is a senior this year and that, after three years of being a writing pair, she's headed off to college next year. Even though I'm (supposedly) the mentor here, Alice has taught me so much: how to design and dress a chibi on my phone, what foods cats can take the shape of when they sleep, and that it's always uncool to eat string cheese. She has explored her Korean heritage in much of her writing, and this is my favorite of her pieces about it so far.

# Lunch Hour

## ALICE KRESBERG

*Every day at school, I get lunch from the same place, just to see the*
*grandma who works there. It's the highlight of my day.*

Smells of many different cuisines hit my nose all at once,
dumplings that gave me food poisoning,
rice bowls that made my stomach churn,
chicken noodle soup that has an artificially yellow broth.

Every school day I come here for lunch.
Despite the poor food selection, there's one thing that's good about this
    place.
"Next. Oh, hi!" the Korean grandma calls out to me with a wave,
    ushering me over.
We greet each other with cheerful eyes, smiles hidden behind our
    masks.

She types the price of the items into the register, and I pay.
I wait for a second before I leave—usually she asks me one question
    per day:
*How long is winter break?*
*Where's your friend today?*
*What color do you like?*
*Do you like BTS?*
She quickly reaches for something next to her.

"What's your name?" she asks as she sets down a receipt, back side up, and a pen.

I write both my English and my Korean name.

She sounds them out, and I'm curious to see which one she'll use.

"이름이 뭐예요?" I ask her the same question, but in Korean.

"Call me Mom."

# EMMA KUSHNIRSKY

**GRADE:** Senior

**LIVES:** Bronx, NY

**BORN:** Hoboken, NJ

### MENTEE'S ANECDOTE:

Robin has been incredibly supportive this year. When I was struggling with my college essay, somewhat last-minute, she met with me twice in two days to help out. She often gets what I'm trying to say in my writing, even when it's not yet fleshed out, and asks questions that manage to pull all of it to the surface. I've loved talking about my week with her and am sometimes surprised by how much we have in common—many of our struggles, strengths, and interests. I am extremely thankful for our meetings and her help with my writing.

---

# ROBIN MESSING

**OCCUPATION:** Teacher/Staff Developer

**BORN:** Brooklyn, NY

**LIVES:** Brooklyn, NY

### MENTOR'S ANECDOTE:

Emma is the consummate artist. When she was working on a fiction piece in our session together, she asked if I could give a short talk on character development. After working further on her piece, she stopped and asked if I'd talk about dialogue. This is how Emma works—with curiosity and a devotion to the art. When working on a poem, Emma took many suggestions when she believed those suggestions were best for the work, sacrificing even ego for art. It's a great pleasure to work with a young talent like Emma who already holds the devotion that art requires.

# my dog spoke hebrew
# and it felt profound

## EMMA KUSHNIRSKY

*The relationship between two deaths.*

I want to tell the reader about a dream I recently had. Then I will also
talk about a dream from less recently because the two are connected
in my mind. Maybe then the reader can tell me what my dreams
mean to me.

It was not the first time my deceased dog had been resurrected. At the
beach she would have leaped among
rivulets of cold salty water
Invade
flat sand planes slope
the gentle aggression of the white sky and
at the edge of the water
the dog—

When I looked at her, I was scared by her gray muzzle. I counted her
age on my fingers. Twenty-one years, but the dream math was
wrong. I found that out when I woke up. My dad's outline next to
me was wavy, his voice nonexistent. Phantom Dad could not
comfort.

I thought of the times we had buried her and the times she had
clawed her way to the surface. She was forgiving of the soil we'd
surrounded her with; she came to us with her tail wagging.
Now, before she lay down to die, finally, she spoke Hebrew,
but all I understood was the *lo, lo, lo* (no, no, no). I wished my mom
was there to translate. Instead, the jumble of sounds dissipated
into the thick air. My dog walked up into the air like she was
climbing a staircase. The horizon was laid out behind her, two
distant islands and a faraway lighthouse that I couldn't focus my
eyes on.

I dreamed about my grandma after she died, but haven't for years. She
was Russian, and I moved through a Russian river. The water
cooled and soothed, parted for my body. It was fresh, even though
there was a city around it. My hair was a pretty brown cloud around
my head. At the edge of the river, my grandma held a comb. I floated
without effort. She combed my hair.

It is strange to me that this is the dream I had of my grandma, when in
real life she was all hard corners and sharp words. I wonder if that is
what she would have wanted, or if a rounding, a softening of that
which had been built up, would have felt like a betrayal to her.
Would she rather I dreamed of her cooking, or criticizing, or
carrying her family across the Atlantic? She did like to do my hair,
but she would pull it tight and tell me it didn't look good the way I
usually wore it.

She combed my hair when I was four too. She told me she had
a magic comb that wouldn't hurt when it hit a tangle. She was right.
It didn't hurt.

There was more to my dreams, but I guess I didn't care to remember
those bits.

It is embarrassing to me that these two dreams feel similar, because no one wants me to compare my love for my grandmother to my love for my dog.

But I wept the same amount. I stood stiffly when dirt rained down on their bodies. I had refused to watch their eyes go glassy. I did not go to the vet. I did not go to the hospital.

# NATALIA LASHLEY

**GRADE:** Junior        **LIVES:** New York, NY

**BORN:** New York, NY

### MENTEE'S ANECDOTE:

I love working with my mentor. Zosha is extremely supportive and helpful. I have grown so much as a writer because of her mentorship. She is always so kind and gracious as well as hilarious. Our connection is larger than writing. It is a personal one, which allows me to bring my whole self to writing.

---

# ZOSHA MILLMAN

**OCCUPATION:** TV Writer

**BORN:** Bridgeport, CT

**LIVES:** Seattle, WA

**PUBLICATIONS & RECOGNITIONS:** *Polygon, Bright Wall/Dark Room, Vulture*

### MENTOR'S ANECDOTE:

Natalia instantly impressed me with the sheer variety of her abilities. She was interested in not only journalism but poetry, mixed media, short stories, and everything in between. Perhaps most fantastically, she was good at all of it; an absolute whirlwind, elevating polite observations into impossibly good prose. Her magpie-like collections bundle together small details from our conversations into wonderful new worlds of Bird Women and criticism. To see the world through her eyes is to raise the mundane to the ornate through simple words. She's an unstoppable force, and I for one am just glad to be reading her.

# I used to hate the rain

## NATALIA LASHLEY

*Acceptance comes after the storm. It poured and poured.*

I used to hate the rain, scowling and whining under clear umbrellas, clutching anything I could find to cover my hair. The hair I worked so hard to erase and burn away, resenting its ocean waves and spirals, too tumultuous for me to manage, for me to love. Broiling its beauty away with the crackling heat from my blow dryer and straightener. All my curves and bends crushed in the wide black clamps of ceramic, shining with coconut oil, plugged into the outlet closest to the mirror. Wrapped with silk scarves or holey hairnets secured with bobby pins, or plastic grocery bags or sweatshirts or even bookbags in an attempt to preserve the only thing I liked about myself. The humidity would puff and poof and undo everything I worked so hard to hide, uncovering the burning truth, which stung me deep like a salty wound. I was not like them. I was the other. The black girl. So I hated the rain, cowered when I walked and whispered when I talked, dulled the bright light of my hair, rejoicing in every sizzle and crack, breaking myself into more manageable pieces, and it worked for a while: People complimented me, told me I looked pretty, that I should do it more often, that I looked better that way. I took their words and planted them, letting the hate for myself grow like well-watered saplings. I hated the rain, but also I hated my lips, their size and pout, how they were lined with brown, and my nose, the way it grew wide when I smiled. It was hard to see beauty in something I was taught to despise, to cover, to lessen, to hide, to unrule, uncoil, uncurl. Taught that they were defects and not features. That day I had no umbrella, no hood attached to my coat, no bookbag, and I walked, sulking, under the black scaffolding, feeling my tears like hot candle wax dripping down to my chin. A great sinking feeling began to settle on my heart, beating more and more aggressively as the scaffolding ended. I stood there for a minute looking down at my phone, desperately trying to lift my shirt over my head, but there was nothing I could do. All of my hard work, all of my beauty, would be curled and coiled into what I would learn to love, as I walked away from the white poles and stood under the sky, which cried along with me. I felt the fat drops hit my scalp, watched my hair begin to revert to its original glory, raindrops clustering on my glass frames, blurring my vision. A graying sky with smoky clouds and fog left only the slits of a pale yellow sun. The beats of nature, a symphony let down so heavenly, which revealed again my gift to me: the beauty and resilience of my natural hair. I learned to love the rain.

# ALEXUS LEE

**GRADE:** Sophomore

**BORN:** Queens, NY

**LIVES:** Elmhurst, NY

### MENTEE'S ANECDOTE:

I have greatly enjoyed working with my mentor over this program. I am able to talk to her about my concerns and I am grateful to be partnered with such a reliable mentor. I love having discussions with her, whether it is about my life or hers.

---

# AMBIKA SUKUL

**OCCUPATION:** AVP—USD Clearing and Payments

**BORN:** New York, NY

**LIVES:** Jersey City, NJ

### MENTOR'S ANECDOTE:

It has been a wonderful experience working with Alexus Lee. She is a very talented and ambitious student. I look forward to reading her writing each week because she is a great storyteller with engaging content. I enjoyed our conversations about writing, school, life, and careers. I hope I made a positive impact on her growth and development. I think Alexus is strong with her pen and I encourage her to continue writing creatively into the future.

# The Corpse

## ALEXUS LEE

*"The Corpse" is a found poem based on* The Metamorphosis.

without a word
*Leave at once!*
following
gleeful figures.
And emerged
dreams.

Journey afraid,
eyes bowed in silence.
Three left for warm sunshine.
Quieter
in the corpse room
now fully light.

Flat and dry
without looking back
appeared a certain softness.
They passed the corpse,
giggling amiably,
sorrow bloomed a pretty girl.

Closer,
a confirmation.

*Let us go!*
They deserved a respite
from work.
The shut door,
Forgotten.

Opened morning fresh air
They left him frightful,
a burden,
seen to all.
And departed
the body.

They discussed
the jobs they had got,
prospects for their future,
a good husband for her,
and better things.

All,
without looking back at
The corpse.

# CAITLIN LEVY

**GRADE:** Senior

**BORN:** New York, NY

**LIVES:** New York, NY

### MENTEE'S ANECDOTE:

My mentor, Susan, is brilliant. From our first meeting, I was astounded by her intimate attention to language and deep connection to poetry. Also, she understood my relationship with writing—sharing in the joyous, messy journey of it. Susan taught me how to say what I really want through precision in my words, and courage in the editing. Also, she's helped prioritize my needs, to grow as a poet, but, first and foremost, she understands being a person navigating this world.

---

# SUSAN ABRAHAM

**OCCUPATION:** Law Professor/ Poet

**BORN:** Long Branch, NJ

**LIVES:** New York, NY

**PUBLICATIONS & RECOGNITIONS:** *The Paris Review, The Penn Review, Poetry* magazine

### MENTOR'S ANECDOTE:

Caitlin and I love reading poems aloud together, appreciating how they help us pay attention to small things. We've been revising poems by looking for the heart of the poem—the poem that's trying to emerge. Caitlin is willing to jump in during our meetings to brainstorm verbs, to find the surprising one that works best, to create a simile to replace a bunch of adjectives, or rethink her line breaks. She started out as a strong writer, but now she's an excellent editor too. Her poems are lovely, and her joy at finishing a poem is contagious!

# My Natural History

## CAITLIN LEVY

**Content Warning:** anxiety, depression

*This poem is special to me; it is connected with my own journey of living with anxiety, longing, and what it means to be in my body.*

I take my walk to the Museum of Natural History
dodging the wild tourists.
The sky above me fades
with my own dark.
My body
tightens with air.
The young couple passing,
their calm Spanish tongue.
How easy for them,
to walk, speak with one they love,
breathe.
I want to be the
21,000-pound whale
suspended from the ceiling of the Hall of Ocean Life.
I am as calm and graceful as the dead.
At fancy dinners, purple lights are strung around me,
and below my belly, socialites dine
and chat about the mayor.
I like how they look at me, marveling at how
I hang from the sky.

I feel sure
I will not crash at any moment, up there
above the stuffed lions.
I will not even think it.
But I am not the whale
and make a U-turn toward home,
where I dip my face in cold water,
letting my head hang an inch above the sink.
They told me in the hospital
it was like diving head first
into a pool, my heart slowing
to help me survive
the terrain of frozen water.
I'm not sure how I got here,
knowing only this cool life against my skin,
how to heal the nameless living of my body.

# VIVIEN LI

**GRADE:** Senior

**LIVES:** New York, NY

**BORN:** Queens, NY

### MENTEE'S ANECDOTE:

Working with Beth allowed me to learn so much and made writing and exploring characters super-fascinating. Beth taught me to pay attention to the thoughts of characters and how to flesh them out through exercises such as writing in the first person and imagining my character sitting on my shoulder. Through character-building exercises with Beth, I was able to strengthen my ability to write well-thought-out, realistic, and detailed characters. I'm grateful for Beth's mentorship and look forward to working with her more in the future.

---

# BETH SHAIR

**OCCUPATION:** Director of
Auxiliary Program

**BORN:** Brooklyn, NY

**LIVES:** Brooklyn, NY

### MENTOR'S ANECDOTE:

Vivien's artistic sensibilities, her infectious curiosity, and her openness to trying new creative ideas were apparent from our first meeting. She meets any challenge I've thrown at her, no matter how far out of her comfort zone, with enthusiasm and a smile. I love watching her take the spark of an idea, play with the possibilities, and do the hard work of reimagining and revising to create beautiful writing. I greatly admire her artistic talent and how that informs the vivid, visceral details in her written work. I can't wait to see what she does next!

# Shattered:
# Getting Out of the Tower

## VIVIEN LI

*The first chapter to a longer work, "Shattered" is a reimagining of Rapunzel. It follows Marianne's journey of finding her place in the world and mustering the confidence to push boundaries.*

There was a grandfather clock in the room. Her mother gave it to her as a gift. Marianne had long stopped the pendulum from swinging, finding that the ticking made her feel lonelier. From the sweltering heat of summer, which left her languid and unwilling to get off the floor, to the frigid air that drew her closer to the fireplace, and then the musty smell of grass touched by rain, she saw less and less of Mother as time went on.

That cold rainy day, when Marianne looked out the window, she realized that Mother would not come back to find her. The realization crept, inch by inch: sometimes in the darkness of night when she lay in bed counting the tiles on the ceiling or sometimes in the morning over her food.

The food was left every morning by a young maid that scurried away in fear, but a different one every morning. In and out they went, never uttering a word. The one in red with freckles, the old stiff one who carries buckets twice her weight. The maids walked past her, never acknowledging her. Why did it seem like everyone else was walking, while Marianne could barely get on her feet? They were walking ahead without her. They had places to be, no time for her, and their dizzying forwardness left her behind in the dust.

That rainy day, the feeling of being ignored stifled her and threatened to snuff out her breath. Without Mother, did she even exist? Hands clenching, she approached the door to her room, waiting.

When it opened, she reached her hand out to grab the first moving thing that came through, pushing the young redheaded girl assigned to place that morning's basket of food on the floor. The maid shrieked at the sudden attack.

"Speak!" Marianne cried.

The young maid was sprawled on the floor, food all over her clothes, tears streaking down her face, cowering with her hands above her head, shielding her body.

Marianne softened at the sight.

"I'm sorry," she said as she bent down to get a better look at the girl's face. "Please, I just want to know where Mother went."

The sobbing girl opened her mouth. There was no tongue.

Marianne fell back in shock. Nothing could be heard, except the maid's sobbing. Silence—cut by the sound of sobbing—holding time still and dragging the moment.

She turned around, stumbling to get out the door. When she finally found her footing she ran out. Out the door. Trying her best to get away from the ghastly sight.

Who did such things to the young girl? Why would they? Tripping on her clothes, she ran down what seemed a dark unbending hallway. The image of the empty mouth haunted her, sending an eerie feeling down her spine, like a stranger was watching her and judging her every move. In an instant, the comfort of her room in the tower felt foreign.

Too wrapped in her thoughts, she was oblivious to the path ahead. Suddenly, she was no longer in the tower and the ceiling opened to the expanse of the sky.

She stopped from exhaustion and fell, breathing heavily. She had never run before in her life, spending all her time in her room in the tower. The air was wet, and she found it hard to breathe with all the humidity. There was a thick fog around her. The lack of vision alarmed Marianne. She was suddenly aware that the tower was nowhere in sight.

She saw ugly trees, not at all like the ones outside her tower window that she painted. These trees were all curled and sharp, peeping out of the fog and slipping back in, as if twisted in agony. She lifted her bare foot off the ground, which was sore and caked with mud. She took a step forward.

Where was the tower? She had only run down the tower. Where else would a hallway from the tower lead?

She tried to look for a way back, but to her dismay, it was as if she never ran through the forest. The ground was untouched, as if she had never existed.

Marianne moved forward, trying to maintain her balance. She tried to keep herself from tilting over by grasping her dress. She looked down at her pristine white dress, now a light shade of yellow and brown from the stains of plants and dirt. The hem was tattered from being caught on vines and thorns. It was unsightly.

It was unnatural for her to be out and about, something she wasn't supposed to do. She had overstepped her bounds and gone beyond her abilities.

This had to be the way back. She felt it.

As she melted into the fog, fresh footprints followed Marianne, marking every new step she took. New steps that would never bring her back to the tower again.

# SOPHIA LUO

**GRADE:** Junior

**LIVES:** Staten Island, NY

**BORN:** Staten Island, NY

### MENTEE'S ANECDOTE:

My mentor and I enjoy discussing our lives each week, sharing book and movie recommendations, and reading each other's writing. We love to figure out the Wordle of the day, watch interesting movie trailers, and rank the songs on Olivia Rodrigo's *Sour*. Currently, we're working on an alien love triangle story, inspired by our discussion of the popularity of love triangles in books and their occasional unoriginality (which is why we chose an alien-based love triangle). I feel like I've gained a new friend and support in my mentor. I'm extremely grateful.

---

# AMY PARLAPIANO

**OCCUPATION:** Deputy Managing Editor, NFL

**BORN:** Brooklyn, NY

**LIVES:** Brooklyn, NY

### MENTOR'S ANECDOTE:

Sophia and I are in our second year of mentoring together. I've been so impressed with her creativity and the vivid imagery and language she uses in her poetry. When we're not writing together, we enjoy doing mini-crosswords, trading off book recommendations—Sophia is always reading something new—and reviewing Taylor Swift's latest albums.

# least favorite season

## SOPHIA LUO

*an ode to winter, but not exactly a commentary on the coldest season.*

frigid cold
warms my face,
a biting wind
caresses my cheeks.

winter hardens
and continues
and so do I.
I've always been meaner
in the colder months.
the weather and I
reflect each other.

an aura of intimacy—
all of us gathered together
bundled with warmth,
yet not intimate at all.

the winds are
careless, callous
constantly blowing.

windows closed,
doors shut—
winter questions why
everyone has abandoned
him.

those who remain outside
he tickles,
saying, "Come play
come dance in the cold."

they shiver and cuddle,
complaining,
"It's so cold out today
I wish I was inside."

winter settles for indifference
for ice and wind and snow
indifference is the opposite
of love
and yet,
winter is content to be alone.

# NOOR MAAHIN

**GRADE:** Senior

**BORN:** Staten Island, NY

**LIVES:** Staten Island, NY

### MENTEE'S ANECDOTE:

Truthfully, I was really nervous that I wouldn't get along with my mentor. Imagine my relief when I met Sam Fox for our first pair session. It felt as if I were talking to a friend rather than someone older than me. Before our sessions, Sam and I talk about school, work, likes, dislikes, and more! Sam is understanding and funny, and I feel that we relate to each other. Along with being someone I can turn to, Sam also helped me improve my writing and get out of my comfort zone. I'm glad to have a mentor like Sam.

# SAM FOX

**OCCUPATION:** Director, Digital Marketing

**BORN:** New York, NY

**LIVES:** New York, NY

**PUBLICATIONS & RECOGNITIONS:** Condé Nast Marketer of the Quarter, Condé Nast Culture Division marketer of the year

### MENTOR'S ANECDOTE:

Noor is the friend I wish I had in high school! We start every session talking about our school/work week, our families, and our passions. We have the same taste in books and text each other outside of our sessions to discuss what we're reading. Noor is truly a natural writer, and it's a privilege to watch as she uses her unique voice to make her ideas come to life. Her writing is funny, smart, inclusive, and exactly what the YA community needs.

# Felicity's Guide to Falling in Love and Not Getting Murdered

## NOOR MAAHIN

*Felicity Quinton never would have thought babysitting her sister's children would result in a wild-goose chase around New York City. But life is full of surprises (tall, dark, and handsome surprises).*

Felicity Quinton has always been the most responsible of her siblings. She's dependable, smart, and a raging perfectionist. She does not have the mental capacity to fail.

She's also standing in the middle of an almost empty subway car, left hand clutching her niece's hand so tightly she thinks she might break her bones, right hand gripping the subway pole. She's acutely aware of the lack of weight in her left jacket pocket where her wallet should be and decidedly is not.

Felicity stands there with dread in her stomach as she takes in the fact that she lost her sister's other four kids. In short, Felicity Quinton is absolutely screwed.

There's only one decision that led Felicity here: agreeing to babysit her sister's demonic children. Unlike Felicity, Amelia Quinton is adventurous and clumsy. Felicity and Amelia were never close, with their contrasting personalities and great age difference. But there was nobody else but Felicity to watch Amelia's kids when she and her husband, Trent, scheduled their sixteenth wedding anniversary in the Philippines. Being the people pleaser she is, Felicity accepted without regard. Babysitting five kids under the age of fifteen shouldn't be too hard, she thought. How completely wrong she had been.

Friday night hadn't been too bad. She'd kept them in the house and watched movies. In fact, she was never planning on leaving the house. Though, when she was faced with five pairs of puppy-dog eyes practically begging her to take them outside, she had to relent. Felicity never would have thought that they'd rob her and run away.

Amelia loves her kids more than her life. If she finds out Felicity lost them, there's no way she'll make it out alive. She feels a tickle in her nose and her eyes begin to gloss with tears. *Oh, God, now is not the time to be crying.*

"Whoa," says her five-year-old niece, Alana, snapping Felicity back to the present. Alana has wandered away from Felicity, stretching her arm out as far as it can go with her hand still clasped in Felicity's. "You're pretty."

Felicity follows Alana's gaze to see a tall man across the aisle. His dark hair is mussed from the wind. His sparkling eyes are a dark shade of brown. Now Felicity's even more mortified. Because he *is* pretty; like he was designed to make Felicity incredibly flustered.

"Do you want to get married?" Alana continues, wide eyes searching his incredibly gorgeous ones. Felicity goes red. There is absolutely no way her niece is hitting on a complete stranger.

The Greek Adonis lets out a breathy laugh at Alana's questions. "I think you're a bit too young for me, sweetheart, but thanks for asking."

"Oh." Alana blinks up at him. "Is being old important?"

"Yes, ma'am," he says as he nods sternly.

"Okay, will you marry me when I am older, then?"

"Alana," Felicity scolds, "stop it."

The Drool-Worthy Stranger looks at Felicity for a while, a small smile playing on his lips. Turning his attention back to Alana, he says, "Tell you what, when you make it to eighteen, we can revisit that question." Felicity isn't drooling. She's not. His gaze finds Felicity's again, then he says, "Now, how about you? Is—"

"I don't want to marry you," Felicity bluntly cuts in while Tall, Dark, and Handsome quirks a brow.

". . . I wasn't going to ask that," he says. Felicity turns an unattractive shade of red. The man clears his throat before speaking again. "I was going to ask if you were okay."

"I'm fine," Felicity says shortly. She most definitely is not fine.

The man narrows his eyes at her skeptically. "Are you sure? I mean, you look a bit . . . frazzled."

"Frazzled?! I do not look frazzled! I am perfectly fine," Felicity huffs in exasperation. She's not about to let some random stranger comment on her appearance. No matter how drop-dead gorgeous he is.

The Stranger rolls his eyes. "Well, if you're not frazzled, then what's up with that hairstyle? Is having a bird's nest for a head the new thing?" Felicity's hands go straight to her head while Alana laughs.

He's right. Her hair *is* a mess and she's totally *not* okay. Tears prick at her eyes. *Stop. God. Do not cry right now.*

Tears begin to stream down her face. She's frustrated and there's now a perfect target to direct her anger toward.

"Well, sorry for not worrying more about how my hair looks when I've lost the other four of my sister's kids! I mean, we're in the heart of New York City, there's no way I'm going to find them by tonight! I'm a failure, my sister is going to hate me, my parents are going to hate me, and I'm probably going to go broke because the kids stole my wallet. Okay?! Is that a good explanation for you? Or do you want me to go into detail on what these kids are like? Huh?"

Felicity Quinton is not one to lose her shit. But, boy, did she just lose her shit.

# WAGIHA MARIAM

**GRADE:** Senior

**LIVES:** Bronx, NY

**BORN:** Bronx, NY

**MENTEE'S ANECDOTE:**

My mentor, Brigid, has challenged me to become a better writer, and motivates me to take my writing to the next level. When I was having difficulty with writer's block, Brigid taught me specific methods to reinterpret a piece and make it your own. This has been incredibly helpful for me, because I have been writing from the most interesting perspectives. I am continuously inspired by her work ethic and talent, and I look up to her both as a writer and as a friend. With her help, writing "Hills Like White Infirmaries" has been a rewarding and a great learning experience.

---

# BRIGID DUFFY

**OCCUPATION:** Associate Creative Director

**BORN:** Brooklyn, NY

**LIVES:** Brooklyn, NY

**MENTOR'S ANECDOTE:**

Finding a way into very personal material can feel paralyzing. As Wagiha and I talked about how to approach the sensitive material within her story, the wisdom of Oscar Wilde came to mind: "Man is least himself when he talks in his own person. Give him a mask, and he will tell you the truth." I encouraged Wagiha to try on the "mask" of Hemingway's voice in "Hills Like White Elephants" as a way into telling a personal story. The result is a beautiful and honest story that could be told only by its author, Wagiha Mariam.

# Hills Like White Infirmaries

## WAGIHA MARIAM

*The story focuses on the point of view of a young girl watching her mother get treated for a cold at a local clinic. After her mother is treated, she is unrecognizable.*

The cobblestone ground and tall streetlights of uptown Manhattan remained luxurious for an eleven-year-old. On this side of town there wasn't any heavy marijuana scent, nor were the sidewalks littered with fast food and plastic bags. Close to the side of the 6 Train station, office workers began to pour from buildings. My mom, who was silent the entire train ride, squeezed my hand, and said that we had to enter through the back door. I asked her if Dad would pick us up, and she said he refused. I thought that the building looked to be the same size as my middle school, about two floors tall and quite wide. I saw the figure of a woman storming at us, angrily shouting at my mother.

*"JESUS LOVES YOU; DON'T DO THIS. YOU'LL REGRET IT!"*

My mother kept her head down and continued to walk quickly while gripping my hand. I turned around to look at the scowling woman as she tried to claw at my backpack. I quickly jerked forward, petrified, and clung to my mother as we darted to the back door. A man pulled us into the entryway and forced the door shut. I heard the woman's screams again before we were guided to a seating area to wait.

I watched them wheel my mother into a medical room. Mom told me she'd been going through an awful cold recently. She said it was a really bad cold and if she didn't take care of it soon, the doctors said it might even kill her. I had pneumonia when I was younger, but it was nothing like this.

Two doctors walked side by side. One wore a long white cloak. She clicked her pen against her board.

"We should check the echocardiogram to make sure she doesn't have tachycardia."

"She says she's been dealing with paroxysmal nocturnal dyspnea at home."

"She's dealing with orthopnea right now."

"It's fine. She'll be all right when the treatment is over."

The staff told me to sit in the waiting area because it wasn't safe for me to be around my mother right then. They told me my mother would be treated in an hour, which was really long to treat a cold if you ask me. I couldn't explain it, but the very thought of us staying there made me uncomfortable.

The entryway was blocked with security officers. All of a sudden, two teenagers began shouting at one of the ladies at the front desk.

"What do you mean I can't get it done without a doctor's approval? If I wait another week, then I'll have to get it done in another state. I need to get it done here, right now." One of them shoved the lady and walked to the door behind the front desk.

"Ma'am, you are over five months. You know you cannot get it done here." The yelling became muffled, and the couple was forced out the entryway, where I could still hear the screams of the lady outside.

Her voice croaked and I felt her trembling from across the room. Something about her—bloodshot, unfocused eyes, her dress hanging off her body as if it were a clothing rack, giving the appearance of something there—made me feel like there was something wrong. Even in this place, where everything indicated it was a regular hospital. There were hand sanitizer dispensers on the wall, but no one was using them. There were beds with rooms, but they were packed and I heard arguing from inside of them.

In the middle of my thought process, my mother came from the room. A nurse was holding on to her. I couldn't read her face, and I couldn't tell if it was a blank expression. Her walk was a step slower, and her hands were weirdly placed, as if they wouldn't leave her stomach. Her mouth was pursed shut as if she had surrendered her ability to speak. She looked sicker than she'd been when she had entered. Incessant streams ran down her cheeks when she saw me.

I didn't know if it was proper to ask her if she was okay. People always say it's rude to tell people to "feel better," but to rather say things like "I hope your symptoms get better." But I didn't even know what her symptoms were. At this moment, it felt like the entropy of the hospital stopped.

At this moment in time, I felt like I could not recognize my mother.

I knew we would go home by train again. Would we sit in silence the entire time? The nurse tilted her head at me and frowned. She told me to hold my mother's hand while she brought out some papers.

"Do you feel better?" I asked.

"I feel fine," my mother said. "There's nothing wrong with me. I feel fine."

The end.

# ISABEL MARKS

**GRADE:** Sophomore

**BORN:** New York, NY

**LIVES:** New York, NY

### MENTEE'S ANECDOTE:

Jackie is so fantastic. The exercises and activities she brings to workshop push me out of my comfort zone and encourage me to try new things within my writing. I've found the quiet moment to push myself as a writer each week to be both so valuable and so enjoyable. It's also been really great to share poems with each other! Our meetings have been such a great time to explore writing in new ways.

---

# JACKIE HOMAN

**OCCUPATION:** Content and Community Manager

**BORN:** Cincinnati, OH

**LIVES:** New York, NY

### MENTOR'S ANECDOTE:

Every time I read Isabel's poetry, I can't believe that it's the work of a high school student. Isabel writes with such a strong grasp of language and has already carved out a signature poetic voice that shines through in every piece. With this poem, she went out of her comfort zone in format and still managed to produce something that sounds so uniquely true to herself.

# All the girls,

## ISABEL MARKS

*I wrote this piece about growing up and being surrounded by other
girls based on my notes app.*

**All the girls,**
in their different dusty pinks,
    coloring their shirts and their cheeks.
How real everything feels.
      Lost, forgotten things,
        all of it.
   Just sneakers,
   fish and flowers.
      Different humor,

how that makes them all
    downright invisible weapons.

You build your ships for yourself.
Do better things.
Refill your water bottle.

# DEWOU GLORIA MINZA

**GRADE:** Junior

**BORN:** Lomé, Togo

**LIVES:** Yonkers, NY

### MENTEE'S ANECDOTE:

Have you ever met a person who just exudes confidence and will always be the first to extend a helping hand? That's Nicole—she's that person 😊. Being able to read, write, and talk with Nicole is something I look forward to every week; I find myself thinking, *Oh, I have to tell her that,* on more than one occasion. Each encounter brings with it the promise of knowledge and laughter. I can't wait to finally explore New York City in person!

---

# NICOLE MARIE GERVASIO

**OCCUPATION:** Festival and Public Programs Manager

**BORN:** Trenton, NJ

**LIVES:** New York, NY

### MENTOR'S ANECDOTE:

Dewou and I have been meeting for two years now. We talk about everything—her writing, her aspirations, favorite foods and memories of her home in Togo, tips for handling difficult men in our lives, and so much more. I wish I had known her when I was her age so that I might have been way less insecure, angsty, and cynical; she is the brightest, most colorful, absolutely most self-actualized ray of sunshine I know. Someday, we will meet in person, and it will be glorious—a pun on her name I most certainly mean with the utmost intention and love.

# What's Buried Deep

## DEWOU GLORIA MINZA

*Desires work in mystifying ways. Actions based solely on these impulses turn back on us in unexpected ways, too.*

INT. BROTHEL—NIGHT

**Detective Jack** and **Officer Dykeman** stand before the door, waiting for the manager to retrieve **Madame Joy**'s keys. Even from that distance, the unmistakable stench of decaying flesh wafts through cracks in the wood. Jack lights a cigarette, hoping to overpower the noisome odor.
**Madame Joy** returns with the keys and her sleeve over her nose.

JOY

We don't know how long she's been here. It wasn't until one of our girls noticed the smell a few days ago that we realized something was wrong.

As she opens the door . . .

INT. SQUAD CAR, PRECINCT PARKING LOT—NIGHT

DYKEMAN

*(lighting a cigarette)*

You can't keep doing this, man. There's a limit to how far my influence can get me. What're you gonna do when I can't protect you no more, huh?

The car starts to fill up with smoke.

JACK

(opening a window)

You just worry about what's in front of you right now, Dyke. Just know I won't be the only one going down if you fail. You've got more at stake than I do, remem—

DYKEMAN

(slamming the car horn)

Damn it, man! Don't go around sayin' stuff when anyone could be listening with that window down.

(throwing his hands up in frustration)

I never said I wouldn't do it, just that you crossed the line this time. It's gonna be harder to throw off the investigation with that woman making a mess of everything.

JACK

(staring at the blinking lights of patrol cars around them)

Hmm.

> Dykeman leans back on the brown leather seat, loosening his tie. He opens his own window to throw out his cigarette and looks back at Jack. In his starched shirt and suspenders, hair swept back, he looks more like a detective than a murderer.

> They sit in silence for a while, watching police cars drive in and out of the parking lot. The flashing lights

bathe Jack in an accusing scarlet and
Dykeman in a deep blue of betrayal.

JACK

(clearing his throat)

It's not good to linger. We best be on our way.


INT. CAR—2:43 A.M. NEXT DAY


DYKEMAN

(tousling his hair and mumbling under his breath)

Ugh, why do I needa protect him just cuz of a little
secret? Doorknobs, fingerprints, CCTV, witnesses. How
am I supposed to get rid of 'em all? Acid? No, too
dangerous. Fire? Nah, same problem. Toss the body?
Shit—that just creates more evidence. What, what,
what . . .

(He freezes)

No way am I really doing this.

> Dykeman exits his car in disguise with
> his bag and heads to the security room.
> After breaking in, he cuts all the
> camera wires and erases a week's worth
> of footage.


DYKEMAN

(muttering)

Body, body, gotta get to the body . . .

> He rushes to the back of the brothel and
> climbs the fire escape into the crime
> scene. He slides the screen upward and
> shuffles through the window into the
> grisly room. Without a light to guide

him, Dykeman fumbles, letting his eyes
adjust to the gloom.

DYKEMAN

Don't freak out, don't freak out, don—

His shoes land on something, and he
hears a subtle crunch. Stumbling back,
Dykeman's eyes land on a hand that could
once have been described as delicate.

DYKEMAN

What in the . . .

A few steps from him, her muted eyes
stare beyond him. The girl's body can be
described only as utterly broken: limbs
sticking out in awkward positions, nicks
and scratches visible through tears in
her robe, clumps of hair pulled out. The
wooden floorboards are steeped in dried
blood.

DYKEMAN

(covering his nose)

What a sick guy.

INT. DINING ROOM—8:54 A.M. SAME DAY

Jack pulls out a chair and sits down for breakfast.
His wife, Clemence, fries bacon, her back turned to
him. Jack gets ready to take a bite of his pancakes
when Clemence speaks up.

CLEMENCE

Don't forget to pray.

JACK

*(letting his fork clatter on the table)*

Pray? Why, did you poison the food?

CLEMENCE

*(silent)*

JACK

*(grunts out an apology)*

I went to church this week, Clemence.

> They stay in silence, the unctuous smell
> of sizzling fat wafting around the room.
> Her back still to her husband, Clemence
> tilts her head and punctures the
> silence.

CLEMENCE

How much do you want to bet he'll use fire?

JACK

*(looks up abruptly)*

What are you going on—

CLEMENCE

Why? Don't you think bacon fries an awful lot like
human fat?

JACK

Clemence.

> The smoldering scent of burning meat
> replaces the buttery aroma of pancakes.

CLEMENCE

I don't like playing games, sweetie. You know that.

JACK

Woman, you're not making any sense.

CLEMENCE

(whispering)

Really, would it have killed you to pray first . . .

# MUNA MIR

**GRADE:** Senior

**BORN:** London, England

**LIVES:** New York, NY

**PUBLICATIONS & RECOGNITIONS:**
Cover of *Portal Magazine* for New
York Public Library

### MENTEE'S ANECDOTE:

Toni is dedicated, hardworking, and a joy to be around, and it was no small pleasure to discover her willingness to discuss everything from Thoreau to the Kardashians. She has consistently pushed me to work outside of my comfort zone (something I will surely have to thank her for in the acknowledgments of my first book), which has improved my writing greatly. No matter how hectic life got, she always made time to share her expertise in topics from life experience to comma usage, although I know I will have to continue to seek out her help with semicolons.

---

# TONI BRANNAGAN

**OCCUPATION:** Copy and Content
Manager

**BORN:** New York, NY

**LIVES:** Astoria, NY

### MENTOR'S ANECDOTE:

I'll be honest, Muna intimidates me—when we talk, I constantly find myself wishing I had a fraction of her self-awareness, intellect, and ability to not only read but comprehend very old poems when I was her age (also now). I'm so excited for Muna to graduate and move on to college in Europe (!!), but I'm selfishly sad I don't get to be her mentor another year. I consider us lucky that the overlap in our bookshelves and Netflix queues helped us develop a shorthand quickly, and I know we'll keep each other updated on gothic media for years to come.

# We Slink into the Wilderness

## MUNA MIR

*This piece chronicles a drive upstate across the Taconic, feeling each
bend in the road, looking for familiar trees out of my window.*

The road to the estate winds like a string around my finger, curving between white pines that stretch to meet the sky. The house looks the same
as I imagine it must have when they lived here, wealthy and isolated from
all but the wind.

The other day I visited a museum where paintings hung in gilt frames.
Clouds blow gently and dew rests on baby-soft leaves. It was a history
painted by the winners who got to live outside the confines of the concrete
jungle and feel the sun kissing their skin.

The water is silent, rushing miles below my feet, too far away for me
to hear, but I imagine it. I feel the sun kiss my cheeks and it brings a soft,
angry feeling to the base of my throat. No matter how many times I blink,
the light continues to wash over me, and it must have been Phaethon's fall
that punctured the heavens and let warmth glaze the valley.

I stare into the sky, with the heat on my face, and remember faces
belonging to people whose names I've long since forgotten. The sunset
burns over mountains and glades, a match dropped on an oil-soaked
horizon.

The city lies loud and brash and dimming in the distance. Swerving
up roads and around bends that push me into the passenger door, we slink
into the wilderness, cutting through the earth until the only sound left is
the hum of rubber on asphalt.

I've always liked this part of the drive, where highway erodes moun-tain, and trees loom from above cliff faces and grassy hills. The cars zoom after one another, racing to stay above the speed limit, like ants crawling between panes of glass.

The mountains could fall and crumb by crumb dirt would rain onto our metal machine until our wheels would spin in the ground and churn up the soil that covers every window. Breath would grow shallower until four people became none and there'd be no oxygen left. I watch the tun-nel become road and the world opens up into fields of corn and grass and trees and I can breathe.

My father turns the knob of the radio and it jolts to life full of static and scratchy voices. Sound reaches into each corner of the car, but beyond the windows the air stands still. The guardrail that trails our path is a barrier of sound and life; the woods remain quiet. Clouds crowd together above the treeline and the sun lights them a painful, fluorescent white. I stare at them static in the sky long enough for my head to hurt and it is instinct that turns me away.

I close my eyes until the glare staining the walls of my eyelids fades to black. The music in my headphones crescendos and for one second my life does too.

We miss the driveway to the house twice: The highway stretches on forever, winding around and around until I feel pressure in my throat and an overcast of pain in my temples. We drive on roads that grow emptier at each intersection until we reach a fork in a dirt road and my mother's con-fidence wavers alongside the signal on our GPS. Everything is gray and barren here. I can't hear the highway anymore and I think for one minute that maybe there isn't a highway. Maybe we have been on this dirt road forever, alone and astray, maybe we always will be.

We go straight over a little wooden bridge, and each muscle in my body tenses. The bridge holds, and I force muscle after muscle to unwind as the car continues to amble along on gravel and dirt. The trees here lie naked, thin, and tall. They bump up and down in sync with the car and I watch them until we turn and the house comes into view.

There used to be a pool around the side. It sits now filled with concrete and covered in goose shit; puddles of ice form in the dips.

My mother comments on the temperature, asking how I'm not cold. I am, I say, freezing. The hike we had planned has been discarded, I was careless and haven't worn the right shoes and my coat is thin and flimsy and my skin is not thick enough to protect me from anything.

# SHAILA MOULEE

**GRADE:** Sophomore       **LIVES:** Elmhurst, NY

**BORN:** Jessore, Bangladesh

## MENTEE'S ANECDOTE:

Annie is a flower that blooms in a garden of imperfection. Whenever my heart is weighed down by despondent moments, Annie is always there to paint my world with a palette of sincerity. I've learned a lot about myself in the pursuit of this new friendship. Most important, I have found my soul sister who is the guardian of a beautiful heart. Annie armors herself with humility and speaks as though love is perched on her lips. I feel safe under her guidance and extremely grateful for her presence in my life. Her face is forever engraved in my heart.

---

# ANNIE PILL

**OCCUPATION:** Brand Marketing Manager      **BORN:** Los Angeles, CA

**LIVES:** New York, NY

## MENTOR'S ANECDOTE:

I often forget that Shaila is my mentee—she is a mentor in her own right. Shaila navigates this complex world with grace and grit. She is wise beyond her years, though keenly appreciative of the joys of youth. Shaila is humble, though achievement comes second nature to her. She is empathetic, innately absorbing and honoring nuanced feelings. And she is bold, questioning authority with gentle yet effective command. It's my absolute privilege and pleasure to learn from her. I'm comforted in knowing she will change this world for the better, and that she'll always be in my life.

# Walking on a Shortened Path of Time

## SHAILA MOULEE

*The love that you have given me shall not perish even if time separates two souls that were destined to meet. This is a love letter to you, my beautiful Ammu.*

Mom,

How many nights did you spend peeking through the windows
That open and close with each breath of the howling wind?
Are you still searching for the rainbow that curves over the meadows
Hiding timidly behind clouds that dare to veil its smile?

I remember watching raindrops stain the glass windows
As I stood atop your feet, tiptoes evading broken glass
Cloaking the echoes of your cries in the name of laughter.
We danced through nights that were lit
With a thousand fireflies aglow
When the rain slipped into my eyes, you were always there
To raise your trembling palms over my closed eyelids
At that moment I was unaware of the pain lingering behind your smile
And the sorrow that had invaded your heart
As you cast your gaze upon the shadows dancing on the gray walls

I thought I had closed my eyes for only a brief moment
But now that I look at you,
I can't help but shed tears at the sight of your white hairs
And the golden bangles that are now covered with rust
With sleepless nights that govern your time in this world,
Mom, please hold on just a little longer.

As life goes on, I'm still unsure of how to find my way home
But I know you'll be there waiting for me
While I walk in search of the secrets that you buried
In our blooming garden, doused by rain that falls in your eyes with no
    relent.
If I were to stop walking, would you hold my hands?

I'm sorry for not knowing that your feet are bruised
From walking on roads that are pebbled and narrow
Mom, I know that you are still searching
For the warmth in the cold world of adults
And I'm sorry for remaining silent that night in December
When I witnessed the weighty breath you released
Evaporate before me in the room
As you grieved the loss of your beloved father

Though I may not say it often,
I hope you know that I admire your strength to lower your wings
You saw my inner child drowning in the sea of adulthood
And with each wave of a rising tide, you held me closer
For that I truly thank you and I promise to be a better daughter
So that you as a mother can feel content
With the flower road that trails your quiet footsteps

If you ever find yourself lost in the essence of fear
Take a moment to reminisce about our love that is written in the stars

Even if your vision is obscured by the sudden downpour
You can hold on to my fingers the same way I held on to yours
The very first moment I met you

Now that I'm getting older, I've gotten used to the nights that drown in
    silence
But if I were to stop dreaming,
Would you cradle me in your arms like you once did before?
You've taught me that acts of love transcend the boundaries of language
So please don't stray when my heart bleeds through your wrinkled
    clothes

You give me a reason to believe in myself and I sincerely thank you
For watering my soul with the tears that rush from those tired eyes.
You've seen my feet limp along a darkened path.
I see yours too.
May Allah have mercy upon your soul and grant you the strength
To be patient with yourself in the same manner you raised me

Even if our footprints evanesce
Along a shortened path of time
And our eyes become quenched from an eternal storm
I will always love you,
Mom

# MAIESHA MUNTAKI

**GRADE:** Senior

**BORN:** Saidpur, Bangladesh

**LIVES:** Corona, NY

### MENTEE'S ANECDOTE:

It's lovely to write with my mentor, Deb! Discussing our writing pieces and sharing my concerns with my mentor play a very significant role in my life. I love receiving suggestions from my mentor. Writing just feels more fun with my mentor. Without my mentor, it would have been very difficult for me to finish working on my college writing pieces. I appreciate the support from my mentor and the bond we have.

---

# DEBRA REGISTER

**OCCUPATION:** English Tutor

**BORN:** Beaufort, SC

**LIVES:** New York, NY

### MENTOR'S ANECDOTE:

Each week we would meet on our video call and start with a wonderful chat about life and what was happening at school and how Maiesha felt about everything that had gone on. It was always filled with funny and poignant stories, and her honesty always inspired me. Her depth of feeling about everything in life, big or small, and her caring nature always showed through with each shared moment and revelation on life. I loved those relaxed conversations so much, and then we ended our meetings with spontaneous writing exercises, which highlighted her incredible talent and her boundless imagination. One afternoon we were talking about superpowers and so we decided to focus on character development from stories we were each working on. I gave the prompt of "What superpower would your main character want and why?" She was as perfectly astute as ever and her work impressed me on so many levels as a writer seeing a young woman who senses and articulates feelings far beyond her years. The prompt also gave my character a new dimension I'd never considered, which was a cherished gift. Working together, but also separately, was so powerful, and the unplanned nature of the writing elicited a bounty of amazing material for us both.

# My Hometown

## MAIESHA MUNTAKI

*What is your hometown? A place you return to with joy and feel comfort from. My poem will remind you of all the little elements that help us create our hometown.*

My hometown is the sound of air
I hear while riding my bicycle
So is my hometown
The mangas I read
So is my hometown
The k-dramas I watch
So is my hometown
The moment I hit back the tennis ball
So is my hometown
Every lustrous plant, flower, and tree I see
So is my hometown
The studio ghibli music I get lost in
So is my hometown
The silly and beautiful drawings I draw
So is my hometown
Every word I write on my journal
They are the little delights that
Just give the comfort of home
Ammu's cooked warm curries and desi dishes
Are the best at making
My hometown whole

At times my hometown is an escape
Escape from reality
My hometown feels consoling
From the comfort of tears
Nothing can ever replace them.
My hometown is serene and a haven
There's no one needed
To fulfill it
All I need in my hometown is
Just perfectly set

I want to be home
when my feet and socks are wet
I want to be home
when I have to choose between which friend I can be with
I want to be home
when I'm distressed about deadlines
I want to be home
when I feel disappointed and compare myself
I want to be home
when I'm not the one she chose
I want to be home
when the day feels long as if I've been seeing sundown the entire day
I want to be home
When I'm rejected over and over
I want to be home.

# TESS NEALON RASKIN

**GRADE:** Senior

**LIVES:** Brooklyn, NY

**BORN:** Brooklyn, NY

### MENTEE'S ANECDOTE:

Since the beginning of Girls Write Now, I've been looking forward to Thursday meetings with Maddie every week. With her encouragement, editing, and support I was able to write in ways I didn't believe I was capable of. The screenplay I wrote with Maddie's help is the longest and, in my opinion, best piece I've ever written. Our meetings and her belief in me have infinitely built my writing ability and my confidence. I feel limitless.

---

# MADDIE BROWN

**OCCUPATION:** Junior Analyst

**LIVES:** New York, NY

**BORN:** Hartford, CT

### MENTOR'S ANECDOTE:

Working with Tess for a number of months, it has become clear that her love for art and writing, whether it be screenplays or in this case a poem, transcends our weekly sessions. I always enjoy hearing which scary, thrilling movies Tess has watched, analyzed, and then watched again. She has taught me a new game that I love playing: Imagine what actor would play the characters you have created. I am so excited to see where Tess's work as a writer takes her in college next year and beyond that in her career.

# liar's job

## TESS NEALON RASKIN

*A self-reflective, nearly narcissistic poem about being a writer.*

it's to catch flies with honey, not vinegar.
pull the sweet out of the bitter and package
deepset ache in brown-paper boxes
To sell. it's to lie for the pillow-feather sugar
of words and the
Currency of clouded eyes and little smiles.
it's a liar's job, you know. to martyr the dead
ants in the bathtub instead of cleaning them
up
to feel their sticky limbs cling to your body as
they swirl around your feet
it's a mortician's job, or a necromancer's.
priestesses and priests of small death alike
cut off their own heads
and watch themselves in the mirror.
it's a farmer's job, or a pest's. watching the
apples ripen
Red in the sun until they fall to the ground
and open themselves to the salty earth
and their sweet insides.
but most won't let them fall, for the sake of a
bite
because above all,
it is a liar's job.

# ISIOMA OKOH

**GRADE:** Sophomore

**BORN:** Queens, NY

**LIVES:** Cambria Heights, NY

### MENTEE'S ANECDOTE:

Katie is really the best! We clicked instantly, and I really love working with her. Every meeting we have, I learn something new about writing and techniques I can use to help my readers interact with my work better. I can't wait to work more with her (and see her cute puppy, Bird) in the future!

---

# KATIE LEE ELLISON

**OCCUPATION:** Editor

**BORN:** New York, NY

**LIVES:** Seattle, WA

**PUBLICATIONS & RECOGNITIONS:** *Jewish in Seattle, Manifest Station*

### MENTOR'S ANECDOTE:

It's been a blast and an honor to support Isioma in her writing work. We have laughs as much as we talk and learn about writing together, and having a Gen Z perspective on my old Millennial hot takes is truly a special treat. I only hope that goes both ways.

# Chapter One of
# Untitled YA Novel

## ISIOMA OKOH

*This is the beginning of a book I am planning to write, based on a true story of my realizing that I liked a girl for the first time.*

It's 5:45 on a Monday morning, and I'm smiling like an idiot.

And no, it's not like I am about to embark on a major milestone—like, say, it's my freshman year of high school, or I have tryouts for a school sports team I've been dying to be on, or it's the first day of a new school year.

'Cause one—I'm a junior.

Two—I'm not coordinated enough to even throw a paper airplane.

And three—it's March 8 and I don't know any school years that start in winter.

So my excitement/eagerness/nerdiness/whatever-you-wanna-call-it, is just because I *really* like school (and, of course, making my parents proud, *wink*).

So, probably unlike the hundreds of other students that attended my high school, every morning I (in this exact order) happily brush my teeth, shower, get dressed, do my hair, greet and kiss my dog, Jammy, get lunch at my local deli, pick up my friend at their house, and venture off to another beautiful day of school.

※

"Shit. I *really* hate Mondays, Kaya. I feel like our school walks are always the longest. And it's like—that *should* be good because it's longer till I have to get to the actual school building but it's like, make my day better, not worse!"

June says this *all the time* when I walk with them to school on *any* given day of the week, so I couldn't help but roll my eyes. Honestly, they just replace "Mondays" with any of the four other options. I chuckled at my friend continuing with their dramatics, now leaning back on their rhinestone/pride-flag/punk-designed cane, trying to show a convincing "I'm-really-an-average-teenager pain" look.

"June, please know, you're annoying. And *very* dramatic." They stuck out their pierced tongue at me.

"Just 'cause you, like, jerk off to the sound of your school alarm doesn't mean you can come at me for being in understandable distress for hiking at seven in the fucking morning."

June playfully hit my shoulder. Then, in a more purposefully condescending tone, they whispered, ". . . and if I'm being honest with you, it feels kind of homophobic of you to even come at me like that. Like the *privilege.*"

Despite my dark, cinnamon-brown skin, it wouldn't take a genius to know I was blushing in embarrassment.

June sensed this and cackled.

"Oh my *god* you're so cute! Babe, I was kidding! You're my fave hetero!" And I'm not gonna lie, that always makes me smile a bit, even if I know June's comments are always glazed in friendly sarcasm.

"Well, anyways, to what I feel like would be to your delight, we are only five minutes away from the school," I said to June, hoping to hide that I wasn't 100 percent sure we were about four and a half minutes from the school's front doors. But they only snickered and stuck up a neon-yellow stiletto-nailed middle finger at me.

Rolling my eyes, I looked down at my phone to switch my music playlist to something more upbeat. After all, I was approaching the school building and that only made me more excited to—

"Oh, *shit*, my fault, my fault."

I was unpleasantly surprised by the resonance of the deep voice belonging to the person towering over me to help pick up my now *very* cracked phone.

I tried looking up at them, but I couldn't bring myself to make eye contact. They were at least six feet tall, with *really* long hair and smelled quite, well, good.

"Shit, did I crack it?"

"No *shit*, Sherlock. You should really watch where you're going, dude," June said, as they snatched my phone from the stranger's hand.

I still mustered up my best "this-is-oh-so-definitely-fine-and-totally-didn't-ruin-the-trajectory-of-my-whole-day" response with my best fake smile, waving my hand dismissively.

"Hey, it's fine, June. And you know, it's really just the screen protector so, it's, like, whatever."

But I actually don't have a screen protector. Made unusually nervous by this tall stranger, I couldn't bring myself to make eye contact, but I did notice their toned biceps protruding from a black, long-sleeved top.

Distracted, I rambled on for, like, minutes about a thing I don't have.

"Oh, a'ight. Well, sorry 'bout that, miss," they said.

As they turned, I watched their long, dark wavy hair sway slightly past their waist.

June woke me out of my trance.

"God, that's so annoying. Don't worry though. I know a guy whose cousin could fix it for you for like forty bucks."

I mumbled, "If it's quick, let's do it."

June smiled. "Okay, dork. Let's go."

# IFEOMA OKWUKA

**GRADE:** Junior

**BORN:** Bronx, NY

**LIVES:** Bronx, NY

**PUBLICATIONS & RECOGNITIONS:** Deputy Director of Teens for Press Freedom

## MENTEE'S ANECDOTE:

Shanille is an incredibly talented and easygoing mentor! During one of our weekly meetings, she presented a prompt that I instantly loved for its creativity and nuance. It required me to explore any component of the phrase *mind, body, and soul* in the context of a story. That day, I devised the beginning of what would later become a fully developed piece about the imperfections of the human experience. More specifically, the following is a carefully woven story that highlights the "body" by exploring the concepts of aging, youthfulness, and liberation through a relationship that transcends generations.

---

# SHANILLE MARTIN

**OCCUPATION:** Assistant Writing Instructor

**BORN:** Kingston, Jamaica

**LIVES:** Brooklyn, NY

## MENTOR'S ANECDOTE:

Working with Ifeoma has been such a fun adventure. Though our schedules have been busy this past year, we always find the time to come together and use our sessions to brainstorm, write, and vent about the busyness of life. It's been awesome getting to see Ifeoma grow and grow over the course of the past months. I'm so excited for the rest of our journey together!

# I Like the Look of Freedom on You

## IFEOMA OKWUKA

*"I Like the Look of Freedom on You" is a fictional piece that examines the intergenerational relationship between a great-grandmother and her great-granddaughter.*

### *Anwuli*

My great-grandmother Ebere says that there's something magical about my freedom, the vigor with which I trudge through life. She's nostalgic for the days when she wasn't confined to a wheelchair, and when her words weren't intertwined with painful coughing spells. Her frame is not what it used to be. She's much smaller now, a bit shrunken like a slowly shriveling flower.

I look to the corner of our living room, where she cautiously runs her fingers through the beads of a plastic rosary. There's an eternal scream encapsulated in her eyes, amplified by the rivers of light that so often penetrate our windowpanes. When juxtaposed with her tranquil demeanor, she becomes something of a walking paradox. Two stories merged into one being—the being I've always loved and forever will love. It is noon and I am just arriving home from school. If my early return surprises her, she does not show it. There is no greeting or sign of acknowledgment, only the hushed sounds of conversation between her and her God.

I find her voice to be warm and all-encompassing like the sun, and she takes major pride in this. Its ethereal murmur gives the illusion of ecstasy even in moments of undeniable pain. She says it's a coping mechanism, but I have yet to decipher what she means by this. I'm told that my strength liberates her, but my strength is a fluid thing. I am left wondering how one could possibly find hope in something as fleeting as butterflies.

The other day she told me that I was fearless. "Egwu adighi atụ gi!" She cried before proceeding to finish a horrendous tale of her own making while I stood transfixed by the kitchen door. I managed only a weak laugh, but it seemed to do the trick. She was convinced that my courage flowed from an infinite source, and I didn't want her believing otherwise. What I really wanted to say, but didn't, was: "I'm scared of losing you. I dread the day your lungs will give out, and my love will prove insufficient to revive you. Don't you know that the death of you will also be the death of me? You must understand that I love you, but I cannot save you."

This morning she watched as Mama transformed my tight coils into finely braided cornrows. There was something about her presence that moved me. Although the intensity of her gaze was unnerving, I could tell that there was much love behind the stare. I was confined between Mama's thighs and attempted to read Ebere's mind. Maybe if she could claim me as her daughter she would? I doubt I would object to that. I doubt I could object to anything she did.

I now move slowly toward her, deciding how best to approach her. Her sunken cheeks are stained by tears that glisten like metal under the sunlight. I can only conclude that she is thinking of Chiamaka, my late grandmother, whom we lost to lung cancer five years ago. I resort to awkwardly kneeling down beside her and make an attempt to join her in prayer. Her face remains mostly unchanged, except now her lips are pursed. I maximize the distance between us, wondering if I have crossed the line between reassurance and intrusion. I retrieve the rosary tucked in the corner of my schoolbag, and utter the next decade. A faint smile unfurls across her face, and I can now feel her eyes on me. Once I am finished, I motion to her to continue. Now it is my turn to stare. I watch her movements carefully and search for fragments of myself in her being.

She says I am a replica of her younger self, albeit a little taller. She finds my strides humorous, the way I always bounce off my toes as if ready to take flight. I'm different from my mother in that way. Mama's steps are often quick and constrained, as if she were safeguarding something of sacred importance. I've been told, however, that I give the impression of levitation. It's not just the walk, but the way my arms hang freely at my sides, ready to embrace whatever comes my way.

Mama says I've always been a curious child, perhaps too curious. She often recounts the pure horror that enveloped my eyes as a toddler when I clasped a rose for the first time. The thorns pricked my delicate skin and sent blood, the color of red wine, streaming from my left palm. When she and Ebere realized what had happened, they searched frantically for the medical kit. Ebere claims that I didn't shed a single tear, but instead appeared puzzled by the biology of my intricate little body. I suppose there was a hint of betrayal too. *How could something so incredibly beautiful be so incredibly menacing?*

# L. OLIVIA

**GRADE:** Senior

**BORN:** Brooklyn, NY

**LIVES:** Brooklyn, NY

### MENTEE'S ANECDOTE:

I've always struggled to share my writing with other people, and Ally was able to help me open up more with it. She's helped me tremendously with improving my grammar and exploring ideas and themes I'd never taken into consideration. Although I wish that we were meeting in person, our pair sessions have become flexible for my schedule, and we always have fun talks and discussions. I'm so glad Ally has helped me explore my passion for writing, and I can't wait for what the future holds for us!

---

# ALLY BETKER

**OCCUPATION:** Deputy Editor

**BORN:** Brooklyn, NY

**LIVES:** Brooklyn, NY

**PUBLICATIONS & RECOGNITIONS:**
*Departures, Here, Vogue*

### MENTOR'S ANECDOTE:

L. Olivia's passion for writing is infectious. It's a pleasure to work alongside her because she brings so much joy to the writing process. Carving out time to write together (through a screen) each week has been a source of inspiration and reprieve. L. Olivia brings her point of view on complicated aspects of being a young woman today to all of her work, and I feel quite lucky to have an inside track to her ideas and perspective!

# Disney Princess

## L. OLIVIA

**Content Warning:** body dysmorphia

*Mia, a sixteen-year-old girl, struggles with body dysmorphia when her friends ask her to be a Disney princess for Halloween.*

"Do you want to be a Disney princess for Halloween?"

Mia looked up at Livia. "What?"

"You said you didn't have a costume for Halloween yet. Do you want to be a Disney princess with me, Jaya, and Scarlet?"

Mia loved Halloween because it was the one day a year when she didn't have to be herself, when she could mask herself from the world. Her best friends Jaya, Livia, and Scarlet always came up with costume ideas for Halloween. However, Halloween was two weeks away, and they didn't have any ideas until now. Mia felt a little uneasy with the Disney princess idea because it wasn't her style, but she didn't want to be the one to break the tradition.

"Yeah." She shrugged. "I guess so."

\*

*"I'm going to be Rapunzel, Scarlet is going to be Mulan, and Jaya is going to be Ariel."*

Livia had long, blond hair and loved to paint. Scarlet was fierce and independent; she didn't need anybody to tell her what to do or be. Jaya loved exploring and was one of the sweetest people to exist. It all made sense for them. But Mia didn't have a connection to any princesses. She just decided on Belle because they both had brown hair and brown eyes.

Mia stared at herself in her mirror. She never really paid attention to her body, but now that she did, she realized she hadn't noticed her hips were so . . . wide. And that the lower part of her stomach bulged. She held out her arms and turned toward the wall and saw the bulge in her lower belly grow larger from the side. She frowned and furrowed her brows. Belle and the other princesses didn't look like her. All of her friends looked like princesses, but Mia felt like she didn't.

*You're not beautiful.*

*

Scarlet convinced Mia to go shopping after school the next day, even though Mia didn't want to. Her mind was still occupied with the thoughts from yesterday.

*Why can't I look like them?*

Mia aimlessly stroked a pink dress in front of her, frowning. *You wouldn't look pretty in that.*

"Mia, would I look good in this?"

Livia held the sweater toward Mia, and Mia read the tag. XS. She glanced over at Scarlet and Jaya. Jaya had on size 4 jeans, and Scarlet held an S tank top. Mia was an L, and most tank tops made her arms look big. But Livia, Jaya, and Scarlet could get any size they wanted. They didn't have to disregard clothes because there weren't enough Ls or because they looked bad.

*They look good in everything. They can pull off anything. They are perfect.*

"Mia?" Livia asked one more time, concerned.

Mia rolled her eyes. "It looks terrible," she snapped without much thought.

Mia hadn't meant to let it out. It wasn't her. It was the voice in her head that said it to her. The voice that made her say it.

*And now your friends hate you.*

Before Mia could make the situation worse, she left.

*

At home, Mia threw her backpack against the wall and sobbed. She didn't mean to hurt them. She didn't mean to upset her friends and push them away. She couldn't help feeling insecure about herself and the way she looked. She didn't know why it was eating her up now. She couldn't bring herself to look in the mirror out of fear of seeing her reflection. A monster who could never look like Belle.

*You aren't pretty enough to be Belle.*

Mia held her face in her hands as she let out another sob.

*You're not beautiful.*

*

Mia loved photography, but rarely took pictures of herself. She was the kind of person who would take a selfie and immediately delete it. To distract herself from the thoughts inside her head, Mia went for a walk and found herself sitting in the park across the street from her house. She wasn't sure if it was the smell of fresh autumn or the way the leaves and trees danced with the light breeze, but she felt compelled to set up her tripod and balance her camera on it. She held up her hand to a withering branch with just a single leaf hanging on, and she smiled.

*Click!*

Mia examined the picture, getting ready to delete it, but stopped. She loved the way her hair curled and rested on her back and how long her eyelashes looked. She liked how the sunlight brought out the glow in her hazel eyes and how warm her skin looked.

She looked beautiful.

At that exact moment, the voice in her head, the one that had been tearing her apart for the past few days, was gone. She found Mia's voice again, and it was so very beautiful.

*I'm beautiful.*

On Halloween, Mia twirled in the yellow dress, letting the ruffles swing around her legs as her friends cheered.

"I said you'd make a great Belle!" Livia exclaimed.

"No." Mia smiled. "I'd make a great Mia."

# ALESSANDRA OLIVIERI

**GRADE:** Senior

**BORN:** New York, NY

**LIVES:** New York, NY

**PUBLICATIONS & RECOGNITIONS:**
Scholastic Art & Writing Awards: National Gold Medalist

### MENTEE'S ANECDOTE:

Melissa and I have explored many genres together, and I always look forward to our time together to grow as writers and people. One of my favorite activities we have done was an exercise experimenting with screenwriting, in which we both wrote about the events of our day from the perspectives of three of our favorite characters from a TV show or movie. Each time we meet, I leave having learned something creative and exciting about literature or just life in general!

---

# MELISSA LAST

**OCCUPATION:** Production Coordinator

**BORN:** West Palm Beach, FL

**LIVES:** Scarsdale, NY

### MENTOR'S ANECDOTE:

Working together with Alessandra this semester has been a blast! We've had the chance to explore different writing formats and styles, ranging from poetry to screenwriting, and gotten to learn more about each other every week. In addition to our more academic writing conversations, our pair sessions have served as a space to discuss everything from the trials of the college application process to what happened on last week's episode of *Euphoria*! I look forward to each session and really enjoy the relaxed writing environment we've created.

# Memory Lane

## ALESSANDRA OLIVIERI

*This piece addresses the duality of memory—how it can be beautiful
but also hold us back from embracing the future.*

I watch the TV burst into a blur of confetti and plastic gold glasses, New
York City in pixels of sparkling lights. My graduation year flashes on the
screen, overlaid on a crowd of smiling faces as my chest tightens with a
familiar breed of panic. The new year marks a milestone in the progres-
sion of a blossoming issue: I'm getting older, barreling toward adulthood.
It's a sentiment that has been blazing in my mind for a while, and this crisis is appropriately tracked on my Notes app. In the fluorescent pages of
the simulated journal, I have meticulously collected pieces of my life thus
far, documenting my favorite moments with my friends, reviews of meals
I've indulged in, feverish existential rants, descriptions of sunsets—the
list goes on. I frequently return to these notes and allow the flickers of experience to flash fresh in my mind, finding comfort in the fact that what I
deem meaningful from my past will remain intact.

But what started as a means of sparking gratitude has newly devolved
into a more frantic attempt to contain these slices of life out of fear of losing them forever. I've started reaching for my phone to jot down joyful
times as they're unfolding, worried about my ability to perfectly replicate
each detail later. As my eighteenth birthday and graduation day creep
nearer, I can't help but feel on the cusp of being thrust into a world that
I'm not prepared for, yearning to turn around and run toward the grade-
school days of soft innocence. I'm struck by the lack of control I feel as I

forget the younger versions of myself. As I lose them, I think, I must be suffocating crucial aspects of my current identity.

I let this thinking entrap me despite knowing better. I've seen the way memory can consume people; I circle back to stories of who my grandma used to be, before her joints stiffened and she stopped waking up early to make pancakes. In her recounting of her own girlhood, she tells stories about glittering prom nights and first loves, which I can only visualize playing out in black and white with the grain of a silent film. She resents this changing world, or maybe she just resents her knees hurting too much to keep up with it. Her husband died before I was born, a man I only knew through passed-down memories—a person who is now only a yellowing picture in an attic and a gravestone that my mom cries in front of as I avert my eyes. Seeing visions of the past ensnare the adults around me, I naïvely vow to celebrate memories instead of mourning them; there is no room in my life for all this antiquated pain.

But as I age out of my adolescence, I'll admit I'm tempted to break that promise. I find myself struggling to fight the human urge to look back. *I remember it like it was yesterday,* we say—not because we actually do, but because we're terrified of acknowledging the ever-growing space between us and our memories, desperate to affirm that we are still connected to expiring moments. There's no way to reconcile the possibility of forgetting the people who make up my world now. In daydreams, sometimes I'm sixteen forever. Sometimes I'm younger. I still have all my baby teeth. The world is just three feet tall, yet limitless and supercharged with possibility. The future is something distant and enticing. A far cry from the truth, where razor-sharp realities descend, adults giving me bad news like I can take it. Magic not being real anymore. How one day my body morphed into something suddenly visible, my introduction to womanhood swift and unstoppable. Growing up seems to come at a price: sacrificing the wonder of the past for the uncertain, shadowed expanse of the future. My inner child bursts into tears at the idea of these becoming the good *old* days. Can't we just stay in the good days forever?

Ultimately, the key to navigating this jumble of past and present is striking a balance: There are ways one can shape the other without swallowing it. While I still can't bring myself to delete my old notes, I have resolved not to add any new ones, choosing instead to focus on the beauty of my experiences in the current moment. I can reminisce about the memories that naturally stick with me, and enjoy the rest without forcing them into permanence. It's far too easy to get caught in the sticky web of memory, hyperfixating on who I have been and how she may be at odds with who I am becoming. The hard thing is the healthy thing: to ignore the ghosts of past lives haunting the empty spaces and forge a pathway to the future. Heavy with the weight of inevitability, this burgeoning adulthood still looms in my peripheral vision like a threat—but soon, I know I'll be ready to take a step forward and shake its hand.

# ALYSSA OLMEDA

**GRADE:** Senior

**BORN:** Jersey City, NJ

**LIVES:** Bronx, NY

### MENTEE'S ANECDOTE:

The first time I met with Carina, we were brainstorming writing genres we'd like to try. I was interested in journalism but had never written an article, let alone interviewed anyone for a piece. I have now written two amazing pieces that have given me the opportunity to explore my interest in marine biology and talk to experts in the field. Carina has taught me so much about not only journalism, but also about interviewing and being persistent!

# CARINA STORRS

**OCCUPATION:** Science and Health Journalist

**BORN:** New York, NY

**LIVES:** New York, NY

### MENTOR'S ANECDOTE:

I can't believe it's only the second year that Alyssa and I have been working together. It's been full of exciting news for Alyssa—going back to school in person *and* getting into her dream college! I'm amazed by how Alyssa has taken it all in stride and stayed laser-focused on her ambitious writing projects. Sometimes we chat about the New York City things we'd like to do together—sadly, because of the pandemic, those plans have been only aspirational. But I feel like I know Alyssa so well that it's like she's with me in so much I do!

# Winter the Dolphin: A Tale of Loss, Love, and Strength

## ALYSSA OLMEDA

*I have been interested in Winter the dolphin since visiting the Clearwater Marine Aquarium last summer. She lost her tail to a crab trap and is the first-ever dolphin to wear a prosthetic tail.*

This past summer I had the opportunity to visit Winter the dolphin at the Clearwater Marine Aquarium. Like many other tourists in Florida, I knew of her story from the 2011 film *Dolphin Tale*. The film tells the story of Winter, a young dolphin who loses her tail in a crab trap and becomes the first dolphin to ever wear a prosthetic tail. Despite the film being based on a true story, many events were exaggerated and distorted. I came to learn this upon my visit to the aquarium, where workers and diagram displays within the exhibit told Winter's true story.

I was touched by the resilience this young dolphin was able to have after such a life-altering tragedy, but I was even more inspired by the love Winter received. The love people had for Winter became even more evident after her passing in November 2021. Not only did the members of the CMA adore her, but she personally touched the lives of many in Florida and around the world.

While it is true that Winter did lose her tail, the process and the reaction she had to her new prosthetic tail were very different from what was displayed in the movie. In order to truly understand Winter's legacy, I needed to know the full story beyond the cinematic experience. I reached out to Dr. Kevin Carroll, vice president of lower extremity prosthetics at the Hanger Clinic in Sarasota, Florida, who helped create Winter's tail, and Camelle Zodrow, animal care program manager at the CMA, who worked with Winter.

While Carroll did have experience creating prosthetics for other animals like dogs, as well as prosthetic flippers for turtles, the idea of creating a prosthetic tail for a dolphin was something entirely unheard of up until that point. Still, Carroll had a positive outlook.

"We can put arms and legs on people, why not put a tail on a dolphin?" Carroll told me.

He would find himself developing this prosthetic tail for the next eighteen months. Carroll and his colleague Dan Strzempka, manager of the Hanger Clinic, started by spending "nights and weekends coming up with ideas and concepts," Carroll said.

Having a supportive, hands-on approach and team, which included marine veterinarians at the CMA, was crucial to the success of Winter's prosthetic.

As depicted in the movie, Winter was introduced to the tail slowly.

"We showed Winter the materials just like we would a child . . . and then let her feel the material . . . until eventually we had a full piece of this on her body," Carroll said.

After Winter got used to each of the materials, which included a soft silicone and rigid material, the team was ready to put the prosthetic on her. The team started by introducing a smaller tail to Winter, about one-quarter the size of a full, anatomically correct tail, to get her accustomed to swimming with it.

However, the movie did embellish Winter's reaction to the tail, showing her rejecting it at first. Carroll explained that Winter never had a negative reaction to the tail and that that was all Hollywood.

Still, there was a bit of a problem. Dolphins cannot verbally communicate if something is wrong, and they will try to conceal any pain because they don't want to show signs of weakness. Carroll and the team needed to ensure that the prosthetic was not harming Winter. To execute this, he says, the team "used thermography to determine the heat around the material, and we found hotspots (like pressure points) that were causing concerns—if we left it on long enough, it would hurt the skin."

"We went back to the drawing board, and we came up with a very soft gel material," Carroll said. "To this very day we call it Winter's gel."

The team took their time developing the gel.

"Today, across the world, there are now thousands of humans [that use prosthetics] that are walking around with Winter's gel," Carroll said.

When I spoke with Zodrow at the CMA, she shared the difficulties of putting on the tail for the first time.

"We'd have to use water-based lubricant and roll it on like pantyhose or socks," she said.

Zodrow told me Winter was very patient during this process.

She noted that the aquarium is "very quiet without her, because she talked all the time, to the very end she would tweet . . . It's kind of weird and eerily quiet without her."

Zodrow showed me the old tails that Winter had outgrown, along with her old toys that are kept at the CMA.

Despite Winter's passing, Zodrow said that people still visit to learn about her. It's clear that Winter's presence is missed beyond the walls of the aquarium.

Winter's company provided great comfort to not just the members of the aquarium, but also to children and families. People would talk about how Winter provided the inspiration for them to wear Winter's gel to make their prosthetics more comfortable, Zodrow explained.

"She represented so much to so many people," she said. "People would connect with her and feel drawn to her."

# ESTHER OMOLOLA

**GRADE:** Senior

**BORN:** Queens, NY

**LIVES:** Springfield Gardens, NY

### MENTEE'S ANECDOTE:

Stefanie is a friendly and kindhearted person. She is someone I have learned a lot from, and I can apply these lessons to both my professional and personal life. I always look forward to catching up with her and working on projects with her. I consider myself extremely fortunate to have been paired with someone as supportive and reliable as Stefanie. She understands me and encourages me to stay true to myself.

---

# STEFANIE WEISS

**OCCUPATION:** Senior Director of Communications

**BORN:** Silver Spring, MD

**LIVES:** Silver Spring, MD

### MENTOR'S ANECDOTE:

Esther is so ready for the world beyond worksheets, textbooks, and dopey assignments. She already speaks up on issues that matter to her, no matter the topic or the consequences. She already deals with complexity and nuance in her studies and in her life. She's eager to tackle Toni Morrison's toughest novels—and anything else college throws at her. She's got moxie, gumption, grit, resolve, courage, nerve—in a word, confidence. Oh, and a great sense of humor, too. It's such a pleasure to listen to her, to read her words, to watch her fly.

# Still Her Words Come

## ESTHER OMOLOLA

*I've got a lot of opinions, and I want to speak out. Still, I struggle to deal with doubts, to find the right words, to steel myself for the comments from those who disagree.*

She is soon to speak
In the center of eyes
And her mind is anything
But empty

She is plagued with the perplexity
Of a particular concept
A feeling so turbulent, so erratic
Filled with anything
But nothingness

She thinks
And comes to a resolution
For every time she holds her tongue
She is the one who pays for it

She searches
A frantic search
For a sense of direction

She anticipates
The stares that will soon burn into her
And despite her desire to delay
The inevitable
Her words still come

Because in her thoughts
And her words
Lies the power
To make others follow

I doubt you'd be calm
If you were in my shoes
An unbridled anxiousness eats me
And in a desperate attempt to silence it
I remind myself that docility is a color
I will never wear

Still, my courage and conviction
Wrestle with passivity and doubt
In the struggle of my own desire

Anoint my tongue
And assemble my words
So I can be perfectly clear
For each of us participates
In the struggle of our own desires

# MADYSON ONEIYA

**GRADE:** Senior

**BORN:** Brooklyn, NY

**LIVES:** Brooklyn, NY

**PUBLICATIONS & RECOGNITIONS:**
Artwork featured in NYC
Educational Literary Magazine

### MENTEE'S ANECDOTE:

We haven't been paired for long, but it's definitely been one of the high-lights of the last year. We have a lot in common and a lot to learn from each other. We both love traveling and we've shared traveling tips and memories. But our styles (of most things—especially writing) seem to juxtapose each other's, and that's provided a lot of perspective. It's been awesome working with Martine, and I'm happy that we've had this time together!

---

# MARTINE SAINVIL

**OCCUPATION:** Director of
Communications

**BORN:** Brooklyn, NY

**LIVES:** Brooklyn, NY

### MENTOR'S ANECDOTE:

Mady is a bright light who has many stories to tell. As soon as we met I was immediately impressed with their enthusiasm and energy. With a wide and varied list of interests, activities, and goals, Mady is taking life on with bold strokes. Their ongoing contributions are making our world a better place through social justice work and community engagement. And if that weren't enough, Mady is a talented artist whose work is creative, intriguing, and imaginative. There's always something for us to discuss; it's been fun and fascinating learning about horror fiction through their love of it.

# And Here I Breathe

## MADYSON ONEIYA

*Despite everything, time continues to tick on.*

*Eventually, everyone's hourglass runs out of sand, and we run out of time.*

Her hands shook with the tremors of a soft earthquake.

The gates squeaked and groaned with displeasure as she pushed them open. They hit the back with a loud crash and the reverberations vibrated through the floor and lightly shook her feet.

A breeze rippled her clean white dress as she hesitantly glided down the worn cobblestone road. Her mind swirled with anxiety and fear.

Her eyes moved with purpose, flipping quickly from object to object. Staring at the swaying leaves, the vines that wrapped around the trunk of a tree, the cracked and ridged bark that seemed as dead as the rest of its home.

Small, undeveloped blades of grass peeked through the gaps in the floor and tickled the soles of her feet, but ultimately, they were crushed under the weight of her burden.

A feeling she could relate to.

Was this the repercussion? Was this what she had to pay? If she had listened, maybe she'd be wandering in a park instead of in a graveyard. In a warm home instead of in a morgue. Maybe she would still *have* a home to turn to. Now the only company she had were the screams that circled her mind.

That, and the rows of tombs.

She could feel the ghosts of fingers scratching at her dirt-encrusted heels. They picked at the scabs that covered her feet and mind. She felt her body leak red rivers of memories. The blood stained the terrain and left a breadcrumb trail down the worn path, from which she then strayed.

The soil dug its way in between her toes, nails, cuts, and gashes as she forged a new route down a row of small stone hedges. As she walked, her eyes tried to decipher the codes embedded in the gravestones, only to scramble the letters further.

She stopped as the smell of formaldehyde tingled in her nostrils. With her hands clenched at her sides, her head swiveled to the left and her eyes caught on a lonely headstone. She approached the stone, each letter shifting slightly until her own name appeared.

The hands grabbed at her now dirt-caked white dress. They seized her feet, dragging them into the dirt. They gripped her legs, arms, and hips and pulled her farther under the earth. She screamed for help, but no noise seemed to ring into the air. She called and called for someone, *anyone*, to help. A dirty yellow skeleton hand grabbed her neck, squeezing as she sunk farther and farther into the depths.

A figure wearing a black hooded cloak materialized in front of her. She reached out, hoping they would save her. She prayed they'd grip her hand—like the one digging into her leg—and pull her from her entrapment.

*"Please!"* she begged, just before dirt covered her mouth.

But the figure didn't answer. Instead, they silently watched her get dragged below the surface. As she slipped beneath, she caught a glimpse of what hid under their hood.

A skull.

And as the sky became unseen and dirt filled her eyes and ears and mouth, she felt each part of her body being pulled apart. Her skin tore from every angle. All she could let out was a quiet strangled cry. Her eyes were ripped from their sockets, teeth pulled one by one from her dry gums. Her fingernails were pulled from their stations, leaving sad nubs in their wake.

At the surface, the dirt was unsettled. The air was still, yet its energy was agitated and aroused. Blood pooled where her body had disappeared and immediately dried. It invigorated the earth like morning dew or light rain. Bright green stems rose from the depths, bright petals emerging from the stems.

Then the figure vanished.

Before long, the entire graveyard flourished with light blue cosmos flowers and forget-me-nots—bent and beautiful.

*And here I stand, my mind wandering back to the ground from the clouds in which it ran. Here, I stare at the gravestones in front of me, knowing I'll soon join the ones below. Here, I place the forget-me-not on the top of the stone hedge and stand. I feel the dismay weigh my shoulders down, yet I do not sit once more. My mind might wander again, and right now I have a funeral to attend.*

*I dust off the seat of my black dress and begin down the cobblestone road. When I exit the cemetery, I do not shut the gate behind me. I know I'll be back.*

*And like the sand of an hourglass, I continue on.*

*And here I breathe, again.*

# KAILEE ORTIZ

**GRADE:** Junior

**BORN:** Brooklyn, NY

**LIVES:** Brooklyn, NY

### MENTEE'S ANECDOTE:

I've really enjoyed my meetings with Emily, where I can enjoy a sweet treat while writing. She's so patient and empathetic with what I'm going through during my junior year. The workload and stress are no joke, but I know she will support me fully in whatever I choose to do. She's incredibly talented and creative, and I'm so excited to see what her next published piece has in store for the world.

---

# EMILY NEUBERGER

**OCCUPATION:** Editorial Assistant

**BORN:** Garden City, NY

**LIVES:** Brooklyn, NY

### MENTOR'S ANECDOTE:

After our second pair session, Kailee and I took the subway home together. We'd spent the afternoon talking about deep, sensitive ideas, and then when it came time to commute I got to witness Kailee's city skills. Watching a native NYC girl squeeze between the commuters' bags, duck under books and arms, and find a seat was like watching a bird in flight. She zipped through the platform without skipping a beat in the conversation. She truly became one with the city.

# The Downfall of
# the Hopeless Romantic

## KAILEE ORTIZ

*When a hopeless romantic gets into a plane crash, how will their experience with love plague her possible final thoughts?*

I know I am dying. Clear waves of aquamarine are crashing down on me as the sun begins to collide with the ocean. A ringing noise envelops my surroundings as I faintly hear the plane begin to combust, parts falling swiftly across the beach, just barely crushing me. Waves have crashed and the sun has collided with the ocean, darkness shortly following. I drag my knees across the burning sand, the skin on my knees slowly peeling off my body as if it must run away from me. There is no longer feeling in my feet. All I can do is continue to drag my shattered legs away from the plane. My vocal cords rip and tear as a bloodcurdling scream hurls out of my throat, not letting any air enter. Tears streaming down my face, I shout and scream for my mom's help, ignoring her limp body sunken at shore. I wish for my thoughts to be silent, but the panic has overtaken every one of my senses. It feels like the words I wish for are overflowing within my mind and spilling out of my ears along with a taunting ringing. I roll onto my back, finally making it far enough away from the plane to hear the crickets chirp and the waves crashing down, wailing at the dead she must consume. I try to even my breath as the burning begins to spread from my feet up. I avoid looking down as the blood pooling around my feet continues to make me hyperventilate. I watch the sky darken as I begin to wonder if anyone else made it far enough to see the stars shelter over us, even one last time. I wonder if my mom was able to get up from the sand, if she is looking for me now. If she loses me I'm sure it will break her world for a little bit, but I'm sure she will be able to find someone to fill the hole I somewhat left her. I'm really sorry, Mom, for not telling you when I struggled with school, for failing one of my classes, for being mean to you. I wish I could kiss you one last time goodbye. I wish I knew what the taste of a boy's lips were like. I'm sure it would be as crummy as this very moment. I never had that fairy-tale romance that swept me off my feet like the Disney princesses I grew up on. I don't have many stand-up qualities that make me special, other than my passion for love, so without finding it, was my life really all that special? I mean, what else am I good for other than loving? My mom is gone. I will never feel the warmth of her hugs or the sweetness of her praise. Or the taste of her mushy rice and roasted chicken. I made it a point to never get too close to friends, to avoid standing out within my friend groups, so if I ever lost them, it would be like nothing even happened. I'm sure my death will carry out in the same way. Like the waves touch against the coast, the wave eventually draws back. And just as the sand dries, it will be as if I was never there. The love I was so ready to give will go unheard, untouched, an heirloom no one will pass down or receive. Was all this for nothing? All my life I've lived within a false reality where I daydreamed of the different beings who I could possibly cherish my life with, who could fill out the fantasy I always desired, yet the bitter loneliness aches me to my core as I lay on this beach without the selfishness to even have a thought for myself in these final moments. Being a hopeless romantic is absolutely nauseating. I swear, if I ever survive this hell, the first person I fall in love with will die by my hand.

# MARIA OSORIO

**GRADE:** Senior          **LIVES:** Elmhurst, NY

**BORN:** Medellín, Colombia

### MENTEE'S ANECDOTE:

Despite being a difficult semester, it was great to know that my mentor was there for me. We created a safe space where we could decompress from the world and we would have a fun Zoom session instead of just feeling like our meetings were an extra assignment that needed to be done by a deadline.

---

# BARBARA VICTORIA NIVEYRO

**OCCUPATION:** Content Strategist and UX Writer      **BORN:** Buenos Aires, Argentina

**LIVES:** Brooklyn, NY

### MENTOR'S ANECDOTE:

This year we decided to start by making a collage with our goals. It was a very fun activity and inspiring to share our desires for 2022 while listening to music together. Remote life sometimes is hard, but we managed to find space to be cozy and creative.

# The Lifelong Gift

## MARIA OSORIO

*People leave a mark in our lives that will forever stay with us; this essay is a love letter to everyone who has influenced me and put me on the path I am now traveling.*

My city, Medellín, is in a valley surrounded by mountains. I grew up in a city, *sí, una ciudad,* but a city where you are immersed in nature on every street, *desde cada rincón.* Mountains make me feel at home.

*"Hoy vas a mirar pa' lante, que pa' atrás ya te dolió bastante,"* sings the Spanish artist Bebe, and I think of the American Dream. Or any dream. Dreaming is not only floating and fantasizing; it requires sacrifice and transformation. When I was a kid, the possibility of change made my heart race. It made me unsteady on my own feet. But in the spring of 2011, I had to accept new things when my abuelos left Colombia. Growing up, Abuelo Gonzalo and Abuela Patricia were my heroes. My grandma, also known as Patry, is the type of person who earns your trust quickly and is willing to help anyone selflessly. The entire neighborhood of Alfonso Lopez, Medellín, knew that about her. *"Be polite, say good morning and goodbye. Always say thank you. Remember that kindness is the key to everything."* These are some of the things she taught me: showing me the good in others, and, by extension, showing the good in me. I like to think my best personality traits come from her. That she has shaped me.

One afternoon, Patry and Gonzalo asked me to move with them to *los Estados Unidos.* At that moment it was hard to understand how that decision could impact my life. I wanted to be close to what was familiar to me and stayed in Colombia with my parents and friends. After all, I was only nine.

With them gone, there was a whole new Colombia for me to explore. Video calls were our ritual for the next seven years, hoping that seeing each other once a week on a cell phone would be enough. Although Patry wasn't with me anymore, I kept honoring everything she taught me. Every December I continued gathering donations for Christmas, which was one of the most important traditions we shared, and now I had to learn to do it alone. The mountains that had always known me found me under a different light. But it was worth it. Gradually, I came to understand that change, no matter how uncomfortable, was inevitable. I had to accept it and welcome it.

I moved to the United States and reunited with my abuelos in 2018. I was sixteen and during the first months in New York I would find myself seeking mountains from my window. Fun fact: They were not out there, and I started to experience the greatest transformations of my life. I don't know if it has to do with how this transition opened my mind—and heart—or if it has to do with growing up, but I started to care about things that were larger than myself and the valley *que tanto extrañaba*. Issues like intersectionality, food justice, global warming, and civic engagement started to be important in my conversations. Born and raised in Colombia, I was taught to be proud of living in one of the most biodiverse countries. I traveled and saw all these beautiful landscapes, but I didn't know all the consequences of the human impact. I started to be aware of people's actions and how we are destroying our resources. How little by little we are killing our homes, call it Medellín, *llámalo* New York.

In retrospect, I see how my abuelos cleared a path for my future where empathy and kindness are the foundations that influenced me, cultivating this person that I am becoming: a woman who aims to promote meaningful change. After four years of living in Elmhurst, Queens, I still seek the mountains from my window. And I see them. I allow myself to look back and visualize the green fields. It's like dreaming but backward, letting myself walk through the valleys that I call home. These glowing hills give me *la fuerza pa ir pa' lante* and the courage to dream about where I want to go next, even if that makes my heart beat fast.

# SRIHITHA PALLAPOTHULA

**GRADE:** Senior

**BORN:** Fremont, CA

**LIVES:** Fremont, CA

### MENTEE'S ANECDOTE:

Yvette has been the best mentor! Throughout college application season, she was so incredibly kind, supportive, and understanding. She helps me with my writing, constantly pushes me to improve, and is always there for me emotionally. Our conversations are so special—I love listening to her talk about her work. She's so funny and always offers the best advice! Yvette also constantly inspires me by working hard and showing me that becoming an author is not a distant dream but a real possibility. I am so immensely grateful to have someone with such a vibrant, giving personality in my life.

---

# YVETTE CLARK

**OCCUPATION:** Author

**BORN:** New York, NY

**LIVES:** New York, NY

### MENTOR'S ANECDOTE:

One hundred words could never be enough to describe all that I have loved about mentoring Srihitha over the last two years. She is an incredibly talented writer who approaches life with wisdom, grace, humor, and kindness—her strength, creativity, and fearlessness shine from each page she writes. Srihitha has inspired me with her approach to her craft and taken my breath away with her lyrical use of language. I cannot wait to see what she will accomplish in the future, and I will be cheering her on every step of the way. I am so proud to be her mentor.

# I am just a girl

## SRIHITHA PALLAPOTHULA

*This is a poem about Monica Lewinsky. I wrote this piece to reshape the narrative.*

*Some parts in style after Eleanor Wikstrom*

God, you named me Monica.

God, I am asking you to ChanceMe*,
to tell me my fate:
I am seventeen and almost an adult
I have black, shoulder-length hair
Eyes that shine brown in the sunlight
A 3.98 unweighted GPA
I've taken five AP classes
Work the afternoon shifts at Wendy's
My favorite movie is *Titanic*—

God, forgive me.
I am rambling
This is what matters:

---

\* A ChanceMe is a type of Reddit post where users share information about themselves and ask for something to be predicted, usually whether they will get into a certain college.

if a fiftysomething-year-old man
who just happened to be president
dug his hairy paws inside of me
He would find,
resting in my belly,
The daughters of this name:
A black lace thong,
a cigar warm to the touch,
a navy blue dress
with a waterfall of cum
running down the front.

God, define me:
Am I a victim or a vixen?*
Predator or prey?*
Myself or a shadow of that woman,
the other Monica?

God, I cannot find you in the comments
of my Reddit ChanceMe post.

Reddit is not God.

Reddit is the two men,
masked faces in this endless sea of unknowns,
who don't give me what I want:
The first asks for nudes,
pictures of me at my most vulnerable.
The second wants to suck on my toes.

---

* Lines from the *Vanity Fair* article "'Who Gets to Live in Victimville?': Why I
Participated in a New Docuseries on *The Clinton Affair*" by Monica Lewinsky.

Why is there an abundance of creepy men in the world?
Why is it that I am seventeen and none of the boys at school will even
    look at me?
Why is it that she is twenty-one and the entire world cannot take its
    eyes off of her?

God, thank you for the gift of subtraction.

21 minus 17 is 4.
And when I was four,
I committed my first crime:

Aged four, my teacher asked me
What I wanted to be when I grew up,
And I said President of the United States,
And my teacher smiled so lovingly
I believed her . . .
I believed her when she said
*maybe you'll be our first lady president.*

Thirteen years later,
and the only women in the White House are still wives and daughters,
What my teacher should've said instead was
*Maybe you'll be the first young girl to get the president impeached,*
and maybe then the class would have clapped for me.

God, when you gave me this name,
you asked me
To shoulder the burdens of all Monicas.
To slut-shame us
for crimes never committed:
black lace thong,
cigar warm to the touch,

navy blue dress
with a waterfall of cum
running down the front.

To call us
sluts,
whores,
cunts.

God, I don't know
if I'm a misogynist
or a masochist
or both.

God, my favorite hobby is cosplaying broken women.
There is something beautiful, even holy,
about claiming their worst parts for myself.

You know all about holiness, don't you?

Watch as I line my lips with blood red lipstick.
Dab my cheeks with the whitest powder I can find.
Curl my lashes, drown them in black ink.
Draw in seductive cheekbones.

I am invisible,
and I am trying
so hard
to be seen.

Final touches:

Watch as I slide on a black lace thong.

Place a cigar warm to the touch
near my vagina,
the heat spreading across my thigh,
searing my skin,
burning my flesh.

Paint virgin white onto my navy blue dress
and pretend it's his cum.

Watch as I smile into the mirror
the way I think Monica would
before another secret rendezvous.

Watch as I fail to look like her because . . .

I don't feel innocent enough.

. . . I will never feel innocent enough.

I am guilty of trying Monica's face on,
of trying to witness the girl
behind the woman
behind the slut.

Guilty of being a masochist,
Of trying to feel some kind of pain,
the same as Monica,
so that there is something sacred and shared between us
beyond the superficiality of our names,
or maybe not,
maybe I am just the girl rubbing the red off my lips,
smearing it across my face,
the girl who will fall asleep
looking like a crime scene.

God, I am seventeen and almost an adult,
and I am sick of trying to find myself
in NSFW subreddits,
the reflections of broken women,
the silent punishments for my only crime.

Damn it.

Burn the black lace thong.
Stomp out the cigar warm to the touch.
Incinerate the navy blue dress
with the waterfall of cum
running down the front.

God, I am just a girl.

# MARIELLA PARMENTER

**GRADE:** Senior

**LIVES:** New York, NY

**BORN:** Las Vegas, NV

### MENTEE'S ANECDOTE:

Adrian helps me develop my writing ideas and challenges me to refine my writing as much as possible; she validates all my thoughts, which I believe is extremely valuable and important. Our sessions are a safe space to me, and I feel as though I can share my writing openly with Adrian because she gives the best feedback and writing advice. In addition to her impeccable writing mentor skills, we always laugh and have fun together, which I look forward to each week.

---

# ADRIAN HORTON

**OCCUPATION:** Arts Writer

**PUBLICATIONS & RECOGNITIONS:**
Arts Writer for *The Guardian US*

**BORN:** Cincinnati, OH

**LIVES:** Brooklyn, NY

### MENTOR'S ANECDOTE:

This is my second year working with Ella, and still she surprises me each week with the candor of her writing. This year we've been experimenting more with fiction—we've both had some personal situations to work through in writing!—but poetry remains our home base for our pair sessions. A ten-minute free-write session with Ella is like arriving straight to the chorus of a song: peeling back all the feeling, opening up, letting loose. And then we get to talk about our favorite fantasy novels (Ella rescued my interest in reading from the languishing doldrums of 2021).

# Piggyback

## MARIELLA PARMENTER

*I live in a one-bedroom apartment with my three younger sisters and parents, and I wanted to write something that gave an outsider a view on the little details of my interactions and relationships.*

As Ada embraces me, her Lilliputian arms pulsate twice, indicating her eager participation in our silent game. When I hug her tightly once, she repeats; thrice, and she does the same. We continue sharing little squeezes as I savor the feel of her arms wrapped around me. She giggles and narrows her hold as I cover her face in kisses and lift her into a piggyback ride. Sometimes I put her down briefly because her powerful grip seems to block my air, but when I jump around and hear my little spider monkey's laugh, it's worth the temporary pain.

When she asks in her five-year-old voice for a smoothie, I cannot refuse, knowing that her high-pitched voice will soon change, along with our time living together. I effortlessly lift her onto the kitchen counter and gather mango, banana, pineapple, and turmeric. Sometimes she'll ask me to cover her ears, and my "giant" hands relish holding her entire head as the blender roars. The sound does not hurt me as much as it would her.

One night after getting bubble tea with friends, I walk into the bedroom filled with our four beds and two desks. Vivi, my nine-year-old sister, asks, "Ella, can I have the last of your bubble tea?" She isn't upset that I didn't bring a drink for her; she is simply asking for the remaining. Once I share, she smiles and chirps, "Thank you!"

Vivi and Ada were born in New York, while my fifteen-year-old sister Paisley and I were born in Las Vegas. My family moved to New York to pursue educational opportunities for all of us. We lived in Washington Heights while my dad studied nurse anesthesiology, and I can still recall the unceasing desire for coco helado, a frozen dessert sold on street corners. Paisley and I devoured it almost every day, and this memory of home, like thousands of others, helped shape us.

All four of us sisters have differing perceptions of ourselves and society, but one of the most important traits we share is curiosity about our surroundings. I encourage them to find excitement in the random questions that arise, and to view the world as it is and what it could be, rather than what we choose to see. I want to earn my sisters' trust; and for everything that I lack, extend to them to reciprocate. Whether I'm a friend with whom they can joke around, a big sister who makes smoothies, or a mother figure who provides comfort, they can confide in me. Their unconditional love assuages the daily burdens that could otherwise leave me believing I won't ever be enough for this world. I am, somehow, remarkably enough for my sisters, and I know that has value.

# SHERMAYA PAUL

**GRADE:** Sophomore

**BORN:** Brooklyn, NY

**LIVES:** New York, NY

**PUBLICATIONS & RECOGNITIONS:**
Valedictorian of Brooklyn Science and Engineering Academy; Winner of the Congressional App Challenge; UN Junior Ambassador Alumni

### MENTEE'S ANECDOTE:

Morgan has been an amazing mentor to me for the past few months. She is truly a role model of mine and I strive to have her level of skill and attention to detail someday. I admire Morgan's freelance work and her freedom to write about what she enjoys or chooses. I've learned and relearned so much with Morgan and I'm always up for receiving feedback on my writing—especially if it comes from her.

---

# MORGAN LEIGH DAVIES

**OCCUPATION:** Cohost

**BORN:** Sudbury, MA

**LIVES:** Brooklyn, NY

### MENTOR'S ANECDOTE:

Every week, Shermaya and I read a short story and discuss it. I feel thrilled and privileged to hear her sharp and canny observations and insights, which make me think about what we're reading in new ways. She is a deliberate, considered person who knows what she thinks about things but is always looking to grow and improve—ideal qualities in a writer. I've been incredibly impressed by the way that she's applied those qualities to her writing: She's worked hard, written prolifically, and is open to feedback, all while maintaining a strong sense of her own voice.

# The Pearl of My Eye

## SHERMAYA PAUL

*After finding her grandmother's pearl necklace, Roman's life seems to turn upside down. Given the chance to fix everything, will she make it in just the nick of time, or remain stuck forever?*

No one had been to Grandma's country house for ten years. We all seemed to move on from her death—from time to time we reminisced about the memories we had made with her, but it seemed like she was forgotten. So as I walked through the creaky corridors of her country home, all of the memories began to flood back into my mind. Lessons on how to plant seeds correctly, running through the sprinklers, picking fresh peaches from the trees. I slowly opened the screen door that led into Grandma's garden. I walked down the dirt path, dried leaves crunching under my feet. I went through the forest of vegetables and fruit trees, gliding my fingers across the leaves that stuck out. There were bell peppers, heads of lettuce, and tomatoes in every color. But something hanging on the tomato stakes caught my eye.

I moved closer to the bed of tomatoes, reaching into the leaves. My hand guided me toward a necklace, sitting on one of the stalks. I lifted the necklace, inspecting it closely. There were three rows of what looked like pearls, creating one pearl necklace. Grandma rarely ever wore jewelry; the only thing I remember her wearing was her wedding ring. Everything Grandma ever owned was passed down, so where did this necklace come from? I stuffed the necklace into my pocket, locked up the house, and started to drive back into the city.

After I brought those pearls into my house, I noticed something odd.

I couldn't seem to escape them. While I was washing my dishes I found a singular pearl sitting in my sink. I thought it was weird, but I just shrugged it off and threw it away. While watching TV I saw an ad for pearl necklaces in a similar style as the one I had found at Grandma's house. I even found pearls in my washing machine after doing laundry. My friends would come over and show me pearls they'd found in the bathroom sink or in cabinets, but when I checked the necklace, all of the pearls were still there.

I'd been on edge ever since I found the necklace. Something about it just didn't seem right, like it didn't want to be left with me. One night, before I went to bed, I was turning off the last light in my kitchen when I heard the sound of something spilling in my room. Startled, I made my way into my bedroom and turned on my light. There were pearls scattered across the hardwood floor. It seemed like the pearls came from my bedside table, where I kept the necklace. So I walked over to the table and opened the drawer, but the necklace was just how I left it—not a pearl was missing. That night I couldn't even be bothered to clean up the pearls; I just slept on my couch.

Pearls continuously showed up throughout my home until I decided to get rid of the necklace. I decided that the best way to get rid of the necklace was to pawn it—and I got three hundred fifty dollars for it. I told my brother, August, about the necklace and all of the odd things I was experiencing. He simply shrugged it off and said that I was just seeing things, "Pearls would've been missing, don't you think?"

I decided to take my brother's advice and just move on. I bought a new pair of shoes, a new lamp, and a new bedside table with the money. Weeks passed. I eventually lost the shoes, the lamp wouldn't turn on no matter what I tried, and the bedside table fell apart, its handle falling straight off as I pulled it.

I was tired of everything, so I saved up enough money to buy back the pearls. I remember passing by the pawn shop daily to see if the pearls were still there. They were sitting in the display case every time, but I worried that when I'd pass there one day, the necklace wouldn't be there anymore. I entered the small shop and the bell on the door chimed happily, notifying those inside that there was a new customer. There was a woman with a bag from the pawn shop standing at one of the display cases, peering inside. I walked up to the register where the owner sat.

"Hey Olly, remember that pearl necklace I gave you a couple of weeks ago?"

He frowned, looking up before responding, "Yeah, I just sold them. Sorry, kid."

"To who?" I asked.

"Her."

Olly pointed to the woman with the pawn shop bag opening up the door to leave. The sunlight hit the bag and I could see the pearls sitting at the bottom. The bells on the door chimed again as it closed shut. Leaning on one of the display cases, I rested my head in my hand. I took deep breaths, trying to take in what had just happened and what would be in store for me.

# VIKTORIA PAVLOVA

**GRADE:** Senior

**BORN:** Staten Island, NY

**LIVES:** Staten Island, NY

### MENTEE'S ANECDOTE:

Getting paired and working with Nevin has proven to be a blessing every year. She has quickly become a trusted confidant, a friend, and someone who I continue to learn from every day. Nevin challenges me to be the best version of myself in every aspect of my life. She is truly an unparalleled force. I wouldn't want to write with anyone else. I will forever be grateful for this opportunity, and for her graciousness and everlasting kindness.

---

# NEVIN MAYS

**OCCUPATION:** Editor

**BORN:** New York, NY

**LIVES:** New York, NY

### MENTOR'S ANECDOTE:

Viktoria is brave. That's one of the first things I noticed about her. She approaches new experiences with openness and curiosity, a willingness to try hard things. Combined with her intelligence and drive, it means that if we try a new writing technique one week, she'll be an expert by the next. It has been remarkable and inspiring to watch her grow as a writer, and a young adult. She is my role model—someday I hope to be as fierce as Viktoria is now!

# Contempt of Love

## VIKTORIA PAVLOVA

*After five years apart, Aurora and Griffin's lives collide again. Aurora can't see past her anger, while Griffin spends his time hiding his past and trying to ignore his feelings for Aurora, which never left.*

Second and third period went by agonizingly slowly. I had math and physics, both of which I was not equipped to handle so early in the morning. The bell rang and I rushed into the hallway.

I sidestepped nameless faces in the crowd, searching for the one face I wanted to avoid. I slammed into someone and grimaced, grabbing my shoulder. "Sorry," I muttered without looking back.

Fourth period was AP English Lit with Mr. Lewis, one of my favorite classes.

"Hello, hello, everyone! Good afternoon!" Mr. Lewis greeted as students filed into the classroom. "Please take your seats, open up your books, and write a journal entry based on the prompt I've put on the board."

I smiled at him as I stepped inside.

"Good afternoon, Aurora, it's great to see you."

"Hi, Mr. Lewis," I called behind me.

Nala was already in her seat, writing quickly in her journal. I took a seat at the empty desk beside her, and she shot a quick smile my way before returning to her writing. Taking out my notebook, I looked at the prompt Mr. Lewis had written on the board. *Have you ever been in love? What does it feel like? If not, how do you imagine it would feel?*

I'd been writing for only a little while before the door opened. I looked up. Griffin looked around the room. Our eyes locked. He quickly averted his gaze and wiped his palms against his jeans. *Of course he's in my favorite class.* He found an empty seat at the front of the room, *thank god,* and took out his book. His nose was practically touching the paper as he wrote.

I cleared my throat and looked at Nala. What the hell was he writing about? She shrugged.

Everyone wrote for another few minutes before Mr. Lewis told us to put down our pens and asked for volunteers to share their responses.

A girl named Sarah went first. She believed in true love because of her parents, but she'd never been in love before. She thought it would feel like walking on clouds.

Dylan Campbell went next. "Ever since I started dating my boyfriend, it's like the world began to shine brighter."

I raised my hand.

"Aurora, your thoughts?" Mr. Lewis asked.

"I've been in love before, and every time I saw him I felt like my heart would beat out of my chest. I thought he held all of the answers to every question I had about the world and how it works." I looked down at my hands. I knew Griffin was looking at me. "It was like regardless of what happened, I'd be okay as long as he was with me."

Mr. Lewis nodded. "Do you think everyone feels that way when they're in love?"

"No. Love can be one-sided. Just because you feel like this person hung the moon doesn't mean that they can reciprocate those feelings. I think that if two people fall in love with each other, they're lucky."

"I think that if you fall in love it's only because that other person let you," Griffin cut in without raising his hand. "Because they wanted you to be in love with them. I think falling in love is a mutual thing."

I wasn't done speaking. I glared at him, hoping my eyes would burn holes in his head.

"Have you ever experienced being in love?" Mr. Lewis asks him.

I watched him, his face emotionless.

"I have."

"What did it feel like?"

Griffin stiffened. "It felt like she was made for me. Like she was specifically put on this Earth so I could love and protect her with everything I have."

Mr. Lewis raised his hands in mock surrender. "Raise your hand if you've ever been in love, and felt hurt by it?" he addressed the whole class.

I raised my hand, along with Nala, half of the class, and Griffin. For a moment his hazel eyes almost seemed sad. Whoever hurt him was returning the favor. *Karma's a bitch, right?*

I turned to face the front of the room, but I could feel Griffin's eyes on me.

"As insightful as it was listening to your experiences or hopes with love, I wasn't asking you all about your love lives to poke fun. This all relates to the new book we'll be starting tomorrow." He moved toward his desk. "We will be delving into the love life of Elizabeth Bennet and Mr. Darcy in Jane Austen's beautifully written *Pride and Prejudice.*"

Mr. Lewis grabbed copies of the book from his desk and began passing them down the rows of students.

"We will learn about love, the hardships, the pain, and the beauty that is associated with being in love."

# AMBER N. PERSAUD

**GRADE:** Junior

**BORN:** Brooklyn, NY

**LIVES:** Brooklyn, NY

### MENTEE'S ANECDOTE:

Over the pandemic, Rachel and I created and messed around with so many different writing techniques and prompts. However, what I enjoyed the most about our weekly meetings were the conversations and jokes she and I had. There was never a dull moment, and even when we were hard at work she made it fun. I felt like I was working with a best friend, not a mentor, and it made the creative process all the better. Not only that, but I could share the personal hardships in my life and she would always make me feel so much better.

---

# RACHEL PRATER

**OCCUPATION:** Freelance Writer and Editor

**BORN:** Miamisburg, OH

**LIVES:** New York, NY

### MENTOR'S ANECDOTE:

Amber has grown immensely in our second year together. She makes me laugh and she inspires me to elevate my own writing. Her creativity is blooming from within and bursting at the seams! This piece is unlike anything Amber has worked on, and I know it'll blow you away as it did me. I am so proud of the writer Amber has become! Her talent will take her far and I'll be right there cheering her on.

# Infatuation Is a Four-Letter Word

## AMBER N. PERSAUD

**Content Warning:** violence associated with parasocial interactions

*Parasocial relationships are one-sided relationships where one person extends energy and time into another who cannot reciprocate it. Teenage Adam's infatuation with celebrity Vanessa Thompson takes an eerie turn.*

"—Adam? Can we talk, man? It's important, and I've been needing to say it for a while," Joseph shouted from the bottom of the carpeted stairs, slowly heading to the second floor. His heart was pounding.

He continued, "I know you don't want to hear this, but I'm coming from a genuine place. I mean, this whole Thompson thing is getting out of hand, I'm concerned."

In his room, Adam sat on the edge of his bed, playing with the metal twine in his hands. He didn't speak, breathing slow and precise, listening to the soft, almost indistinct footsteps approaching.

"I'm going to come out and say it, and I don't want anything to change between us, bro." Joseph teetered on the edge of the door, his foot just behind the baseboard.

Adam's mind was racing. Joseph was here to take Vanessa away from him.

Vanessa Thompson was the epitome of his delusions. She was an enticingly beautiful actress with ringlets that lined her face and curves that mimicked an hourglass. His walls were lined with posters and paparazzi images of her; related paraphernalia was scattered across his desk.

The door opened and Joseph opened his mouth to speak.

"I think I love you, like *love you*," he said, and as he was about to finish speaking, he saw something in Adam's eyes that made chills run down his spine.

Adam lunged at Joseph. Twine in hand, pressing so hard along his hands that his fingers turned white, and in a matter of seconds it was wrapped around Joseph's neck.

Adam wrapped the twine around once, twice, three times, and pulled in opposite directions as hard as he could. The veins surrounding Joseph's neck began to bulge and he clawed at the skin along Adam's arms. Adam's grip tightened and the twine began to cut and slice through layers of tissue.

The room went black, and when it all became clear again, Joseph was faceup on the ground. Blood littered the floor. Adam stood above him, taking in the scene. It was almost as if he didn't know Joseph at all. He had no remorse for this stranger on the floor who had something tragic happen to him.

Adam spent no longer than half a minute staring at the now cold body. Instead, his gaze drifted to a poster on the wall. The face that once had a bright white smile on it, now conveyed an emotion that could only be described through screams. Vanessa had been backing up from the scene, looking down in horror.

Adam dropped the twine and, as if it had randomly happened, he looked around with the same emotion as Vanessa. He dragged a bloodied hand through his blond locks, then looked to the poster.

"It's okay, baby. He won't be able to tear us apart anymore." Adam trailed his eyes down along her curves, covered by her sequin dress. But when he brought them back up, she was a smiling, picture-perfect person again. In shock, he backed up, slightly stepping onto the arm of his mutilated best friend. He stared at Joseph's face. Adam tilted his head as if he had discovered the secret to eternal youth. His gaze paced back and forth between the poster and Joseph. Every time his eyes darted back at Joseph, he began to eerily resemble Vanessa.

First the nose, then the eyes, it was as if he wasn't Joseph anymore.

"You're here. This is it."

Adam scattered around his room, gathering items branded by Vanessa: foundation, chestnut concealer, orange blush . . .

With a grin the size of the moon, he bent down so that his breath was hitting Joseph's cold temple.

"You just need a little bit of . . . tweaking." He began to unscrew caps and pop open palettes.

He was carefully painting the face of his friend, sometimes taking short but critical looks at the poster above. A guideline.

Small grunts and whispers left his mouth, incoherent to anyone but him. He continued to make small changes.

After a few tedious minutes, Adam pulled back so that he was sitting on his knees and whispered, "Perfect."

He admired his sculpture. Adam could finally reciprocate the feeling Joseph had for him, now that he had his own personal Vanessa.

Seconds, minutes, maybe even hours, passed before Adam felt a pair of eyes on him. Then he heard the breathing, and the whimpering.

His hand crept to the bed where the metal twine once laced around Vanessa was. He turned his head slowly and calmly toward the sound to see a small figure in the doorway—his little sister, Malia.

A small wave of relief washed over him, until he realized the look on her face was one of horror.

Malia teetered at the edge of the door, her foot behind the baseboard. "It's okay, Malia, don't worry about her."

Malia's eyes welled up in tears. She opened her mouth to scream.

Adam had finally gotten Vanessa—he wasn't about to let her get away. Not this time.

The metal twine in his hands was pressed so hard that his fingers began to turn white.

# ALINA POVELIKIN

**GRADE:** Freshman

**BORN:** New York, NY

**LIVES:** New York, NY

**PUBLICATIONS & RECOGNITIONS:**
School Spelling Bee 2018 and 2019 Winner

## MENTEE'S ANECDOTE:

In the past few months, I've noticed that Daria and I are very similar people and we get along really well. In previous pair sessions we've talked, done free-writing, discovered new words, and shared both past and more recent pieces of art and writing. Overall, I've enjoyed hearing some of Daria's writing and sharing my own. I hope we are able to continue brightening each other's days and inspiring each other to write throughout our busy schedules!

---

# DARIA SIKORSKI

**OCCUPATION:** Prestige Account Manager

**BORN:** New York, NY

**LIVES:** New York, NY

## MENTOR'S ANECDOTE:

Meeting and mentoring Alina has been an incredible experience; she is a creative force, dedicated to her craft, and her willingness and ability to grow as a writer and student inspires me! She has an energetic and inquisitive spirit and is extremely accomplished. My favorite moment so far has been her completing this poem! It was an evolution of her writing style and a great example of her ability to take critique to fantastic heights! I can't wait to see what other wonderful pieces she creates, and I treasure the works she shares with me during our weekly sessions.

# An ode to Sandy: Three things I love

## ALINA POVELIKIN

*This poem was written from the perspective of Sandy. The word "sandy" itself may spark memories of your own, but I will leave it to you, reader, to figure out who Sandy truly is.*

### Part 1: I love you, human

I wake up
I bask in the warmth of overhead lights
I open my mouth and smile

It's been a while.

How I long for a new day
Monday, Tuesday . . .
Saturday?

Dampness surrounds my water dish
But, my wish, my truest desire,
All they require
Are diligence

Though I am awake
I need a break
For time is never-ending

You rise from the dead
Or rather
Your bed

I am waiting.

Hello?

You look at me
I look at you
But, alas,
Our differences are clear

Time is a wall
And I've seen it all

But have I?

I can't help but wonder
Is there something more?
Do you also sit in a tank till 4?

I sit
I think
I sleep
I snore

Hours pass
But, alas,
Time is more than that

You leave your tank
I leave mine
And suddenly
All is divine

When I return
I come to find
The glass of my tank is ashine
Brighter than a summer's day

A buffet
Of insects
Awaits me

Perhaps
You do not understand
Patience is a virtue
If time were finite

I love you so
So perhaps time is both
A Bridge
and
A Wall

## Part 2: I love change

My eyelids open
I have awoken
To yet another
Time-filled day

Time is all I ever see

But—wait.

A graceful melody plays
When all is interrupted

I've thought about me
And I've thought about you
But could it be I've misspoken?

An ominous figure stares back at me
As I stare back at it
I move my head
It copies me
I seem to provoke it

Who are you?
*Who are you?*

We say together.

Colorful scales
And a long pointy tail
Am I a lizard too?

I cannot say I love this creature
For it copies my every move
But the end of this monotony
Has made an interesting afternoon

What I mean to say is
When you are gone
I am fond
Of change.

## Part 3: I love hope

I am alone
In the only home
I've ever known

Someday, though,
With diligence
I'll make it to
The mountains

A picture-perfect desert
Lies behind me now
Never changing
Day or night
A familiar little sight

I bathe in time
I sleep in time
I eat in time

Time is all I ever see
But could it be
There's something more?

A never changing backdrop
Sits still as
Well,
Time.

As much as time is stopping me
From making it to the mountains
Perhaps they are united

Perhaps
I'll look
Beyond.

# RIZOUANA PROME

**GRADE:** Senior

**BORN:** Sylhet, Bangladesh

**LIVES:** Elmhurst, NY

### MENTEE'S ANECDOTE:

Ever since I got to know Hanna, she has become my comfort place. She never fails to bring peace into my life and always helps me look at the bright side of all things. I am so thankful to have a role model in my life with whom I can talk about my day-to-day activities as well as gain college advice and so much more.

---

# HANNA KOZLOWSKA

**OCCUPATION:** Investigative Reporter

**BORN:** Brooklyn, NY

**LIVES:** Brooklyn, NY

### MENTOR'S ANECDOTE:

This is our second year working together—it's also our second year working together during a pandemic. On top of that came college application season. Things have been stressful for both of us! And yet, our FaceTime conversations continue to be the highlight of my week, whether we talk about writing, school, life . . . or generational fashion differences. Rizzy recently made me cry laughing when she said, "I see this trend on TikTok, it's, um . . . Y2K fashion? Do you know it?"

# Internal Storm

## RIZOUANA PROME

*This poem explores the feeling of neglecting different parts of your personality to achieve a certain goal, yet feeling incapable of doing so.*

A sudden storm took over me
The type I never knew existed
It made my world dark and gloomy
Swept away my most memorable memories

As I tried to survive
I forgot the sunny days
I forgot the cherry blossoms
I forgot the sound of stepping on fall leaves
I forgot the touch of people
I forgot me myself and I

At times it disappears
I dream for a while
Hoping things would fall into place
Just then it presents itself
Stronger than ever
I seek shelter
Try to find comfort
Until I realize it's inside
Gradually uprooting me

# MARION RAI

**GRADE:** Junior

**BORN:** Darjeeling, India

**LIVES:** Hicksville, NY

**PUBLICATIONS & RECOGNITIONS:**
Long Island Language Arts
Council Kenneth F. Gambone
Writing Contest: Third Place,
Short Story; *Polyphony Magazine*

### MENTEE'S ANECDOTE:

A collection of moments and words splayed around: It's great. Keep working on it. Send it to me anytime. You know I love reading your work. Thank you for sharing your work.

I collect every sentence and contain its fragility in the core of my memory, a jar of thankfulness; gratitude for the amazing person that is my mentor.

---

# EMI NIETFELD

**OCCUPATION:** Author

**BORN:** Minneapolis, MN

**LIVES:** New York, NY

### MENTOR'S ANECDOTE:

I met Marion this year over Zoom. The constant background of her bedroom belies the fact that she has a rich life: past, present, and future. Reading her stories about growing up in Nepal, and her community here in New York, I find a clarity of vision rare in writers of any age. She is hardworking, determined, and strategic. When I suggest new opportunities, I usually find Marion has already applied! Her brilliant work testifies to her unique experience and perspective and will be a beacon for other girls finding their place in the world.

# I am my mother's daughter

## MARION RAI

*An immigrant anthem.*

### I. Beginning

fragile hands hold me firm to the ground,
pressing weight of her heart
we are painted of a
lost, unknown
culture: आमा.
mother and daughter. afraid
foreign land, fleeting fears

### II. End

It begins and ends
there isn't a middle. It's over as soon as it begins, abrupt.
Like broken english that has been left to
scratch the walls of her neck,
choking
in the depths of her throat and then
the deafening silence.

## III. मृत्युः eulogy

haze. haze. haze. her
silent pleas to not bury her culture within her,
muffled like withering flowers in my malnourished body.
Stifling stench of guttural death
and frozen hands.
I climb to the coffin and
lay down
my mother's dreams.
a silent death to all our
unspoken words.

# JAYA RAO-HEREL

**GRADE:** Senior

**BORN:** Brooklyn, NY

**LIVES:** Brooklyn, NY

**PUBLICATIONS & RECOGNITIONS:**
Scholastic Art & Writing Awards:
Honorable Mention

## MENTEE'S ANECDOTE:

In the chaos of COVID-19 and college applications, meeting with Amanda each week has offered me a sense of stability and calm. Wednesdays at 3:30 p.m. is a time for exploration, drafting, editing, and crafting. Amanda has helped me delve deeper into my passions for music and poetry, while also offering support as I tested new genres and mediums. In my final year as a mentee, I reflect on the time I have spent with Amanda and everything she has helped me achieve, and I am so grateful to have her as an incredibly talented music partner, supporter, and mentor.

---

# AMANDA EKERY

**OCCUPATION:** Assistant Director of Academic Affairs

**BORN:** El Paso, TX

**LIVES:** Brooklyn, NY

## MENTOR'S ANECDOTE:

Three years have flown by. Three years of learning, creating, experimenting, and growing as writers together. Three years that will be treasured and missed as Jaya graduates on to brilliant adventures and new experiences! She's constructed a varied and unique portfolio from recorded soundscapes, multimedia immersive poems, and the catchiest songs I've ever heard, to poems, short stories, and essays—some finished, some still simmering. Her pen, voice, and experiences all formulate her personal style, which has been a gift to know and watch develop. Three lucky years, a wonderful way to spend them.

# To What Has Become

## JAYA RAO-HEREL

*Years pass, cycles break, moments shift, but things remain.*

There was something so nostalgic about the smell of pesto to her. Its earthy scent brought her back to the first-grade garden, jam-packed with seven-year-olds, all running around from task to task. Planting, watering, picking, cooking. She was a part of its full cycle: from basil to its blend with oil, pine nuts, and cheese, spread across a doughy baguette. She would run around the garden after eating each piece of pesto-covered bread, trying her best to be sly while breaking the "one piece per person" rule.

As dramatic as it sounds, she thought that first-grade garden pesto was very special. The schoolyard, brimming with the sound of laughter and voices: assigning roles to each person. They were a collective unit, made up of many moving parts: chaotic limbs, a part of one harmonious body.

With age, this chaos gave way to the need for order and responsibility. And with time, the world in which first-grade pesto existed shifted in many ways.

The physical world around her warped. Memories fogged.

The bright overhead lights of Key Food towered over her as she rolled the red-handled basket in her palm. People were scattered throughout the store like poppy seeds, passing by one another in avoidance and distant formations. She stopped in front of the produce aisle, sliding her feet to meet with each other as she turned toward the greens. A man leaned in next to her, inspecting the bunches of basil. "Can I grab this real quick?" His voice was muffled as it fought past the cloth. Her eyes smiled, making space for him to pick up the desired bunch. "$13.78," said the cashier behind the glare of plastic. She slipped her dollars and coins through the opening, giving no thought to how the reflections of lights bent before his face.

The crisp wind met her face as the automatic doors sensed her movement and slid open. The tight pull of plastic handles left white lines on her fingers as the weight of each ingredient shifted in the bottom of the bag. Down the block, she could spot the familiar yet distant dark green fencing of the schoolyard. Her eyes glanced through the diamond-shaped holes, viewing the subjects of her memory. The wind picked up, causing a crinkle in the dried-up leaves that hung to wilted stems.

Comfortably resting within the soft sound of the wind, she was startled by a fragmented bang and the release of tension from her fingers. The bottom of the white plastic was torn open, giving way to its treasures. A puddle of oil sat at her feet, inching closer to her shoes as it spread beneath the metal fencing. Pine nuts rolled on the sidewalk, following the wind as it pushed them into the street. The basil sat still, bound by a thick rubber band, and had landed flat in the puddle of oil and scattered pine nuts. They all mixed, but never lost their form. Unable to become.

# ALICE ROSENBERG

**GRADE:** Sophomore

**BORN:** New York, NY

**LIVES:** New York, NY

### MENTEE'S ANECDOTE:

Kendyl and I have been meeting nearly every week since the beginning of my freshman year, and in these past eighteen months, we've written multiple collaborative stories, (accidentally) read the same book at the same time, and even created a podcast to talk about our shared love of books. I can't imagine a better mentor, and I can't wait to see what we do next!

---

# KENDYL KEARLY

**OCCUPATION:** Food & Drinks Editor

**BORN:** Jacksonville, FL

**LIVES:** Brooklyn, NY

### MENTOR'S ANECDOTE:

Now on our second year of Girls Write Now together, Alice and I have formed a collaborative, supportive style of working on our writing. We spend our time picking random writing prompts; discussing what we're reading on our podcast, *Buckets of Books*; and encouraging each other to keep going, even when we have creative blocks. Alice keeps our conversations entertaining with her many interests (writing, theater, art, music, etc.) and makes me want to take on new creative projects that I wouldn't have otherwise thought of.

# Rising and Falling and Crashing

## ALICE ROSENBERG

*The five "Yearlies" stay on the tiny beach island over the summer, while the rest of their boarding school friends go home.*

Lucy wakes to the sound of an osprey calling to its mate and sunlight streaming in through the cracks in her shutters. When she closes her eyes and holds her breath and blocks out all other sounds, she can just barely hear the waves crashing on the shore and pulling back into the water.

The landing at the top of the stairs will groan underneath the quiet weight of her foot, and hundred-year-old support beams will groan back. The bottom of the screen door that refuses to fit inside the frame will swing open first, boasting to the rest of the house how lucky it is to be the first one outside every morning, and the last one inside every night. The cushions will still be damp with morning dew despite the fact that in a few hours, the sun will make them too hot to touch.

In less time than that, the front gate will swing open, the vines wrapped around it shaking at the impact of warped wood on the rusty metal latch.

There will be a steady stream of people, sandy feet hovering outside the door and dripping bodies leaning in, yelling upstairs at the top of their lungs, only to be met with a reply from right behind them, then loud laughter from both of their mouths.

In less time than it takes for the sun to heat the house, and the cushions to dry, and the leaves to lose their moisture, the island will be awake.

But, for now, there is just Lucy, and the sunlight in her window, and the ocean waves, rising and falling and crashing and rising and falling.

She thinks for a moment how wonderful life could be if this was all there was, just endless summer and soft morning light. She wouldn't have to worry about family weekend, or required readings, or anything else for that matter, because all that would exist would be her, and the four other Yearlies who stayed on the island when everyone else went home. The ones left behind because their parents were too busy with their very important lives to bother with their teenage children, with their—

"Lucy?" a voice calls from downstairs, distracting her from her thoughts. It's probably Max. He's always the last one to leave.

"What do you want, Max?"

"We're leaving! Let's go!"

These not-so-quiet words are just a formality. They both know exactly where they're going, exactly what time it is, exactly where the others are.

Lucy begrudgingly rolls out of bed, moaning and groaning about how it should be illegal to wake up before the birds. She can hear the soft oomph of the peeling leather couch downstairs as Max drops onto it, his gangly legs kicking out in front of him and drumming against the coffee table in a beautifully impatient tune. She can see his arms stretching above his head from the landing, how the blush-colored morning light falls onto his face like silk on a marble statue.

They walk out of the vine-covered house together, arms folded across their chests against the early-morning wind, feet walking in an effortless rhythm with the other. Before they've even reached their destination, voices break through the leaves, and it sounds as if the branches themselves are the ones having the conversation, not their friends waiting for the latecomers to arrive. In just a few short steps, they will call out to the others, smiles on their faces, bare feet eagerly running across the boardwalk to meet them.

# AVELINA KIYOME SANCHEZ

**GRADE:** Senior

**BORN:** Montclair, NJ

**LIVES:** New York, NY

### MENTEE'S ANECDOTE:

It has been so amazing getting to know Adrianna. She is confident, outgoing, and resilient. Sharing my writing with her every week has given me the confidence to put my words out there. We also have so much fun just talking about our lives, updating each other, and sharing our goals. We've had much to bond over, from our admiration of Eric Matthews from *Boy Meets World* to stories of the fish we used to have. I love discussing feminism, food, and what we would do if we won the lottery. I'm so excited to continue to grow our relationship.

---

# ADRIANNA C. KUMAR

**OCCUPATION:** Compliance Analyst

**BORN:** New York, NY

**LIVES:** South Ozone Park, NY

### MENTOR'S ANECDOTE:

Within our first couple of meetings, Avelina and I bonded over our love of sushi, trying new restaurants, and our love for Eric Matthews. During our pair sessions, we often choose prompts from different genres of literature and write short stories based on them. My favorite parts of our meetings include exploring new subgenres of writing and reading Avelina's stories— which always end in cliffhangers. We sometimes go on a tangent and share personal anecdotes, often about animals that aren't conventionally attractive. These things all contribute to our energetic dynamic, and I'm excited to see it grow both professionally and personally.

# The Watchtower

## AVELINA KIYOME SANCHEZ

*Excerpt from the Scholastic Art & Writing Awards Silver Key–winning short story. Two Japanese American twelve-year-olds, in World War II relocation centers, hatch a plan of escape. But something unexpected happens on the day they plan to leave.*

"We're getting out of here."

Riku looks confident, as if there's no question he can get past the guard towers and barbed-wire fences, then figure out where to go once he's out.

"But my parents said—"

"I don't care. Mine probably said the same thing. Some variation of: 'We must stay loyal to our country, show dignity and honor, to prove we are Americans.'"

I'm surprised by the way Riku mocks his parents.

"Kelly, we don't have to do anything we don't want," he continues in a hushed tone, knowing the stable walls are far from soundproof. He asked me to meet him here, behind his family's assigned living space, while everyone's out getting food. "I am not going to spend another minute waiting for freedom that might never come. They're taking away our civil rights, you know."

"What?"

"You've read the constitution, right?"

I didn't know Riku before the war, but he's always telling me about how much he loved to read. But since we were allowed only one bag each, he couldn't bring his books here.

"Uh . . . no?"

"We've been evacuated without any probable cause. No warrant, no evidence, no trial."

"And . . . you really think we can escape?" I ask, coming back to the point.

"Absolutely, Kelly."

I think about my family. Mother hasn't been the same since we got here two months ago. Father yells at us constantly. My older sister Anne is mean now and acts like how Mother is supposed to act.

"I'm in."

Riku goes on to explain the complicated but surprisingly reasonable plan of escape, involving a diversion, crawling under the barbed wire, and then making it all the way to the train station. Once we're out we'll have to hide our Japanese ancestry, pretending we're Chinese or Korean, and we can live regular lives again.

When I come back to my family's tiny stall, I enter a typical scene: Mother scrubbing the floor, Father sitting down and smoking his pipe, and Anne mending a torn curtain. The smoke from Father's pipe fills the single room with a thick fog, and my eyes tear up as I enter.

Anne coughs. "Father, would you mind smoking outside?"

Father looks up from the notebook he's writing in. "Yes, Anne, I would mind," he snaps.

"Good morning," I say.

They all look up for a split second before going back to their business.

The sun shines through the open holes that are supposed to be windows, as well as the cracks in between the wood slabs. I wonder which racehorse used to live here.

There's a small pile of grass and weeds in the corner of the room, which Mother has spent all day pulling out of the ground. We still haven't been able to find more wood to put over the bare floor. Mother scrubs anyway, even though we all know it's pointless.

"Hi, Mother," I say, crouching by her side. "Do you need help?"

Ever since the evacuation, she hasn't spoken much. Today is no different.

The big day arrives. I barely speak to my family, and I stay outside. I didn't expect leaving them to feel as terrible as it does, so I'm hoping that if I avoid them today, the need to hold on to them will stop feeling so strong. I'll find them again when they're released for real.

Rather than worrying more about everything that could go wrong, I imagine what could go right. I'll stick with Riku. Maybe I can ask my best friend Lindsay if we can stay in her basement. She's always been mad about my family having to leave.

Then, once we're settled, I'll start school again. I'll also catch up on my favorite radio shows and Riku will get new books. I'll get a job so that my family can have some money when they're out. I'll use toilets that aren't lined up in an open room and shared by everyone in the block, and eat food that doesn't make my stomach turn. I'll smell the clean air, and when I look to the distance I won't see barbed wire or watchtowers.

When the sun is high in the sky, we meet by the barbed wire to play hopscotch from squares Riku draws in the dirt. No one is around except for the guards in the towers, whose eyes I can feel watching us—just like always.

Then, out of nowhere, a young man rushes past us, panting hard. Curious, we watch him as he runs to the fence, stops suddenly, then looks at the floor as if he's found a lost possession. He bends down.

A gunshot sounds, the blast continuing to ring in my eardrums. All of my senses pause as my ears fill with the sound, burning it into my memory. Then I see the man lying facedown on the floor, red pooling out beneath him.

I'm frozen in place, unthinking and unfeeling, just staring. Until I feel a yank on my arm, and find myself being pulled away as Riku and I run for our lives because we might be next.

# DIANA SANCHEZ VARGAS

**GRADE:** Junior

**BORN:** Queens, NY

**LIVES:** Corona, NY

### MENTEE'S ANECDOTE:

I didn't think I would enjoy myself in Girls Write Now because COVID has sucked me dry of my happiness and my dreams, but meeting Alison and just talking with her brought back some part of me that loved writing. Throughout the months together, we talked and wrote about the most random ideas I had. She always asked the right questions after we were done, almost as if she wanted to know exactly what was in my head. I'm proud to say that she's gotten very close, not just to what I'm thinking but also to my writing.

---

# ALISON LEWIS

**OCCUPATION:** Literary Agent

**BORN:** Brooklyn, NY

**LIVES:** Brooklyn, NY

### MENTOR'S ANECDOTE:

Diana wrote this piece with a kind of freedom that felt new and exciting—she recorded the thoughts on the page as they came to her, without polishing or censoring them to "make sense" or sound "appropriate." It made for an essay that feels poetic, raw, and real—one I've been awed by since reading the first draft. It was a great joy to watch her edit her own work, pruning and rewriting to get at the feelings even more precisely, to get both the sound and meaning of the lines just right. I am very proud of her!

# Cherophobia

## DIANA SANCHEZ VARGAS

*"We are shaped by our thoughts; we become what we think."*

*This piece helped me break free and I will forever be thankful to my mentor for encouraging me.*

**I pick at every little feature on my face.**
Some people self-harm by cutting or scratching,
I do it by picking at every bubble on my arms and face.
The acne on my face can keep me distracted for a long time,
Always itchy and bleeding; I probably shouldn't pick on it
That's how infections begin
**I've thought of scratching myself across the face**
Maybe then I'll be happier. I'll have something to show off,
**The stretch marks across my back**
**The skin on my arms covered in pimples,**
**I don't honestly know why my skin is that way**
**Especially when it used to be smooth.**
The perfect body doesn't exist; the perfect skin is covered by makeup.
My youth isn't going to be buried under the perfection of society.
I won't ever press my own children to cover themselves up,
they [she] will never know my pain. I'm dealing with everything now
   so that she'll never deal with it.
Let's trade places now, maybe then I'll be happier in the future.

I can't decide whether or not to resign my fate to being a mother or to be free forever.

My children's features live in me, one day they'll [I'll] see my face on theirs.

Hopefully I live long enough to love myself and them.

I know I say a lot of things but I've loved children

**[Just never my own sisters.]**

I want to have my own children one day but I know I'll be criticized by everyone around me

college isn't something on my mind anymore; making films and showing my world to the rest of the world

**That's my dream now. To have a family of my own whether adopted or not at whatever age I want.**

I can start fostering children at 18. Yet I'll probably still be here in the same apartment as my parents and siblings.

I want to be able to move on and heal from everything. I have so many open scars that I keep picking at.

I don't know if therapy is going to help me or not; if I'm able to talk about this then something has to change, [right?]

I plan on leaving once I'm in college.

It's not promised but I want to make a name for myself. Not a name I hate or think too little of, but one held with respect.

Diana, you've probably heard of it. Must have been named after the princess, right? Honestly I don't know, my dad chose my name and my mom chose my middle name. Named after an actress.

**Maybe Paola would have been a better person than me.**

They always said I would be a good actress [dramatic and a crybaby]

I've always wanted to entertain, to be seen even if I'm not heard.

The job would keep me entertained for a while.

**I kinda want to be a medical examiner or coroner. Rather deal with the dead than the living. I've had enough for my lifetime.**

# MARZIA AFRIN SEEMAT

**GRADE:** Sophomore

**BORN:** Dhaka, Bangladesh

**LIVES:** Jamaica, NY

### MENTEE'S ANECDOTE:

Madeline and I are constantly learning from each other, sharing our perspectives on life. To be honest, Madeline is the best mentor I could ever wish for. She is always there for me whenever I need to let my emotions out. She is always curious to learn about my techniques for writing and is excited to share her way of writing. She takes her time to understand my viewpoints as she explores my writings in depth. Another reason I love my mentor is that she helps me identify who I am as a person and as a writer.

# MADELINE DIAMOND

**OCCUPATION:** Ecommerce
Writer/Associate Digital Editor

**BORN:** Dana Point, CA

**LIVES:** Brooklyn, NY

### MENTOR'S ANECDOTE:

Every time I log on to our weekly Google Meets, I can't wait to see what Marzia has written, whether it's a short story, a poem, or a personal essay. It's always a fun and inspiring adventure, but when she shared the first draft of "The Princess," we both knew she had truly come up with something special. Certain sentences from that first draft still stick with me to this day, and it's been an incredible experience to watch her process as she finalizes every piece of writing, but especially with this story. I'm already excited to read what she writes next!

# The Princess

## MARZIA AFRIN SEEMAT

*A broken princess discovers a power that she held in herself from the beginning . . . But most important: Who is this princess?*

Once upon a time, there was a princess, with long, dark hair, wide eyes, and a bright smile with a dimple on her left cheek. Unlike any other princess, she didn't have an empire, nor a ton of soldiers, or a prince. All she had was an innocent heart filled with pain. Her misty-eyed tears used to soak her pillow every night as she glared at the stars, quietly, from her small window.

All she wanted was for someone to listen to her; to understand her; to support her; to wipe her tears; to hug her tight; to not judge her like the rest of the world; simply for someone to love her. But all she had were inner demons, constantly fighting with her little heart, as it cried out *silently* inside.

This princess was unique. She was fake to the world, but real to herself; fake to the sun but real to the stars. She used to put fake smiles on around others, pretending to be the happiest soul alive. But only she knew about the deep scars each of her smiles left in her heart. She often found herself standing before the mirror, observing her crystal-clear reflection, where she always stood with a broken heart, a tired soul, and a shut mouth, along with her hollow eyes, which kept dropping blobs of tears. Maybe those tears were the only possible way for her heart to express its pain with her soul. Maybe her soul was looking for the real princess through her eyes, who got lost long ago trying to fit in among the worldly creatures. Or maybe her soul decided to be the one listening to her unspoken pain.

Every morning she wiped away her tears, trying to be wise, to be strong, to hold back her brokenheartedness. But no matter how much she tried, tears always managed to find their way back to her eyes. If pain taught her anything, it was to control her emotions in front of others. Because she knew no one cared. She knew about the self-centered characteristics of humans. She knew about the jealousy her smiles produced. She knew that others wanted her "perfect" life, which she only pretended to live.

At one point, she got tired . . . tired of pretending . . . tired of forcing . . . tired of presenting herself as a different person before her loved ones. It seemed like she became a complete stranger to the people she shared her life with. She wanted to change that. She wanted to reveal herself . . . her pains, her struggles, her insecurities, her true life . . . precisely, the Real Princess. But what could she do? None of them asked; they all got fooled by her forced smiles . . .

What else could she do other than faking those smiles? Ignoring her confusing memories was difficult. Sometimes they left her with a feeling of beautiful warmth. But mostly, with ache and nostalgia.

Those dark memories used to be her weaknesses until she learned to let them fuel her. She taught herself to wipe away her own tears because no one else would. Now she started to look into the mirror without a swollen face but with sparkling eyes. Now she admired the stars at night. After all, the stars were the only ones who had seen her every night, dragging herself to sleep. They were the only ones who saw her without her fake mask. They were the only ones who knew about her deep, dark pains, which she carried all day. They were the only ones with whom she could let her heart speak in its own language. After a long time, those shining luminaries up in the sky got to see this princess sleep without a puffy face or a drenched pillow.

It is often said, when the heart wrings with pain, hatred is the only thing that offers a hand. The same thing happened for her. Those pains crossed the limit of her tolerance. So hatred took the place instead. But this time, she didn't hate herself. She didn't blame herself like before. She didn't force herself to wear a fake mask for others. She didn't let herself run into the life-maze again. This new princess *finally* learned to liberate herself. She refused to let anyone or anything control her besides herself— not even a memory. She repelled everything that would cost her even one droplet of tears. She started to use her inner storms, which she held in herself for so long, as her weapon. A weapon that would let her sleep in peace again. A weapon that would bring her smile back. A weapon that would wipe away all her pain. A weapon that would bring back her innocent soul, but this time with a new version. A completely distinct version of herself who will not get betrayed again, will not get manipulated again, will not get lied to again. Someone who will not get bullied, neglected, or threatened again; someone who will not feel abandoned, played, or hurt again. Someone who will not waste her precious tears again; simply someone who will not allow the world to shatter her again.

# MICHELLE SEUCAN

**GRADE:** Senior

**BORN:** Staten Island, NY

**LIVES:** Staten Island, NY

**PUBLICATIONS & RECOGNITIONS:**
Coauthor of *Songs of Peace* and *Across the Spectrum of Socioeconomics: Issue 1* (published by Google Books and Harvard University); Scholastic Art & Writing Awards: Gold and Silver Keys

### MENTEE'S ANECDOTE:

My Sundays with Stevie are ones I have looked forward to since that fateful October in 2020 when I first met her over Zoom. Since then, we've grown together, as writers and as women. We've shared our life stories with each other through our own written works and have been there for each other through times of stress. Stevie is one of the smartest, most creative, and funniest people I've met in my life, and as we continue our journeys in media and life, I know she is someone I'll keep in touch with even beyond Girls Write Now.

# STEVIE BORRELLO

**OCCUPATION:** Producer/Journalist

**BORN:** Danbury, CT

**LIVES:** Brooklyn, NY

**PUBLICATIONS & RECOGNITIONS:**
"Prisoners Are Going Viral on TikTok," Vice News; "Hamilton's Pharmacopeia"; "Invisible Monsters and Tomato Soup," Short film for *The New Yorker*

### MENTOR'S ANECDOTE:

It's been a joy being Michelle's mentor for a second year and seeing her growth not only as a writer, but also as a determined, motivated young woman preparing for the next big chapter in her educational career. She worked so diligently to craft an outstanding personal essay, which we workshopped during our pair sessions. It's bittersweet that our time together will be ending once she graduates, but I'm so excited for her future successes and will keep cheering her on in the years to come. I'm so grateful for this program and to have met someone as brilliant as Michelle.

# The Step Calculator of Life

## MICHELLE SEUCAN

*A whimsical narrative of my life as my step count increases. Through-
out my journey, I meet different parts of myself, from Curiosity to
Shame. It's a story of how these "people" have helped me grow.*

*Humans take 1.5 million steps yearly, and millions of others in their life-
time.*

I feel the rocks crack underneath my Hello Kitty flip-flops, a pair I've
had since the dawn of time. Whipping out the step tracker on my phone,
a large blue number shines back at me:

**17,000,000.**

And counting.

It gets lonely sometimes, going on this journey by myself.

But Solitude is an old friend of mine.

We first met around 9 million steps ago when I wandered away from
my family on a beach in Punta Cana. Passing by an ordinary sailor near
the coconut trees, She whispered how the sailor was an astronaut lost
across the cosmos, his boat a portal to the Andromeda galaxy.

Together, we learned to paint the world with nonexistent colors, our
works born from the marriage between Observation and Imagination.

But Solitude wasn't my only companion.

The daughter of Romanian and Taiwanese immigrants, I met Curiosity
on the convergence of my Eurasian paths. We'd stroll down alleyways
behind Eastern European castles, conversing with street performers

about the educational disparities in Romania, or traversing down earthy trails by Sun Moon Lake, devouring my grandmother's Chinese dictionaries as we did with her mooncakes.

Together, Curiosity and I studied the architecture of social ladders and aspired to become lexicographers.

**19,000,000.**

One summer's day, I reached a fork in the road, each trail labeled with a wooden sign.

Path 1: Independence    Path 2: Comfort

I saw Curiosity playfully dart His head from the end of the first path. So I followed Him.

I emerged into a church classroom in Italy, surrounded by other students who shared my passion for learning about the world.

A German boy speaking fluent Japanese.

A seventeen-year-old professional photographer.

A girl who started her own clothing business to escape poverty.

Their unique paths inspired an epiphany—I wanted to learn about the stories of others.

I wanted to become a storyteller.

Suddenly, another student waved at me from across the room.

Her name was Open Mind.

**21,000,000.**

At nightfall, I saw Curiosity and Open Mind perched in the moon, illuminating hidden trails of literature and film that deviated from the main path. On these trails, I'd drink from Rupi Kaur's *Milk and Honey* or watch *The Talented Mr. Ripley* do his tricks, falling in love with storytelling through different art forms. I began to carve notebooks from the trees around me, my ideas sprouting from little seeds into gardens of poems and screenplays.

Under the guidance of Curiosity and Open Mind, my stories transformed into spoken-word performances, stage plays, and virtual Scholastic exhibitions in art museums.

As my writing evolved, a new friend began tending to my gardens. Her name was Voice.

**23,000,000.**

The February wind blew in our faces as Voice and I ventured up a hill to the NY State Capitol.

The most important path of my journey.

You see, millions of steps ago, I didn't just meet Curiosity on the convergence of my Eurasian paths—I met Shame too. He'd appear in the form of racist mockery or questions of *What are you?*

For the longest time, I hated my differences.

But Voice changed that.

Stepping up on the podium, I shared my story to empower others. In the crowd, I saw Her smiling at me like a proud mother.

Since then, Voice and I protested injustices at the NYC Department of Education, traveled to Peru and England to amplify the misrepresented sex education stories of students, and interviewed musicians and producers on their experiences with mental health and inequality.

Down these paths, we became storytellers.

**25,000,000.**

My seventeenth birthday.

I follow a rose-colored path to one of my gardens, where a celebratory picnic, thrown by Solitude, Curiosity, Open Mind, and Voice, awaits me.

Together, we raise our glasses of coconut milk, honoring the step calculator of my life.

Here's to 25,000,000 steps . . .

And millions more.

# SHIVANI SHAH

**GRADE:** Junior      **LIVES:** New York, NY

**BORN:** New York, NY

### MENTEE'S ANECDOTE:

I love the conversations my mentor and I have—I learn about different ways to view the world, life experiences, and life lessons every time we talk. My favorite activity we do is analyzing poetry. Our discussions about the poetry and the meaning behind each word have opened my eyes to a new world of poetry and literature.

---

# LEAH KOGEN-ELIMELIAH

**OCCUPATION:** Executive Assistant      **LIVES:** New York, NY

**BORN:** Moscow, Russia

### MENTOR'S ANECDOTE:

Shivani has sort of become part of my household, her voice is recognized by my kids, they know to behave if we are meeting and not ask me for too many things! Our sessions often echo intense discussions and excitement for something we figured out, whether in a poem we are reading or in a piece she's working on. Our dynamic is quite special and unique, there's nothing that feels forced, and for that I am grateful.

# Falling Through the Cracks

## SHIVANI SHAH

*This short story is supposed to represent a phenomenon I see every day—kids falling through the cracks in public school.*

Muddy boots file into Mr. Sterr's eleventh-grade math class, each lining the floor with their own chevron pattern. Whispers of the latest homecoming game and candy grams fill the classroom while he clears the blackboard with a damp rag. Mr. Sterr tries his best to create an environment conducive to teamwork and learning. As he writes "test next Thursday," groans pour out of students, even though another bad test grade won't impact their already failing grades.

Trees surround the school and light honking can be heard from the distant highway. Dampness seeps through the walls of the math class. Mold outlines the intersection of the wall and the floor. Black charcoal dust covers the beige walls. The one bit of color, other than the green chalk Mr. Sterr added to make his class different from the rest, is the yellow-and-blue rain boots worn by the boy who sits in the chair closest to the door in the last row. He likes to think his hair is effortlessly styled knowing he spends more than twenty minutes in front of the mirror. He wears light baggy blue jeans that complement a button-up flannel shirt. No matter the season, he dresses for the fall.

Mr. Sterr states, "You can use the discriminant $b^2-4ac$ of a quadratic function to see if there exists roots of that function. If the discriminant of the function gives you a number less than zero, there exists no roots." His monotone voice drones on and on. Groggy, yawning students don't know the difference between Mr. Sterr's statements or his questions.

The boy in the back thinks, *These roots are invisible on the Cartesian plane, but they aren't invisible on the Argand plane*. He wants to shout it out. *No, I shouldn't*. Last time he spoke up he recalled Mr. Sterr joining the rest of the class as echoes of mocking laughter bounced off the walls of the classroom. He wished to disappear then, never to face this unavoidable humiliation.

The boy was an honors student until sophomore year, when one concept didn't make sense and snowballed into a failing grade. He figured it was best to stick to what he knew best, translating dead languages. He had always been drawn to Akkadian, the language of Mesopotamia, home to the oldest civilization of the world.

To start small talk one day during sophomore year he asked his lab partner, "Do you ever feel like high school is kinda similar to the Tower of Babel? Like no one understands anyone anymore."

"No, we all speak English here, you freak," said his lab partner, piercing the boy's eyes with ridicule. The boy in the back felt less and less visible with each scoff. The Tower did fall because no one understood him.

*Today everything is going to change*, the boy thought. *I'm going to attend the game*, he continued dreaming, as the classroom gossip took him by storm. *I'm going to do what the normal outspoken boys do. I'm going to emulate them. Today, I will walk home with the others, I'm going to be normal. And if they ask me a question, I'll find the right words*.

A few moments after the last bell rings, he can already hear the loud roaring of the pep rally. Before the last period ends, the hallways empty as kids flock to the field. He walks through the hallway where the mausoleum reluctantly greets him as lights tremble with a slight flicker.

Suddenly, he is pushed to the ground by a mob of kids rushing outside. He looks around and sees Mr. Sterr's classroom. He slowly walks in with the dried mud patterns cracking underneath his footsteps. He looks around the room and senses the change in the texture of the air. Tempted to crush all of Mr. Sterr's green chalk, he throws the damp rag out the window and kicks the dried mud. Suddenly, the room begins to move. The floor slowly rises and falls to the breath of the boy. His heart rate accelerates. The rising and falling of the floor follows his every beat. The desks break as metal shards fly on pieces of a broken heart. The rot spills out of the walled veins. The mouth between the walls and the floor starts to open. Teeth grind anything that falls through the cracks. The faster the boy breathes, the hungrier the cavity gets. The boy disappears with the last swallow of the mouth.

The next day students file into the classroom with conversations about the homecoming game. No one notices how the chalk turned from green to yellow and blue; fading, in the shape of a mouth. Horrified, Mr. Sterr attempts to write but finds himself no longer in control of the universal language. The boy scribbles, *There is the Argand plane, stop ignoring invisible roots.*

"It's time I start teaching you about the implications of math," Mr. Sterr states as he trembles, noticing the empty seat in the back.

# OLIVIA SHEN

**GRADE:** Senior

**BORN:** Cupertino, CA

**LIVES:** Milpitas, CA

### MENTEE'S ANECDOTE:

I never knew that I could have so much fun talking to someone years beyond my scope of experiences. Given the opportunity to interact, share, and learn from/with my mentor has truly been one of the coolest and best experiences this year. Most of my social interactions are derived from talks with people my age, so being able to interact with someone who is so different in terms of location, age, and experiences, but still be able to form a connection, has been an amazing experience.

---

# JINNIE LEE

**OCCUPATION:** Senior Copywriter, Content

**BORN:** Queens, NY

**LIVES:** Brooklyn, NY

### MENTOR'S ANECDOTE:

I'll never forget how during our first session, Olivia asked if I knew my personality test results—from well-known tests (*e.g.*, Enneagram) to tests I'd never heard of (*e.g.*, Female Archetypes). How lucky was I to be paired with a mentee who is so curious about getting to know herself and others? To that end, a recurring theme in our sessions was empathy. This concept showed up in her college applications and in her personal writing, and it makes sense that Olivia is looking to pursue human rights law. Dang. I'm grateful to Olivia for opening up my mind, too.

# white woman (crocodile) tears

## OLIVIA SHEN

Crocodile tears *is a phrase that refers to a false display of emotions, specifically sadness or grief. The term is derived from the phenomenon of crocodiles crying while consuming prey.*

white woman tears and crocodile tears are one and the same
when tearstained cheeks cry only for bloody murder

*the crocodile*
wades in the water with jaws snap that cut through my sinews and
    snaps my bones
her gluttony powers her cruelty which smears the water with my red
but when i look, she looks, he looks, they look, the world looks . . .
    she cries,
weeping through her fleshy swallows and crimson teeth, she mourns,
    tear after tear as she devours and weeps me
    her tears fall, marbleizing the blood-stained waters

her appetite is satiated (for now)
    her strikes will subdue (she sinks back into the water)
        her tears will dry (the water is settling)
(and her cruelty which shaped *my* mutilation is hidden in her stomach,
    *my* pain has dissipated into the heat of the air, *my* echoing cries
    smothered)

so it is quiet, because she has been fed, but in death i smile
because the water will always be tainted pink

and when the water calms, she is ~~crocodile~~ woman.

# CATHY SHENG

**GRADE:** Sophomore

**BORN:** Palo Alto, CA

**LIVES:** Palo Alto, CA

### MENTEE'S ANECDOTE:

My mentor has really helped me so much through every process, from deciding on a topic, getting over writing stumps, figuring out the nitty-gritty details, shaping the poem the way I want to but can't fully express. She introduced to me the beauty of poetry, and I found in it a beautiful form of writing to express my innermost feelings and messages. She really helped me polish my work and give the final gloss to it. Also, she gave me a further glimpse into journalism and the writing world in general, and I really appreciate it all!

---

# IVANA RIHTER

**OCCUPATION:** Writer and Reporter

**BORN:** Los Angeles, CA

**LIVES:** Los Angeles, CA

### MENTOR'S ANECDOTE:

Cathy has inspired me endlessly. Her writing is powerful and her voice shines. She is already an impressive journalist: Her profile of her math teacher turned into a thoughtful meditation on the struggles of staying afloat as a teacher in a post-tech-boom Palo Alto. From the initial idea, to the stellar interview, to the impressive final product, Cathy's dedication was a constant. As a poet, Cathy mused on life with her little brothers and wrote a touching ode to teacups, often bringing me to tears and making me laugh in the same poem.

# A World of Glass

## CATHY SHENG

*I've always had glasses; to me it offers separation, protection in a world full of chaos and injustices. This is a poem about overcoming vulnerabilities, seeing the unfiltered world, and molding a better world.*

The world is full of glass
Pairs upon pairs balanced on my wobbling head
   Cowering behind them at school
Making bean-like indents into my nose
Trying to disappear behind them
A shield
Leaking tears outline my face
   Bloody streams from hidden wounds
My insides tighten like a readied weapon
   Battling against the ceaseless storm

Shards of glass slice off my vulnerabilities
Glass grips my heart
   An impenetrable case
Drowning I sink below the weight of
   Glass
      Glass
         Glass

So many glass walls
    Untouchable surfaces
        Unbreakable barriers
           Unchangeable laws

Glasses upon all our heads
    To shut out atrocities
        Bear the wretchedness with a covered eye
           Perceive a better vision in our jagged world
              Mute our presence

Beautiful in each of our own ways
    Our unique cultures, an ornament of pride
        Our ancestry, a story we carry in our heart
           Our language, a mesmerizing song

But glasses are breakable, the world is not static
No need for correcting glasses to adjust our society
The world was not meant to be experienced through plexiglass

We cannot fix our society
By looking through a rose-colored lens
Lose ourselves in false illusions
Dreamy mirages do not mend flaws
A world through warped filters
    Is a glass prism without colors

In the vision of equity,
    Places are carved for us all
No matter our origin, no matter our roots
There's beauty in all identities, we shall
    Discover and share
        Care and empathize

Equalize and accept
Use affection not bigoted division to orbit the world

The world is full of glasses
One by one I yearn to take them off
Step out from the shadowed security of glasses
Perceive the world in all its vividness
   Dims and glows
Stitch a better world for diversity
Vision by vision

# GALIA SHKEDI

**GRADE:** Junior

**BORN:** Queens, NY

**LIVES:** Forest Hills, NY

## MENTEE'S ANECDOTE:

I wasn't sure what to expect when starting out my mentorship with Laura. I was hoping to grow my skills and confidence as a writer, but I have gotten so much more out of this experience. Every meeting with Laura is filled with a mix of laughing, brainstorming, free-writing, and critiquing every word until we end up with a polished piece.

---

# LAURA ESTHER WOLFSON

**OCCUPATION:** Interpreter/Translator/Transcriber/Editor

**BORN:** Santa Monica, CA

**LIVES:** New York, NY

**PUBLICATIONS & RECOGNITIONS:** *For Single Mothers Working as Train Conductors*; Iowa Prize for Literary Nonfiction; translator of *Stalin's Secret Pogrom*, winner of National Jewish Book Award; MacDowell Fellow

## MENTOR'S ANECDOTE:

I actually have two mentees, Galia and Jamie, the adored and adorable black-and-white mini bernedoodle. No session is complete without Jamie sprawling on Galia's bed or on her lap, gazing raptly at the screen. Galia is organized, decisive, and juggles so much, yet never fails to follow through. Like me, she resolutely believes in her work, while agonizing over every word. Today, as we worked to prepare her anthology submission, Galia urgently wanted to continue revising; I urged her forward, with an eye on the deadline. Pensively stroking Jamie for inspiration, Galia always aims high.

# Subway Creep

## GALIA SHKEDI

*An evocative piece of flash fiction meant to draw the reader into the author's encounter with a so-called subway creep.*

"What's your name?" he asks the girl in front of me. This petite girl, standing firmly, holding on to the overhead railing. There's no way her arm isn't tired.

She looks over, with a nervous almost-laugh.

"Why?"

The creep, an oldish white guy, early sixties or late fifties, wearing a slightly dirty, oversized blue coat, looks back with piercing light eyes.

"No reason, just wondering," he says with a pause. "My name's Michael," he adds, with what seems to be a smile under his mask.

She nods and looks away, back at her phone. Her fierceness hasn't wavered, but I think she's nervous. I would be. We all know what happens with these subway creeps.

"This is Jackson Heights, Roosevelt Ave," the MTA loudspeaker booms. People start getting up and I notice an empty seat in the opposite corner. I want to tell her, Go sit there. Get away from him. She gets off instead. I wait to see him follow her and the line of people off the subway car, hoping he'll get away from me. He does not. The guy next to me gets up and off the train. In his place, alleged Michael sits. I feel him staring at me and sneak a look only to catch his unnerving gaze on me.

Please don't talk to me, I think. Do I get up? Do I move to a different seat? The other side of the car? My body on edge, I try to shrink myself away from him.

I grab my calculus worksheet from my bag and plug the last problem into my calculator. As I finish up and write my name across the top, I realize, now this creep knows who I am. Hurriedly, I stuff my folder back into my bag.

"This is Forest Hills, Seventy-First Ave," the loudspeaker finally crackles. I can't get off that subway soon enough.

# ELIZABETH SHVARTS

**GRADE:** Senior                    **LIVES:** Staten Island, NY

**BORN:** Staten Island, NY

### MENTEE'S ANECDOTE:

A renaissance woman, phenomenal educator, and fellow enjoyer of early-morning nature walks, Liz Bengels is electric in every sense of the word. From gushing about Ocean Vuong and Jeannette Walls to discussing educational reform and how spoken word can be a platform for students to thrive in their empowerment, each phone call with Liz leaves me intellectually enriched and unabashedly hopeful.

---

# LIZ BENGELS

**OCCUPATION:** Teacher                    **LIVES:** Staten Island, NY

**BORN:** Queens, NY

### MENTOR'S ANECDOTE:

One of the greatest delights in building a new friendship is discovering what one shares in common. Elizabeth and I were astonished to learn that we are both musicians, songwriters, nature lovers, pet companions, eldest siblings, daughters of Mother Russia and all that this entails multigenerationally ad infinitum, fierce advocates for social justice, gentle listeners, good friends, and last but often least, residents of Staten Island! Elizabeth is vastly cooler than I could ever hope to be. Hers is indeed a voice that you will hear and read and savor—share with those who need to hear her!

# Adonis

## ELIZABETH SHVARTS

*Fusing intricate yet gritty imagery and allusions to Greek mythology, "Adonis" is a reimagining of beauty as a birthright and burden of the first-gen gifted American kid as they reclaim their narrative with humanity.*

the first crime is breath. a soft shuddered Thing
a burbling river a promise so pretty we

call this accident. call this abstract
painting is the second crime. plaster smile bolted

blush like the nettles myrrha and theias first touched
every root every leaf save yours if only

just for show nothing more than less
more laurel than hyssop meaning third crime

meaning scrub harder. meaning wring meaning
leave to dry meaning take up anything

a scalpel a dagger a brush anything. shape
sandpaper rust-bolt smile solid silk ribbon.

people turn a blind cheek to a good mirror
and beauty is a fickle god but at least venus knocked

on the temple. this body is a temple then
your footsteps are crusade tread light don't forget

the laurel trees are bittering and it's not
your fault. prepare offering just in case when

you are born a sin you sing of miracles
until your throat rusts ochre

and wheat-field gold we remind ourselves
this is how you get them through the drought pretty

boy smothered slick with olive oil
boy you are our indulgence
last.

# VICTORIA SIEBOR

**GRADE:** Senior

**BORN:** Brooklyn, NY

**LIVES:** Brooklyn, NY

**PUBLICATIONS & RECOGNITIONS:**
Managing Editor of Townsend
Harris High School's *The Classic*;
Teen Reading Ambassador for
New York Public Library

### MENTEE'S ANECDOTE:

I've really enjoyed getting to work with Stephanie this year and bond over our shared love of odd buildings in our neighborhoods and memories of coastal Maine. With topics ranging from fountain pens to stoop debates and other stories from her childhood, I avidly look forward to our weekly meetings. I strongly feel that Stephanie has helped me and my writing by motivating me to work consistently and dig deep within myself, especially when working on personal essays. She's taught me that my voice is worth hearing, and it's a lesson that I will never forget.

---

# STEPHANIE GOLDEN

**OCCUPATION:** Freelance Author
and Journalist

**BORN:** Brooklyn, NY

**LIVES:** Brooklyn, NY

### MENTOR'S ANECDOTE:

Victoria's a senior, so our first semester was focused on college essays. As we worked I discovered that Victoria thinks in images, as I do, and is eager to dive in and explore the depths of meaning she can find in them. You'll find a lovely one in her essay here. We've had a real meeting of minds, which has been a continuing pleasure as we've gotten to know each other better. Between writing and life we have so much to talk about that our meetings sometimes stretch to two hours—both having a great time.

# A House Sparrow's Song

## VICTORIA SIEBOR

*Even within a crowd, one can discover wings.*

In front of my house there's a discolored wooden bench, naturally dyed by the sun and rain. When the weather permits, I like to sit there and wait for the birds to begin their conversations.

I always hear chirping—it's one of the first sounds that comes to my ear when I step outside or open my window. I'll look to the trees for any signs of movement before gazing at the sidewalk where the house sparrows try to avoid the people walking by. They hop around in their little dance, blending into the screeches of city life. I fixate on sparrows because they're plain, they're generic, and all the other adjectives I would give myself; they fade into the background with all their shades of brown, gray, and black.

I've made sure to notice house sparrows for as long as I can remember, from them hopping around on the pastel chalk drawings in my nearby playground, to the many nests they've created around my house over the years. They've found solace under old siding, gathered twigs from the overgrown grapevines, and used our urban jungle pipes to nest atop our yard, free from the eyes of watchful hawks. They go unnoticed and unrecognized by most. Yet, as minuscule as they are, I admire their ability to fly and to leave the concrete sidewalk.

There are only a few times when I feel the same liberation as the sparrows. When a certain piece of music speaks to me, I can't help but extend my arms and imagine the wings I'm missing. Just as the birds fly, I dance. Having dedicated many formative years to my former studio,

Hamilton Dance, I can't recount the exact amount of time I spent within those purple walls, trying to correct every mistake in the wall-length mirrors. I learned all the contemporary leaps and jazz turns that the intermediate level allowed, even if I couldn't complete the same extensions as my more flexible peers. I polished and perfected each three-minute song later to be performed on a recital stage.

Although my studio is no longer open, I utilize my experience and training as much as I can, both at home and at school. This year, I performed a short solo during an entirely student-run and -created school production, S!NG. When I say short, I mean five seconds consisting of improvisation and a calypso jump, learned years ago, that still remained within every vein and muscle of my body. But those five seconds were mine.

In my eyes, dancing is the natural feat of flight, something that's practiced until it becomes second nature. It's my only passion where I have full control over my movement, where I don't need validation to feel satisfied.

I also get that same liberating feeling when I write. I find myself including birds in almost all my creative writing. There's always a clear distinction between the ground I'm forced to touch and the sky that only extends upward. While the birds can fly to any destination and height they desire, I can simply hope to achieve those same heights through words.

Though I'm still learning to be proud of my writing without external validation, my main goal is to be able to look back on an art piece and feel satisfied with it. I can tell if I'm happy with the metaphor I wrote, similarly to how I can feel my arms lock and extend in the correct ways while dancing. There's a certain energy that exists within the two art forms; I can feel if energy is physically obstructed in my body when I'm dancing, as well as if energy is emotionally obstructed when I'm writing. To me, a straight arm is of the same value as the right rhythm and rhyme in a set of lines. Writing and dancing are embedded in every part of my body, just as singing and flying are coded into every bird and sparrow.

# LENA SINGH

**GRADE:** Junior

**BORN:** Staten Island, NY

**LIVES:** Staten Island, NY

**PUBLICATIONS & RECOGNITIONS:**
Author of the poetry collection
*"things i never said aloud"*;
*Teen Ink*

### MENTEE'S ANECDOTE:

I sometimes believe it was fate that Courtney is my mentor because she is able to deal with my tendencies. I just remember bonding in the first meeting over a few laughs and some K-pop. I'm so grateful that I had her as my mentor for my first year of Girls Write Now, and I hope I can continue with her when I return. I hope she feels the same way, because who else would be able to walk through the fires of my tight deadlines and sarcastic words?

---

# COURTNEY LINDWALL

**OCCUPATION:** Writer and Reporter

**BORN:** Brooklyn, NY

**LIVES:** Brooklyn, NY

### MENTOR'S ANECDOTE:

Lena is technically the mentee, but I'm usually the one who ends up inspired. At the start of the year, we started a shared document for all of her writing, and it's been a joy seeing the document get longer and longer as the year has gone on, with dozens of poems and contest submissions and journal entries. Lena has helped teach me to always push creatively and just put your work out into the world, where it belongs.

# white with a hint of lavender

## LENA SINGH

*My fear of snow was like someone's else's fear of darkness. I now find the snow to be a good subject for metaphors, which I explore in this piece.*

I glanced out of the splintered net of the door
my toes curled at the breeze coming through the bottom gap
I had only a shawl wrapped around my now prickly shoulders
the door begged for me to be merciful and close it
it creaked / sweat / slammed trying to reach me but failed
just like the admiration of the sun did against the need to freeze

the sky was white with a hint of lavender
I couldn't tell if it was the snow that made it so
or the delusion that the sky could be more than colorless
the cotton balls had barely started sticking to the ground
when the flakes touched my hair, my eye twitched
and I was gifted a shudder

snow was so lifeless when I had the eyes of an infant
I was thrown into the avalanche by the weatherman
and a thump of the drop of my body was heard
they couldn't see that I couldn't breathe
that the snow was forcing itself into my little crevices
and filling me up with more water than I needed
"you shall not be afraid," the weatherman whispered

after a few years passed
drowning in snow instead started to feel like
little patches of sugar, so sweet to inhale
rather than like tiny crystals that impaled your heart
but then I was given rise by the weatherman
"you're finally ready," the weatherman whispered

the snow suddenly didn't feel shattering, the sky wasn't gray anymore
no, it was chalky with a hint of lavender
so much so that I leaned on the corner behind the door
listening to the distant piano keys in my ear
all for a weather so predetermined
but unexpectedly ethereal

and I didn't close my eyes when I wished
the weatherman would pluck my teenage body
and throw me back in the white again
-rebirth

# ARPITHA SISTLA

**GRADE:** Senior

**LIVES:** Ballwin, MO

**BORN:** Atlanta, GA

### MENTEE'S ANECDOTE:

Working with Sarah as a mentor has been amazing. She has been incredibly kind and understanding throughout the entirety of my crazy-busy college application process. Her edits helped me transform my personal statement into a much stronger piece. I always look forward to our weekly meetings; Sarah is genuinely such a fun person to talk to.

---

# SARAH ZOBEL

**OCCUPATION:** Senior Writer

**LIVES:** Essex Junction, VT

**BORN:** Arlington, MA

### MENTOR'S ANECDOTE:

For someone who has as much going on as she does, Arpitha is incredibly good-humored. When we first met, she was in the middle of applying to twenty-six colleges. That's a lot of essays! She's involved in show choir, traveling frequently for competitions, and is co–online editor of her school newspaper—but she still found time to get a part-time job. She's got big plans to effect change and I have no doubt she'll succeed. Biggest compliment she ever gave me: We're a lot alike. I'm just trying to keep up!

# different, not wrong.

## ARPITHA SISTLA

*Being the older sister of a younger brother with autism has been both challenging and gratifying. Throughout the years, I've learned many lessons from my brother on empathy, identity, and understanding.*

Digging his fingernails into my arms, my brother embraced me and let the tears run down his face and into the sharp sequins of my dress.

I caressed his head and held him close, feeling Aarush's frantic heartbeat below my own. As he heaved in between muffled screams, I wasn't exactly sure if he was gasping for air or trying to suffocate.

"Stop it!" the bazaar owner screamed across from us, glaring at us, anger in his eyes and disapproval in his gaping mouth. What prompted his sudden outburst was that my eight-year-old brother had just knocked an entire row of paper dolls off of the exhibit table.

My parents attempted to let the owner know that my brother did not have any malicious intent—his meltdown was caused by the loud honking sounds and bright white lights and foreign, sugar-sweet smells of Indian street food.

New and unfamiliar sounds, lights, and smells are experiences that many travelers associate with vacation and paradise. For my brother, however, his autism meant that he experienced these very same sensations as if they were his own personal hell.

As I stretched myself out using one hand to wipe the warm tears off of my brother's face and the other to frantically replace the dolls back on the table, I heard the store manager mumble under his breath a question

I would later find myself well acquainted with—"What is wrong with him, is he retarded?"

That day in the bazaar, twelve-year-old me did not have the words to answer his question.

Over half a decade of questioning, research, and maturing later, I finally do.

The complete and honest truth is, there is nothing "wrong" with him. An autistic brain, which is wired differently and with abnormal sensory responses than a neurotypical brain, is not so much wrong as it is different.

Different. It's different how Aarush has to crack his fingers in a specific order before he gets into a car. It's different how Aarush can respond only in one or two words. It's different how Aarush cannot understand what is socially unacceptable. But it's not wrong.

It's different how I feel a painful twang of embarrassment as I sit down to help Aarush learn how to read and write even though he is in middle school. It's different how I still play games from our childhood even when we are both teenagers just to see him smile after a difficult day at school. It's different how he and I vent to each other not through traditional conversation but through the robotic voice of his speaking device.

The bond Aarush and I share is different, but certainly not wrong.

As I understand more about Aarush's autism, the way others view him because of it, and the way he likely will never be able to fully communicate, my burning passion to use my ability to speak in ways that are meaningful grows in tandem.

In high school, this passion has manifested itself in my pursuits of talking about issues important to me through journalism, public speaking, and performing arts. In college and beyond, I envision myself writing cases, speaking at court hearings, and enacting policies that uplift the often-ignored voices of individuals with disabilities.

Being the older sister of Aarush has taught me that different doesn't mean wrong.

Though Aarush may never quite have the grasp of language to say those words, every moment I am with him, he teaches me this invaluable lesson.

Although the bazaar manager from years ago may not have realized how much those who are considered by society to be without a voice have to offer, it is my duty as an older sister, as an activist, and as a human, to make sure that as many people as possible do.

# TIARA LIZ SOTO

**GRADE:** Senior

**BORN:** Queens, NY

**LIVES:** Queens, NY

### MENTEE'S ANECDOTE:

Writing is much more than a hobby, it is our voices and talent beautifully combined in an artistic form of words. This is something I have grown to value most in my relationship with my mentor. Every time our weekly sessions ended, I would definitely always look forward to the next one. Each session left me even more empowered to continue pursuing my passion for writing. My mentor has been nothing but a supportive, kindhearted, and positive role model. She reminds me of the special power I have in bringing change to our world.

---

# RILEY COWING

**OCCUPATION:** Publications Adviser

**BORN:** Denver, CO

**LIVES:** Denver, CO

### MENTOR'S ANECDOTE:

I was instantly impressed by Tiara's enthusiasm, which not only applied to writing itself but also sharing her voice and ideas with others. During our weekly check-ins, I've noticed something new—total openness to the creative process. Whenever we discuss goals or pieces, she is entirely open to new genres, ideas, directions, etc. Even for this anthology submission, she shared a desire to try the poem in a short-story format, just to see where it took her. This is such an incredible quality in creative individuals—nonattachment to the way things "should be" and letting our voices guide the way.

# Beauty by Heart

## TIARA LIZ SOTO

*There are many stigmas surrounding body image and beauty standards, to the point where it has become underestimated. This poem is written through the lens of a girl who experiences it but finds strength to overcome it.*

Eyes set on the defining shards of glass
"This is beauty, I'm beautiful," painfully wished
Happy little girl that appeared in her outer world
But what is beautiful?
An illusion of perfection pressed onto the souls
The souls of our young girls, our young girls who hold the world in
    their hands
Her powerful way of words, her curvy body, and her tight shoulder-
    length curls
All with a warm smile that shines in the dark for those close to her
But no confidence fills her lovely soul
The beauty that lies in every piece of her, the beauty she wears
    unknowingly
Working out until every bone aches
Counting calories excessively in order to fit the mold
Baggy clothes to hide her fears
Straightening hair to avoid natural embrace
Little girl, yes me, beautiful you shall see
Promise to not hurt me and change you a minute longer
Promise to love me a little more each day

Promise to show me kindness just as you do in the outer world
No more mask, no more shame
My story, her story, to every girl in doubt of her shine
We are beautiful stars aligned by heart and scars
Eyes set on the defining shards of glass
"This is beauty, I'm beautiful," confidently proclaimed
Happy little girl that appeared in both her worlds

# OLIVIA STRIPLING

**GRADE:** Senior        **LIVES:** Brooklyn, NY

**BORN:** Brooklyn, NY

### MENTEE'S ANECDOTE:

My mentor, Jules, has morphed my brain in the best way possible. In the beginning of our time together I couldn't sit and just write. I told her this, and ever since she has provided me the space to grow. I would never have known where to start without her. I'll never forget her telling me that my writing makes her emotional, and her telling me she was proud of me. The endless support that flows out of Jules is something I will always love. She is the foundation for this piece, truly, and I am forever grateful.

---

# JULES VIVID

**OCCUPATION:** Copyeditor        **LIVES:** Brooklyn, NY

**BORN:** Brooklyn, NY

### MENTOR'S ANECDOTE:

Liv is incredible—creative, open, honest, and funny. She surprises me each week with some of the deepest and most moving creative work I've ever read. I'm so grateful to have been able to connect with Liv, to cowrite pieces, and to share and expand in our creative writing journeys together. It's been such an honor to have witnessed her process with writing "Palms." I am forever inspired. Liz is someone I wish I had had as a friend when I was her age. But that I can be her mentor today is a true gift.

# Palms

## OLIVIA STRIPLING

When I was born, I didn't have hands.
My father gifted them to me on my first birthday.
We held hands before dinner, kissed knuckles before bed. He held my
    wrist and he held my neck and he held my esophagus with expectancy.
He made me promise to hold caverns of quiet in my palms.

But my palms are empty.
Never have they not been empty.
I trace earlobes and spines.
I try to grasp my brain and poke my own eye.
Nothing holds. No, nothing stays.

My father and I have the same fingerprints. They bleed together like
    inky residue. Often I feel the need to stick my finger into his skull
    and test the fragility of his brain.

A boy I used to know stuffed dirt under his fingernails. White hot
    knuckles pressed into my cheeks, burning away my tears. Clammy
    child hands fought wars with my own. His fingerprints were
    someone else's. Mine. Or yours.

If the light shone too bright, he balled his hands into instruments of
    anger and punched blood into my nose.

He never thought of ripping his own skull out.
He would never think of taking his own eyes out.
Maybe he could if he tried.

.

When the girl I love is intoxicated she holds my hair and twists it into
    braids. Squeezing my scalp and passing drinks, her melting
    indignation encircles my own. We have only held hands once, but
    she holds my shoulders and cleanses my cheek with silk palms.

I wonder if her hands should be more scarred than they are.
I've borne witness to feet pulled, tugged.
To candles that softened into eyes, burning irises.
I've heard whispers of pain when her tongue licks salt off my palm.
And yet only during the inauguration of the moon does she threaten to
    kiss my ear, leaving it ringing.

.

My palms are empty, but not without pain.
Yours are forced to stay open, to catch and hold whatever's near.
Still I think the pain comes all the same.

Your spine was cracked before mine was held. The words you write
    become my fingerprints, and Dad's. Ink on ink on ink, until the
    corners of our existence spill onto the floor, and our spit is black with
    words and thought. Sometimes you can't follow my footprints in the
    sand, so I'll turn us around and follow you instead.

.

Follicles of breath tracing along sweating temples. Gushing blood held
    in sacred palms. The first drink is passed to my love, and I lick its
    sweet syrup dregs.

I imagine feet in silt.
I think of ink-born eulogies.

My father is left with my hands, as a parting gift. He is given a kiss on his knuckles. I can only hope the quiet caverns I so desperately clung to were good enough to leave behind.

My hands bury themselves into a memory, hollowing out my head and searching, quietly, for remains.
They find love in the deepest cracks of my brain.
I grab on to my mind, and it stays in my hands.
It fills my palms.
My body is mine.

# ALBA SUAREZ

**GRADE:** Senior

**BORN:** New York, NY

**LIVES:** Astoria, NY

### MENTEE'S ANECDOTE:

Just as I did last year, working with Zoë throughout the course of this year, I feel like I have grown so much in the way I express myself. I always look forward to meeting with her because I have so much fun trying out all the different writing prompts we do together, and in addition to being creative together, we have also learned a lot about each other.

---

# ZOË WEINER

**OCCUPATION:** Beauty and Fitness Editor

**BORN:** Providence, RI

**LIVES:** New York, NY

### MENTOR'S ANECDOTE:

Alba and I have worked together for the past two years, and this year it's been so much fun watching her flex her muscles in essay writing. I've learned so much about her in the process, and am so proud of the work she's done. We've also played around in poetry and fiction writing, and have spent quite a few sessions deep diving on Taylor Swift lyrics.

# Moving On

## ALBA SUAREZ

*I wrote a love letter (kind of), but not to a person. It relates a lot about realizing that your childhood is gone and that the place you grew up is changing forever.*

For quite some time now, both my most profound appreciations and sharpest pains about us have stemmed from how impossible it is to anticipate the swelling tide of our next moment. Right when I think we have both moved on, I stumble upon you running across the street to catch the icy cart or hanging out by the swingset at the Steinway playground and I join you for a few untainted, peaceful moments. Within the span of milliseconds, we can fall right back into the place where we left off.

In many ways, I have resigned myself to the roller coaster that the oscillating nature of our relationship entails, and I have accepted not having a pristinely defined plan for what may lie in our future. However, that does not come without its momentary heartbreaks, because when I indulge in the memories of our past, I cannot help but feel my heart become entrenched within the depths of our history.

I have a fantasy that even when I leave you behind for what comes next, you will never stop being here, waiting for the day I choose to come back for a visit. Is that selfish of me? Perhaps. But I still hold on to the idea that when I do return, you will invite me on a walk through Astoria, and we'll stop by the park with the bear and seal and turtle statues where we used to spend summer afternoons writing our names in chalk until our sweaty fingers turned dust into clay. Or maybe we'll marvel at the giant hole in the pavement in front of our old elementary school that we turned into an impromptu swimming pool after a rainstorm before heading to Natalia's house for pickle soup.

But in the depths of my mind, I know that these romanticized ideals I have thus been admiring from afar will only ever be viewed through the barrier of a steel door left only slightly ajar—painfully close, yet undoubtedly out of reach. Because the crusty animal statues got torn down three years ago when the park was renovated, and the giant hole got paved over the year after we graduated, and our friends' parents probably won't be able to keep paying for their places here when the Trader Joe's store opens.

It feels as though I took too long counting to ten in a game of hide-and-seek and opened my eyes to find that the place where we grew up has disappeared with you in it.

Every time I think I still have a grasp on you, I am falling right into a trap that will end only in heartbreak all over again. And I can't help but think that maybe you've known that our time together would end this way since the day we met.

Maybe it's time to move on.

# ALEHA SYED

**GRADE:** Junior      **LIVES:** Brooklyn, NY

**BORN:** Brooklyn, NY

### MENTEE'S ANECDOTE:

Donna Hill is a professor and a guider. Through her words, she shows sympathy and power. Every time she has helped me with my writings, the suggestions she has left me help empower my writing and create an even stronger message than before. She is also very family-oriented and always talks about the time she spends with her children and grandchildren. Every meeting I have with her is a window into her life and it connects us even more. Her vacations and the stories she shares always make me excited to hear about her experiences through them. Her collection of powerful feminist books also shows her essence as an empowering writer.

---

# DONNA HILL

**OCCUPATION:** Assistant Professor      **LIVES:** Brooklyn, NY

**BORN:** Brooklyn, NY

### MENTOR'S ANECDOTE:

Getting to really know someone is not always easy. Getting to know someone virtually even more so. However, this first year pairing with my mentee, Aleha, was more than I could hope for. Aleha is fun and genuine, and her imagination astounds me. Her work ethic makes me feel lazy, as she is the one that always keeps us on point! With all that she has dealt with this year, she is still able to push forward and smile. I am humbled to know her, and so look forward to our next year together.

# One very long day

## ALEHA SYED

**Content Warning:** death of parent

*A journey of acceptance and yearning.*

"He's gone!" my little sister exclaimed the moment my dad walked out the open door with his suitcase in hand. It was December 2021. This was the first time in eight years that my dad was returning to his home country of Pakistan. That also meant this was the first time in eight years that my dad left us without his watchful eye censoring all that we did. For us, this was exciting. My dad is strict, he would be cautious of letting me out because of my safety and was always stern about my education. So him being gone for two weeks was a new beginning for my sixteen-year-old self, even if it was for only two weeks.

The night he left, I hung out with a friend of mine at her house. We got dressed up and acted out the life of the iconic teenage girl you see in movies. The corner pizza delivery and the cookies we baked tied the night together. With my dad gone, I felt a weight lifted off my shoulders. I no longer had to carry the stress of being "watched," as a teenager would dramatically say, by my father. Being from a background with strict cultural enforcement, especially on women, not having my father's eyes piercing my every move wherever I went was relieving. It felt freeing.

The two weeks went by in a blur, from going out and being relieved of the stress of strict cultural pressures. The weeks were a breeze. Until the last day.

The day before my dad was due to return, I suddenly yearned for him.

I realized I missed him a lot, which was unexpected. I thought I would have wanted him gone for longer, which was true in the beginning, but as one week turned to two weeks the days felt oddly unending. You see, my dad coming home at night was the shift in our days that made it feel like night. His entrance brought the family together in the living room to greet him and to have family dinner together. After these dinners we would all go to bed. That was our routine. Him waking up and being ready before us was the shift from night to morning. My dad's presence brought stability, security, and regularity to our lives. Without him, time wasn't passing as it usually did.

Finally, Dad was coming home. It was a Friday. I came home as the bustle of my apartment was in full swing again. The aroma of my mother's spicy chicken biryani flooded the hallways, and the apartment was sparkling clean. The TV was tuned to his favorite channel: the news channel. I walked into the room my sister and I shared with a glimmering smile. Friday was always a fun day. It was the day to wind down from the hustle of the week and relax. I started ranting to my sister about the things that had happened. I told her about how I had aced my calculus test and was excited for the weekend. I started taking off my jewelry and brushed out my hair as I had begun to destress from the school week.

My brother came into our room and sat down with us. The three of us hung out in the bedroom, sitting on the floor, and stretched out across the bed. There were then two loud knocks and screams coming from the living room. We all jumped. My heart raced. I pulled open the door and my mom burst in. Tears filled her eyes and streamed down her cheeks. "He's gone!" she cried between sobs.

I felt like I could not breathe. Time stood still. My dad was gone. He'd died.

He died on January 6, 2022. The day before he was supposed to return home. I cried for him, missing him. Maybe I was feeling what was to come and didn't realize it. I may never know.

Earlier in 2021, we lost my aunt. Grief wasn't something my siblings and I knew how to deal with. My mother lost her mother at a young age so she had some idea of it. But my siblings and I didn't. When my aunt died, I remember my siblings telling me how they didn't know how to react since no one close to us had passed away.

We still don't know.

It's been a month. As I'm writing this, a month has felt like a very long day. Very long. Time doesn't pass the same way it once did when my dad was with us. Life seems to be one continuous loop. The two weeks are now an eternity.

My hope in writing this piece is perhaps my way of not getting *over* the grief, but to recognize it, to understand that the weight I thought I carried around was not really heavy at all and the weight made me strong, made me who I am. Recognize the change, and instead of replacing what I considered the switch between day and night and night and day, to *challenge* it.

# PAROMITA TALUKDER

**GRADE:** Senior　　　　　　　　　**LIVES:** New York, NY

**BORN:** Sylhet, Bangladesh

### MENTEE'S ANECDOTE:

Although I mainly focus on poetry writing, Carmen has helped me open the doors to journalism and news reporting, which I am taking much more seriously now. It is very easy to communicate with her about my interests and struggles, and we often spend the majority of our meetings discussing topics ranging from creative works, forms of media, politics, and more. These conversations not only help fuel my writing process, but also prompt me to think more critically about the world and myself.

---

# CARMEN REINICKE

**OCCUPATION:** Reporter　　　　　　　**LIVES:** Brooklyn, NY

**BORN:** Janesville, WI

### MENTOR'S ANECDOTE:

In one of our earliest sessions, Paromita and I worked on an essay she'd written that incorporated some of the books that impacted her as a child. One series, the *Magic Tree House*, was also one of my favorites! For me at least, it served as a reminder of one of the reasons why I write and read—not only to be imaginative, creative, and escape a bit from daily life, but to connect with others across the page or screen.

# Blackout

## PAROMITA TALUKDER

*This poem is a climate change activism piece that follows Mother Nature's crystalized tears as they pelt down on Earth, causing a blackout in a hospital where a guilt-ridden man awaits death.*

the manifestation of mother nature's sorrow
thunders across the sky as her beads of tears
   coagulate,
    turn to slivers,
     firing
pricks on her own membrane.
Each shell plotting
a revenge,
in hopes that a civil war
may transpire
once they strike the ground—a blizzard.
a battle
   between
     progeny.
The storm wreaks havoc,
plundering, pillaging, pulverizing.
a perpetual game
of mimicry
   between
     posterity.

It is a pain strong enough to pick oneself apart,
chewing one tooth at a time, carving out one eyeball at a time,
stretching apart the belly button to take a peek
at what your body is doing to itself.
A rancid boiling of stomach acid, gurgling
up pipes and down cavities, cooks
tender flesh until there's nothing left to suck on but bones.
Bones that are used, by the womb, like skinned sticks and branches
to light a fire that cremates the womb—by the womb.
The apoptosis of an organism.

All the while—a man lies covered in sheets as white
as the fossilized fluids outside.
I will die of natural causes, he thinks,
as he remembers sucking the sap
from the fathomless flesh of the Earth.
Rocks he turned to oil
turned to gas
turned to asthma.
I will die of natural causes, he thinks,
as his body sips blood from a bag,
and white and blue rubber ribbons bolt
to a screen display the electricity
coursing through his body.
I will die of natural causes, he thinks,
as the bullets of the storm outside sink
into power lines and encase, flood,
man-made generators of energy.
I will die of natural causes, he thinks,
as he seeps into darkness,
the whirring of machines goes mute
and the pumping of blood and air
from plastic bags
rests.

Perpetrators turned bystanders—
dependence for
   wealth
turned dependence for
   survival—
grants no exoneration.
Blame is a burden
staining the shadow
that follows the soul
through reincarnation.

# CARMEN TAN

**GRADE:** Senior

**BORN:** Brooklyn, NY

**LIVES:** Brooklyn, NY

### MENTEE'S ANECDOTE:

Honestly, Nicole and I get along so easily, it feels too good to be true. We bond over a multitude of things, including K-pop, our sweet tooths, and our latest interests. Every meeting, we discuss our recent reads and places we want to visit for sweets. It's an extended list already. Aside from that, Nicole has been like an older sister for me, helping me with the college process and (still) helping me with time management. I learn from her every meeting, and she gives the best advice. Here's to more talks and future dessert outings!

---

# NICOLE GEE

**OCCUPATION:** Senior Learning Designer (Editor)

**BORN:** Boston, MA

**LIVES:** Astoria, NY

### MENTOR'S ANECDOTE:

Carmen and I are similar in many ways. We appreciate the same books, Netflix shows, K-pop music, and—most important—desserts! We've also bonded over our shared Chinese culture. Asian discrimination and hate are topics important to us; we wish to change the statistic of Asian representation in publishing. However, it's Carmen's curiosity that surprised me from the beginning. She doesn't hesitate to ask probing questions. Instead, she investigates and researches for her own knowledge and understanding. Carmen impresses me every week with her evocative writing and her methodical work ethic. I look forward to reading her work one day!

# Waking Up to You

## CARMEN TAN

*Some people would run ten miles instead of confessing to their crush. Some people would never let that ridiculous thought enter their brain at all. If I don't ask, I'll never know the answer.*

Ripe orange sunlight streams into the classroom, illuminating our desks. As the teacher continues his tale in a sonorous voice, I can only keep my eyes on the enby sitting next to me.

The rays fall onto their crimson hair, glinting off the strands and making them look . . .

I can't even find the words to describe it.

Three months ago, I moved into a new town, new neighborhood, and new school. And even through all my worries of coming here and being different, Fenix was there. They helped me on my first day at school and didn't treat me differently for my narcolepsy disorder. We connected over books and offered recommendations to one another. We studied together. We hung out after school. Whenever one of us felt down, the other always swooped in to help.

I now know this feeling in my stomach that I get when they smile at me. The fireflies that warm me inside out until I can feel it in my ears. I like Fenix. And I want them to know that.

I'm going to tell them today after class.

It'll work out. I'm sure it will.

Right?

There's no way it'll turn out too poorly. People are still friends even if one has a crush on the other. I think. It's okay if they don't reciprocate. I'm not planning on it. I admit it would be nice if they have the same feelings I do.

What if they want to stop being friends?

Will they be disgusted at me for liking them?

Do they really enjoy the time we spend as much as I do?

We're good friends; we laugh and have plenty of fun.

But what if they looked out for me only because I was the new kid?

Do I mean as much as I thought I did?

Is this the wrong decision?

As the bell rings and students pack up to leave, this stream continues. The thoughts rush in like ocean water, choking my throat and burning my lungs. What if I mess everything up between us? My emotions are crashing in waves too strong for me to handle.

I can see the teacher exit the room, leaving Fenix and me. I want to confess my feelings now. The words stick in my throat and it's like they're blocking my breathing. Fenix starts saying something. The sounds float into the air, muffled and incomprehensible. I can hear them, but can't at the same time. My arms suddenly go slack from my shoulders down. I slump forward, and my head lands on the table with a soft thud. Fenix seems to be calling my name. I can see my shoulder and feel my limbs making movements I didn't ask them to. I'm having a cataplexy attack.

I'm not moving my limbs.

I'm not in control.

"Fenix . . . can't move," I manage before my muscles completely slacken, feeling like they weigh a ton each.

"It's okay, I got you, Matthias." Their words hang in the air briefly. Fenix had helped me before when I first had an attack in front of them. Though they had panicked, they could stay calm. Back then I had guided them and explained the attack since I could still talk.

This time, I can't. My arms, my mouth, my neck . . . every part of me is jittery. My lungs can't take in enough oxygen. I don't have control of my body at all.

I'm scared.

The worry remains on Fenix's forehead and in their eyes. Their hand starts rubbing my back in small circles. The warmth from it sinks through my sweater.

My fear still lingers in my bones despite Fenix's comforting me.

It doesn't feel like it's ending.

Gradually, my limbs grow a little lighter. I begin to twitch my fingers on my own, the feeling starting to return. I think Fenix notices because I can feel their hand leave my back. Their fingers hold and intertwine with mine instead, rubbing the skin above my thumb. As they continue, it's as if they are restoring the feeling back into me from my hand.

I test out my neck, trying to prop myself back up. My limbs are parts of a puzzle that I'm trying to rebuild piece by piece. Fenix holds their arms out to create a protective ring around me.

I stumble slightly. They pull my body to lean against them. As I gain more control of my limbs, I grasp their hand back with the little strength I have. They don't pull away.

"Do you need to nap?" they say against my hair, continuing to rub my hand.

"I don't want one." I fidget and shift to meet their eyes. I wait a beat. "Are you okay with this?"

"Of course."

"And what if I asked us to be more than friends?"

"I would like that."

# THE 17 MOONS

**GRADE:** Sophomore

**LIVES:** Brooklyn, NY

**BORN:** Brooklyn, NY

### MENTEE'S ANECDOTE:

Building connections with the public has been a challenge for me throughout many years, but when meeting with my mentor I was able to overcome such a challenge. I felt as though it built a part of me as I opened and shared my writing in a safe environment, building trust with each other as time passed on. Our interests varied and we discovered more about each other as we both went through a process of "self-growth." Feelings are never ignored or put to the side; they are required and always heard with an open ear. The journey continues on.

---

# ANALYSA VIVANCO

**OCCUPATION:** Senior Barista

**LIVES:** Brooklyn, NY

**BORN:** Costa Mesa, CA

### MENTOR'S ANECDOTE:

One of my favorite attributes of The 17 Moons is their constant positivity and zest for life! Whether they're talking about their passion for cleaning, music, or where to find the most authentic cuisines in NYC, their enthusiasm is contagious and always makes my morning better and brighter when we speak. The 17 Moons is uplifting, resilient, and empathetic, and I am so lucky to be mentoring them.

# THE 17 MOONS

## THE 17 MOONS

*A poem in the hope of having the audience grasp the meaning of a love letter. Not your usual love letter. As you read, the writer begins to build trust with the reader, the environment breathes, building the impact of the letter.*

Write a love letter
Meet the standards
Express the love of this thing, place, item, person
Go in-depth of these emotions
A love letter
Must not lack these emotions
But sometimes can cause a commotion
In your mind
My love letter
Must be taken and flown with the wind
We must read it across the deepest length of the oceans
It must be sung to the swaying of the trees
It must run through the wind blowing the love away
The animals must imagine it so they can connect to it all day
Although I shouldn't forget the people
It must be described with imagery to the people so they can feel
    emotions from away
And
Visualize
But to the moon, it must be written

Written well
Because it shines, providing, it's listening to the poems, to the
  breaths, to the cries for help
It's there
Staring down

We haven't met, but I often see you
I take pictures to remember what phase I discovered you in
From new, waxing crescent, first quarter, waxing gibbous, full
  moon, waning gibbous, third quarter, waning crescent
There's never an exact feeling I can delineate you as
You make the goose bumps along my skin rise
You make my cheeks turn red with all my acne, scars,
  and oily skin
My body turns cold becoming paralyzed at the moment, as the
  sweat drips off my palms
My fingers tremble all at once
All causing a stop in my pulse
This brings me to a high degree

Pulling you closer
A moment you build awareness, finding truth
A door you open
Built with my imagination, turning different colors, with
  different textures, shapes
My eyes flash with lights
Ready to explore
Knowing I felt like this before
I always feel this connection within my soul, spirit, emotional
  being, physical being
You don't see me from the close but you know me from the far
You influence a character in me
Within me, to me, and through me
You hold my eyes with all your light

Capturing me in a moment
I neither run nor hide from these feelings but build
    a sense within
We are mature lovers
Deeply in love
Showing, sharing, expressing it every time
There is no doubt that we are beyond the years of ink I press on
    paper writing a love letter to you
Our love is timeless
But all needs to end
As my planet ends
Your planet is never-ending, your start is your end, your end is
    your beginning
We are a chemical reaction
Burning others around
The moon eclipsed
The human heart feels you
Surrounding yourself with more stars
You are my light
The stars around me
My sight of freedom
You are the moon
In a crescent

The love letter is written

# ELLEIGH W. TODD

**GRADE:** Junior

**LIVES:** New York, NY

**BORN:** New York, NY

### MENTEE'S ANECDOTE:

I've enjoyed meeting with my mentor, Julia, and I look forward to us meeting every time! She's super-fun, sweet, and always understanding. Julia really helped me come up with unique and creative ideas along with building on whatever ideas I had and giving very good feedback. She's amazing to work with, and I can't wait to continue working with her in the future!

---

# JULIA CARPENTER

**OCCUPATION:** Reporter

**LIVES:** Brooklyn, NY

**BORN:** Atlanta, GA

### MENTOR'S ANECDOTE:

I cannot wait for the day I finally meet Elleigh in real life! Every time we FaceTime I find myself smiling and laughing. She's such a fount of ideas and I am so excited for people to read her creative and original writing.

# GUARDIANS OF THE SPIRITUAL GIFT

## ELLEIGH W. TODD

*The fantasy land of Catrossau, Oseka, in 434 BD tells the story of travelers struggling to survive making their living by killing demons. This tells the story of an unlikely group of people working together.*

### 434 BD: CATROSSAU, OSEKA

Kiyoko couldn't help but admire the beautiful land of Catrossau as she walked through what was known as Heaven's Forest. Legend has it that when one of the Goddesses of Heaven, Alectrona, came down to Earth to visit her lover Cybele, Goddess of the Wilderness and Nature, Alectrona was so excited to see her that she came crashing down to Earth so hard that the forest she landed on absorbed some of her Heavenly energy, purifying the forest itself and giving it magical powers. The forest Alectrona landed on became known as Heaven's Forest, rumored for its magical properties.

By the time you step even one foot into Heaven's Forest, you can already feel the purifying, magical energy that engulfs the forest and not only feel, but see it too. Heaven's Forest has a golden iridescence that makes the forest look like it is surrounded by golden fireflies. The trees are tall, the plants glow with a stunning light, and even the animals seem to glow too. To the untrained eye, the forest would look just like a normal forest but the magical energy is so captivating that anyone can feel it.

This place felt comforting and warm with such a distinct energy Kiyoko would know it from anywhere. She practically grew up here, as it was where she would spend her time when she needed to escape reality. Kiyoko continued down the unmarked path with her long black hair flowing through the wind as she took a moment to look up at the sky, which blinded her enchanting deep blue eyes that seemed to have a golden glow whenever she looked up at the sun. Kiyoko always had a special connection to the sun since she was a child. Taking a breath, Kiyoko continued on her way, wearing her signature red hakama and white kosode with her yumi on her back and a pack of arrows as well. This was the outfit Kiyoko typically wore as she was a priestess who used to attend to her family's shrine though she hasn't been back there for quite some time.

"Kiyoko! Kiyoko!" A female voice called out.

Kiyoko looked toward the direction of that voice. She recognized that voice all too well.

"I'll be there in a second!" Kiyoko called back with a warm smile.

Kiyoko walked faster toward the voice and quickly arrived to see two people standing there, a man and a woman. The woman was average height, with long black hair that shone in the sun and brown skin that complemented her entrancing brown eyes. The woman was wearing a black outfit with detachable sleeves that ran to her fingertips and had green details all throughout, with a bow and arrows on her back. She had a black mask below her chin and a hood that was also down. The man who was standing next to her was a bit taller with even darker skin that almost had a blue tone to it, with short curly black hair and wearing ragged clothes. He had on a long-sleeved, tattered white blouse and a light purple petticoat with baggy black pants, a big black scarf, a long baggy light blue jacket, and short black boots with a very large and intimidating sword on his back.

"Kiyoko, you're always wandering off and making us late. You need to manage your time better or else one day we're gonna lose these bounties," the woman said sternly.

"Pîsim, I can't help that the spirits always call out to me. I'm just following along, so I don't get on their bad side," Kiyoko replied with a smirk. Pîsim rolled her eyes with a smile, used to Kiyoko's excuses.

"Well, let's leave before someone else gets offered this bounty," the man stated as the trio started walking along the marked path.

"Chuk is right. I'd hate for it to go to those monks again. They're always so smug, not very holy like if you ask me," Kiyoko complained.

"You think they're even real monks or just scammers?" Pĩsim asked.

"No, those monks are definitely real ones, powerful too. They just happen to be assholes," Chuk replied.

Pĩsim and Kiyoko nodded their heads in agreement as they all continued to walk in silence until they reached a large white mansion with four huge columns in the front.

"This the place?" Kiyoko asked.

Pĩsim pulled the crumpled piece of paper out of her pocket and looked at it for a second.

"The address is the same. I didn't think the place would be this big though." Pĩsim chuckled.

"Well, they wanted the best, so here we are!" Kiyoko said confidently.

"Don't let your pride get the best of you, we have no idea what we're going to face," Chuk reminded.

"I'm not getting cocky. I am simply remembering what the bounty said," Kiyoko replied, taking the paper out of Pĩsim's hand. "'One hundred and fifty bronze coins, a hundred silver coins and fifty gold coins to the best demon slayers who can expel the demon that has been wreaking havoc on our humble abode.' I mean, to me it just sounds like a rich family who has no idea what they're dealing with and nine times out of ten ends up being a little demon who doesn't have the power to go after anyone powerful like us!" Kiyoko stated confidently.

# MAHDIA TULLY CARR

**GRADE:** Sophomore

**BORN:** New York, NY

**LIVES:** New York, NY

**PUBLICATIONS & RECOGNITIONS:**
Mali Rising Foundation—Middle School Case for Caring Award Winner

### MENTEE'S ANECDOTE:

I have really enjoyed connecting with my mentor. I got the time I needed to just write or discuss with another human, and I really value that. I feel like I can go to my mentor for almost anything, and she will hold space for me and listen, as well as aid.

---

# NORA RITCHIE

**OCCUPATION:** Senior Producer

**BORN:** Albany, NY

**LIVES:** Brooklyn, NY

### MENTOR'S ANECDOTE:

Mahdia is whip-smart, creative, and organized. I am constantly amazed by her imagination and her ability to build fantasy worlds and plot lines. She is a big reader and also likes to write songs. We often start our sessions with a free-write and then chat about the week or writing ideas. Mahdia is also empathetic and kind. It's been a wonderful honor to work with her this year.

# The Eldritch Crown

## MAHDIA TULLY CARR

*This is an excerpt from a book I am writing. In simple terms, it is a taste of the very beginning of my character's journey, and I hope you will enjoy it.*

### ONE

"Did you leave out the apples again?" Aerilyn called from the kitchen.

"No," Dalia responded. "Why?" Dalia appeared in the doorway, broom in hand. Her curls were already freeing themselves from their braid at the temples.

"Something must have gotten into them. They've got holes again," Aerilyn explained.

"How could there be holes? Nothing is alive in this weather. It's too cold to even go outside," Dalia whined.

Aerilyn smiled. Her sister had never been one for household work, or for cold weather.

"I wish it was warm again."

Aerilyn pulled her shawl tighter around her shoulders. "And you wonder why I have all the responsibilities this time of year. You always get cranky in the winter." Aerilyn dusted off her hands on her apron before untying it from around her waist.

"You're just older. Grandma never trusts me with anythi—" A knock sounded from the front door. Aerilyn and Dalia exchanged glances. "Who could that be?"

"I-I'm not sure," Aerilyn admitted, moving toward the door. Even with the fire crackling behind her, it helped little when the cold rushed in. Aerilyn's mouth dropped open.

The woman on the poster looked exactly like Aerilyn. They had the same nose, the same eyes, the same dark curls and brown skin. The woman on the poster *was* Aerilyn. Or at least she could be.

Beside her, Dalia's face had gone pale. Only yesterday everything was normal: the skies had been winter gray, the air had been cold, though not painfully so, and people still acted as if time was precious—and it was, with the first snow sure to arrive any day.

But today there were five women in full suits of armor in the square of Wallo Village. Their hair had been cropped short, and most of them were not from the Jann Province, some even appearing to be from Murto, the Province directly north. At the very least, they weren't from Wallo. Winter held strong in the village, yet the women hardly seemed cold in their suits of armor. Most didn't even wear scarves. Aerilyn tried to contain her jealousy for their warmth, but the circumstance of their arrival only compounded it. They seemed so *important*, so carefree. Aerilyn crossed her arms as a shiver ran down her spine, the cold seeping into her bones.

"I-I'm not sure what to say," the dark-haired woman got out. The soldiers looked over Aerilyn and her sister, Dalia.

"I can't blame you. I'm sure you were not aware. May we come in?" one of the women asked. She was a light shade of brown, lighter than most got in Wallo, even during the winter.

"Of course." Aerilyn stepped aside to let them pass.

# VICTORIA VILTON

**GRADE:** Senior

**BORN:** Brooklyn, NY

**LIVES:** Brooklyn, NY

### MENTEE'S ANECDOTE:

All I know is there is no other person in the world I can talk to about a Hall & Oates phone service and my obsession with the Beatles than Amy. Amy is equal parts brightly encouraging and refreshingly honest, and I feel like my work is better for it.

---

# AMY MACLIN

**OCCUPATION:** Features Director

**BORN:** Nashville, TN

**LIVES:** Harrison, NJ

**PUBLICATIONS & RECOGNITIONS:** *Real Simple; O, The Oprah Magazine; Whole Living*

### MENTOR'S ANECDOTE:

After sessions with Victoria, I feel, as my grandmother might say, "lifted up" (and not only because I'm a Gen Xer who's also into Hall & Oates). She takes such joy in creativity and artistry, yet brings such sharp attention and intelligence to her revisions—such a big portion of the hard work of writing. I love talking with her about her work, and I'm always delighted by the directions in which she takes it. Also, I couldn't hope for a better person to discuss topics ranging from the cultural significance of *The Simpsons* to the magic of George Harrison's lyrics.

# Baggage

## VICTORIA VILTON

*High school friends have a surprise encounter in an airport a few years after graduating.*

I'm walking to my plane when I see her. She looks so different, I almost miss her. Almost. But despite the golden braids and nose ring, I recognize the glasses and soft dimples. I pause and people move around me, cursing under their breath.

She's listlessly eating a sandwich, eyes drifting around like she's looking for something. I realize we haven't spoken since our high school graduation.

*We were friends*, I think to myself. Or something like that. I was fond of her, I think I recall.

Suddenly I'm shouting her name. I feel myself making a scene, but I'm agitated. Why has it been so long?

She looks up at me, her eyes widening. She hesitates, then gets up.

"Oh, wow." Her voice is friendly, but her eyes dart away. I think she'd rather be anywhere else.

"How are you?" I ask. It's all I can think to say. Closer, I realize she's nothing like the seventeen-year-old I knew. She is so much more elegant. I only ever remembered her as a somewhat immature teenager.

"I'm fine." Her answer comes so quickly that I'm still talking when she finishes.

"That's cool. That's nice." The silence hangs, and my bag slips off my shoulder. I let it fall.

"How are you?" The question is strained.

"I'm fine too. Flying back to school."

"Me too."

The conversation is so awkward I feel my knee jolting, urging me to get out of there. I never should've said anything.

The airport feels hot, and I tug at the hem of my shirt. I glance down at my shoes before I can look back at her. She looks older. Much older than I feel.

"What have you been up to?" Her mouth pinches at the corner.

"Nothing, just college." I try not to think too hard about the fact that she seems to be doing so much better than me. The weight of my still-undecided career path grows ten times heavier.

I want to ask, *What's going on? We're still young. We shouldn't be this awkward!* but instead I say, "Do you still make those necklaces?"

She laughs, and it's genuine, and it lightens my heart. "I can't believe you remember that. No, not so much anymore. Too busy getting ready for law school."

I don't bother with surprise. Even from our short acquaintance, I knew she'd be a lawyer. She was passionate back then. Arguing like every little word mattered.

"That's great. Where are you studying? What kinda lawyer do you wanna be?"

She looks at me, perhaps taking her time to process my questions, but I doubt that. Then she bends her head, focusing on the floor.

Around us, the airport continues to push. Someone's suitcase clips my ankle, but I barely notice.

"I'm sorry." She looks up at me and she is laughing, but her eyes are wet and her hands are shaking. "I'm really sorry, but I can't talk to you."

I pull back. "What?"

"I don't want to talk to you right now." She still has a smile on her face. I feel like some important memory has been stolen.

"What? Why?" This comes out harsher than I intended.

She turns, her braids whipping around her, warning me away.

"Did I do something?" I follow, chasing gold in a sea of dark, shuffling bodies. She stops and I bump into her, coconut filling my nose. A small part of me wishes that smell was familiar.

"Are you that stupid?" I fall silent, like someone who's just been punched in the throat. "Do you *really* remember me from high school?" People begin boarding her plane, pushing past us, but I hardly notice.

"What do you mean?" I stare like an idiot.

"You're kidding." She throws her hands up in the air and the sandwich flies. We watch as someone tramples it. "You had no idea?" She glares back at me.

"Had no idea of what?" I'm grasping at the straws of my memory but nothing substantial comes up. Everything just slips through my fingers.

"That I was in love with you." She says it very matter-of-factly, like I should've known all along. A tear falls and the surprise of it makes me quiet. All I notice is how it slides down her cheek. "I've spent these last few years trying to forget everything about you. Everything." She breathes heavily. "I'm in a relationship with someone who loves me, so I don't want to see you. You were always blind, but I'm happy now. So please. Go."

She stares at me like I should leave, like it would be effortless after hearing that. When I don't move she shrugs, wipes her face, and turns around.

I watch her go.

Has *she* been in love with me? I don't believe it. And for some reason, I don't want to. What does it say about me that I never noticed? Perhaps I didn't care. Or I was just stupid. Either way, she's gone now. And I suppose it'd be best if I just forgot about her.

# GRACE WANG

**GRADE:** Junior

**BORN:** New York, NY

**LIVES:** Rego Park, NY

### MENTEE'S ANECDOTE:

Danielle was extremely supportive, engaged, and interested in my process. It felt nice having a separate pair of eyes to read over my work, especially with such an encouraging mentor.

---

# DANIELLE KOLODKIN

**OCCUPATION:** Manager, Speakers Bureau

**BORN:** Hackensack, NJ

**LIVES:** New York, NY

### MENTOR'S ANECDOTE:

Working with Grace throughout 2021–2022 has been the highlight of my year. I look forward to meeting each week and talking about writing. I'm continuously blown away by Grace's talent. Her writing is vivid and gripping, leaving the reader hanging on to each word—watch out, world, for what's to come.

# Dissociation

## GRACE WANG

*Dissociative amnesia. One man and his wife.*

The wooden palette adorned with a taste of the rainbow, from fiery orange to milky white, was placed firmly on his lap. His spiky, slender paintbrush had a blob of hazel brown that drizzled off his brush as he lifted his careful wrist to the canvas. The lightbulb flickered from a warm yellow to complete blackness from time to time. Surrounded by gray floors stained with the footprints of bare feet, he wondered when his house had ever had gray floors. He dismissed this thought, knowing he had a portrait to complete, and turned his attention to his subject. His wife, Marta, sat poised on the creaky wooden chair situated directly in front of his easel. Her skin, paler than it usually was, made her appear like a ghostly being.

"Marta, dear, would you move your body to the right?" he grunted.

No response.

He sighed, wondered what he had done wrong again, and forcefully began to stroke his fragile wrist over the empty canvas. He began with the outline of her eyes, the very eyes that held endless aspirations never to be seized. Focus never leaving the canvas, he began to paint her eyes that were as green as the grass of the meadows, with streaks of gold like the sun rays of golden hour. He scribbled on her eyelashes, always an intense carbon black from her ever-lasting tube of mascara, with a ballpoint pen that made her eyes seem rather large.

None of it was doing her beauty justice, but he needed to get a rough draft done. He moved on to her nose that was pointy, with narrow nostrils, and straighter than his. He carefully outlined the shape of her nose with soft pencil shavings until it somewhat mirrored her nose. Half of it, at least. He still had not lifted his gaze from his canvas once. He found it odd that not a single word had been muttered from Marta's mouth. She always complained when he forced her to be another "lab rat" for one of his strange portraits.

He knew that this would be one of his last portraits of her, at least for now. She hadn't been too enthusiastic apart from their constant fighting every day. He missed the spark in her eyes whenever he'd tell her he needed her for a portrait. Something he never thought would come back.

Everything he sketched so far had been partial. The nose had one nostril, the eyes missed Marta's golden spark, and he had not added much color onto the canvas despite his palette that spanned the whole rainbow. Restless and confused on why everything was going so corruptly, he decided he would move on to her mouth, the one part of her he had spent countless hours gazing at. His gaze was not focused on them today, though, as his eyes were still fixed on the art. He once again lifted his slender paintbrush, now dripping with the same hue of pink as her hot pink tube of lip gloss.

Gently, he rested his eyes. It was not enough to fade into complete oblivion, but enough that the humming of the radiator and the world around him faded. He reminisced about that very last kiss he had with Marta. Her lips roughly chapped from refusing to use ChapStick contrasted against his lips that were velvety and soft. The memory of the tingle of her tongue against his, and the blood of her chapped lips rubbing against his made him whimper and flinch. Feeling rather disturbed, he was interrupted as he felt a distant, chilly hand placed on his bare shoulder, sending a shiver down every vertebra of his spine. Expecting to see Marta, he jolted his eyes open, his eyebrows shot up, and his jaw dropped so far down that his wisdom teeth were visible. It became apparent that the chair was empty, and there was no Marta in front of the easel. All he examined were metal bars with more rust than should be permissible, a damp ceiling light that dripped with a mystery liquid, and a man in a white coat who kept muttering the words "dissociative amnesia." Without being conscious of it, he shrieked her name with a bloodcurdling yell.

The kind you'd only hear in horror movies, the ones that never truly erased from your brain.

The man in the white coat glared at him up and down. He warily opened his mouth.

"Marta died last month."

# KAYLA WANG

**GRADE:** Senior

**BORN:** Queens, NY

**LIVES:** Elmhurst, NY

**PUBLICATIONS & RECOGNITIONS:** Staff Writer and Digital Media Strategist for the "Politically Invisible Asians" newsletter, Regeneron International Science and Engineering Fair Finalist

### MENTEE'S ANECDOTE:

Girls Write Now allowed me to find someone I deeply admire and am inspired by. It gave me an outlet to look forward to every single week to grow and allowed my artistic expression to unravel. We can laugh and make jokes about pop-culture references while simultaneously diving into deep, pressing topics. Priyanka is my role model who I can depend on and is making an enormous impact on me as a young adult as I step forth into the real world. She supports my hopes, dreams, and aspirations beyond what you could imagine a mentor could do.

---

# PRIYANKA CHANDRA

**OCCUPATION:** Brand Specialist

**BORN:** Orlando, FL

**LIVES:** Orlando, FL

### MENTOR'S ANECDOTE:

I wanted to be a mentor to be a guide for someone who needed to find their way. What ended up happening is I found a friend. She is someone I learn from more than I teach. We start each session with a question such as *Which cartoon character would you bring to life?* and end with talking about topics such as what it is like being an Asian American woman in this country with immigrant parents. The conversations and connections are endless, as is the creativity. I am so lucky to know Kayla and watch her journey unfold.

# Where Love Grows

## KAYLA WANG

*A glimpse of how my best friend and grandfather mold me into the woman I am today as we bond in our backyard garden filled with a cornucopia of vegetables and a sense of community.*

A forest grew in my bedroom with vines adhering to every iota of white space. My youthful wonder transported me to a different world. In that moment, I was Max, leaping from one page to the next on an exhilarating voyage in Maurice Sendak's *Where the Wild Things Are*. The pattering of my grandpa's footsteps became my favorite intervention, snapping me out of my reverie as he called for me: "Bao bei, would you like to help?"

I grasped his cozy, inviting palm. My baby-soft skin felt the contrast of his thick, blistered world—every crevice and memento of Guang-dong, China, every vein of tribulation as an American immigrant, and every creasing line of my green-thumbed hero. Holding on to his radiating warmth, I felt our stories intertwine.

Those hands were usually buried deep in the soil of our backyard garden. I enjoyed chasing his shadow as the scorching sun bounced off our backs. We spent hours at a time together, tucking seeds, watering them, and making compost out of banana peels and the pits of avocados. As the day slowly dimmed, he would tell me about the passersby who stopped to admire the greenery. We would talk about "white hat" who went to church on Sundays, "golden retriever" who waved when picking her kid up from school, our Bangladeshi neighbors who had a beautiful garden filled with tomatoes of their own, "shopping cart," who always offered me jelly beans, and many other characters. These afternoons watching the melons ripen and pumpkin flowers blossom allowed me to witness the unwithering respect, civility, and patience my grandpa had in listening to the narratives of people. My grandpa taught me to have the courage to want to make a difference and fostered my connection with the Earth by getting our hands dirty together in the rich, fertile soil.

When the cucumbers, pumpkins, and green peas ripened, he would be thrilled to give them as gifts to friendly strangers. I was a spectator to his unwavering kindness and generosity, and it evoked a complete sense of gratitude in me. Although as a child I wondered why my grandpa hesitated to turn up the thermostat, and I questioned the overflowing Salonpas patches in our cabinets—serving to mend the sores of my parents' blue-collar jobs—resilience was a constant factor in my life. To see him give so much when living in frugality instilled in me a sense of purpose, not only of thankfulness but of the magnitude of sacrifice.

Despite not speaking English, my grandpa never allowed language to be a barrier in communicating and establishing himself as part of the community. All I ever heard him utter to one-time strangers was "Hi, my friend," followed by hand gestures. His pride in being Asian American did everything to bolster my own, and I grew to have honor in my culture and Chinese roots. I was not ashamed to bring him to chaperone my school trips or to have him attend my parent-teacher conferences because I was lucky to have him by my side. He stood as my example in learning to dissect the nuances of my heritage.

Hearing the distant voice of my grandma calling for dinner, we walk back into the house hand in hand. Returning to my seat, I flip to Sendak's last page. Max returns from his independent excursion to a home full of love and a hot supper. The jungle of vines steadily vanishes. I exit my bedroom and sit down to a pleasant, boiling bowl of winter melon soup and an array of vegetables freshly picked this morning. I was home.

# TRACY WANG

**GRADE:** Sophomore

**LIVES:** Brooklyn, NY

**BORN:** Brooklyn, NY

### MENTEE'S ANECDOTE:

Working with my mentor, Keydra, has been such an insightful and inspiring experience. She is totally open with me about her own personal background and when she expresses her thoughts as we have more serious discussions. Meetings with her are meaningful and a great learning environment. Our pair relationship extends to something more than just limited to what's going on inside this program. Keydra listens to me, supports my voice, and gives wonderful advice to my concerns of day-to-day life.

---

# KEYDRA MANNS

**OCCUPATION:** Writer

**BORN:** Brooklyn, NY

**LIVES:** New York, NY

**PUBLICATIONS & RECOGNITIONS:** Craig Newman School of Journalism graduate; *HealthCentral*, *TheGrio*

### MENTOR'S ANECDOTE:

Working with Tracy has been refreshing and inspiring. She is always so candid and thoughtful through our writing prompts and Sunday Funday conversations. When we were first getting acquainted I shared with her that I wanted to grow my social media following for my small business and considered using Instagram Reels. Tracy candidly let me know that if this was a real goal I should consider TikTok. We took the Girls Write Now TikTok workshop and my first video went viral with 18,000 views. This is just one of many ways working together has brought me joy.

# Living in Gratitude While Missing My Native Tongue

## TRACY WANG

*It's easy—almost far too easy—to just say where we are from. A country. A place. A word. But where we really come from is from our parents and our culture. A history.*

I lost connections to my homeland when I was brought to America at the young age of three. As a child of immigrant parents, my sister and I had to worry about our English speaking skills to survive in this new country. We spoke English every day, whether we were at home, at school, or just taking a walk. But all that practice left us in a complicated position. We started to excel in English but gradually began to lose our native tongue.

Yet, I'm grateful. I am grateful because the foundation my mother has set in me is strong. I'm also grateful for my mother and the sacrifices she has made for me and because of her, I will never really lose my native tongue.

I am from a place I don't understand because I don't speak the language fluently. I don't know many places there, not even a single unique landmark, and I can't tell you precisely where I used to live as a child. But sure, allow me to show you the geography of China and tell you where I'm from. I don't trust in my full capabilities to deliver an origin story but this is as beautiful as it can be.

I belong to a small city in a southeastern province in China with a population of 7 million people, and that is where generations of my family grew up and lived out their overworked yet amazing lives. This blood, the Fuzhou blood running in my body, separates me from so many other Chinese descendants, and it's a beautiful concept to belong to a smaller and more distinct community. Fuzhou is part of Fujian, which is the real province, and it belongs to the river basin, which makes us surrounded by glorious mountains. And oftentimes when I travel back in the summertime, I visit the loud and awake areas of the city then to the more remote and peaceful mountainous regions that are farther out.

My immigrant mother was raised in an impoverished family so she didn't receive a high school education. She had to work odd jobs in middle school after she got out of class. She would come home exhausted but had to take care of the house, cook dinner for her fatigued parents, and care for her younger brother. She did this with nobody by her side and no emotional support. She did not get the chance to eat foods that were nutritious and tasty because she couldn't afford them. She taught me not to be wasteful of food and to always live a humble life as well.

My mother came to the Americas in hopes of finding a new job and a better life. And here in this free country is where she chose to have us, so we can have a better life, unlike her. School for youngsters like us means busy mornings; she would be waking up in the early morning to prepare breakfast for us and walk us to school in the frigid winter weather, to make sure we were warm and all bundled up. She prioritized our education by helping us with homework to the best of her power. She made us lunch and dinner and always remembered my favorite foods like stir-fried cabbage and Chao Mi Fen, a delicious noodle dish. Her actions were the constant motivation to keep us learning and show us that we're loved and cared for, and that although we are kids we work hard too.

My mother also makes life fun for us. She would agree to chaperone on field trips so she'd be able to watch over me, and put me in swimming classes. She also put me in a Chinese class so that I would know life skills. We hung out at the Bronx Zoo, aquariums, Brooklyn's Prospect Park, amusement parks, supermarkets, the beach, and the Botanic Garden. We also traveled to China and Canada. She made it all possible to ensure we had a memorable childhood. She also supports me emotionally.

After school, I would come home and cry because I was made fun of and harassed by little kids in my grade. This is just a drip from a bucket of everything she's done.

Today, I stand as a sixteen-year-old girl who has skin the color of sun-kissed desert sand. I'm grateful because through the help of my mother I'm regaining my native tongue and learning about my culture. My mother has been there for me and made so many sacrifices so my sister and I can have a future, live stably and independently. Where exactly is someone with yellow skin from? This is an easy question, but for some reason we, being humans, usually overthink it. Or more like overexplain it in efforts to make it more complicated and meaningful. And even so, that complexity is just as beautiful as our simple origins. I'm just grateful for everything in my life.

# AMAYA WARD

**GRADE:** Senior

**LIVES:** Bronx, NY

**BORN:** Bronx, NY

### MENTEE'S ANECDOTE:

This is my second year with Girls Write Now and it's been quite incredible. I feel so honored to be a part of this community of talented people and to share my work. I remember when I was around nine years old, I would write and illustrate my own short stories. It started with little strips, but as time continued, I became more obsessed with narrative writing and wanting my work to be shared. I've been writing seriously since I was about eleven or twelve, which is when I started working on my current novel, *The Mysterious Reappearance of Princess Amantdeiylaia*. It's been a long time coming, and I'm so happy to see my childhood dreams come to life right before my eyes. I'm sincerely grateful for the opportunities given to me to help make my dreams a reality. Thank you!

---

# ELIZABETH C. CROZIER

**OCCUPATION:** SEO Writer

**LIVES:** Barrington, IL

**BORN:** Auburn, IN

### MENTOR'S ANECDOTE:

Working with Amaya and being part of this program have been incredibly rewarding. I love learning about her life and getting to see her art. She's so far ahead of where I was at that age that I can't wait to see what she does with future opportunities. Though we live halfway across the country from each other, we've found ways to communicate and still stay connected.

# Excerpt from *The Mysterious Reappearance of Princess Amantdeiylaia*

## AMAYA WARD

*An excerpt from my novel that is a work in progress! The excerpt is about an alien princess who is ostracized from the outside world and is forced to be isolated by her controlling grandmother.*

It was about that time when Princess Amantdeiylaia was taken away to a small cottage with her grandmother. Although there wasn't much to do, her favorite part of the day was when the wind hit the window's curtains. The princess sat in her room, though not always alone. The birds landed on her windowsill, giving her company until she'd get too close to them. This startled them, making them fly away—just like everything else in her life . . .

It was something that would bring her joy, but it only lasted for a couple of minutes before being taken away.

Sitting comfortably on the bed she was given to rest on when forced to be with her grandmother, she overheard her name being called. Dreading the person who called her, she tried to ignore it, opting to watch the birds outside.

The girl heard her name being called once more, and her eyes avoided the door where the voice came from. She hoped that if she pretended she couldn't hear it, then she wouldn't have to face what was waiting on the other side. She instead diverted her attention to the wooden floors, her eyes scanning the cracks and scratches. The wood was rough on her feet, and she noticed that they probably needed to be fixed, since they gave her terrible splinters. The voice only grew in volume, causing her to finally break her avoidance.

"Yes, Grandmother?" Amantdeiylaia, the blond princess, mumbled. Her voice was soft and held no pride or confidence, and its only good quality was how it was hushed and how it never got any louder than this. Footsteps approached the wooden door where she was locked up, and the door opened, revealing an incredibly tall woman.

"What have I told you about ignoring me when I call for you, Amantdeiylaia?" her grandmother scolded, her voice much louder and deeper than her granddaughter's. She towered over the princess, her shadow casting down on her face and causing her to lower her head in shame.

"I'm sorry, Grandmother," Princess Amantdeiylaia meekly responded. She realized in her thirteen years of life thus far, her grandmother was impossible to please. It was better to just answer her the way she wanted or else she'd face severe consequences.

The princess's eyes naturally drifted off to where the window was, the only source of lighting in the room besides a candle that was nearly finished on her nightstand. Recognizing the hold she had on her granddaughter, the grandmother immediately grabbed the princess's face, forcing her to keep her eyes on her. She clicked her tongue, her eyebrows furrowed.

"And what have I told you about not maintaining eye contact when someone is speaking with you?" She awaited a reply from her granddaughter, but only silence followed. The princess's eyes naturally gravitated toward the wood, or the walls, or the door . . .

Anything that wasn't her grandmother.

"Do you hate me? Do I anger you?" her grandmother inquired, her voice becoming softer, luring her granddaughter into a false sense of security.

"No, Grand—"

"Then why do you disobey every teaching I give to you? You must hate me if you don't think what I'm teaching you is of any value," her grandmother argued, slapping her granddaughter. The sound reverberated off the walls, and once again silence filled the room. Tears brimmed around the princess's eyes, her lower lip wobbling. As if her grandmother wasn't the cause of her tears, she comforted the princess.

"Don't cry, my granddaughter. It's unbecoming of your visage," she said sternly, making the princess want to cry even harder.

"Why can't I go outside, Grandmother? Am I so terrible that I don't deserve to see the world I live in? I don't like it here in the cottage! I want to be able to see the world, touch the trees and the grass with my own hands," she cried out, her voice strained from the yelling. The princess hated loud noises; however, her grandmother acted like a catalyst, igniting all the ugliness she buried deep down inside of her. Her grandmother sat beside her, feigning sympathy for her pleas.

"I realize that you want to see the world, but for people like you—" Her eyes scanned her granddaughter's body, before scoffing at the idea. "You wouldn't stand a chance! You're so weak, my darling. You lack basic social awareness and would only cause more harm than good. Don't forget, this cottage keeps you safe. The world outside is much too dark for a young, dimwitted girl like you. You're much too simple to go outside," she said, her voice stern as per usual.

Her grandmother stepped back, leaving her to be alone with her thoughts. When she felt as though she smashed her granddaughter's fragile confidence to pieces, she left her to wallow in her own self-pity. However, Amantdeiylaia was determined this time, for she refused to stand idly by whilst her grandmother spoke down to her. This time, she would prove to her that she was deserving of happiness.

This time, she would be free.

# ZUZANNA WASILUK

**GRADE:** Senior  **LIVES:** Brooklyn, NY

**BORN:** Brooklyn, NY

### MENTEE'S ANECDOTE:

Just after *Dune* came out in theaters last year, we read *Dune* to discuss with each other as a small book duo rather than a club. These discussions were short because they were usually at the end of our meetings, but it was very enjoyable to read *Dune* knowing that I could discuss it with someone each week. We were inspired by *Dune* in our writing and even began a creative writing piece using lines from the book. Bonding over *Dune* helped us examine the new attitudes toward its themes and characters.

---

# APHRODITE BRINSMEAD

**OCCUPATION:** Product Marketing Manager  **BORN:** London, England

**LIVES:** Brooklyn, NY

### MENTOR'S ANECDOTE:

It's been wonderful to work with Zuzanna as a mentor for a second year with Girls Write Now. Over the last few months, I've watched her develop and tackle different styles of writing. Her nonfiction pieces are filled with humor and written in a unique style, teaching me about the world. Zuzanna's wonderful college essays gave me a glimpse into her life growing up in Brooklyn. I'm looking forward to learning more about Zuzanna through her writing.

# Outsiders Do Their Best:
# Soviet Mapping

## ZUZANNA WASILUK

*The U.S.S.R. military undertook a secret global mapping program that endeavored to create maps of areas around the world. These maps were incredibly detailed yet the cartographers in the Soviet program made mistakes.*

The U.S.S.R. military undertook a secret global mapping program during the twentieth century. Some of the greatest talent in the field of geography endeavored to create hundreds of thousands of maps of areas, from cities to small towns. This effort started with Stalin during World War II and continued through the Cold War by his successors. Cartographers included a *spravka* with each map, an essay of 2,000 to 3,500 words describing the city's geography and geology, the ethnicity of its citizens, climate conditions, public transportation, and industry. These essays display remarkable attention to detail for the multitude of places being mapped under this program's initiative. American pilots invading Afghanistan in late 2001 even relied on Soviet-era military maps because they were more detailed than other maps of the area. Despite the attention to detail, mapping various towns and cities from other countries is a difficult task, and as a result, the cartographers in the Soviet program made mistakes. They convey the significant impact locals have in shaping their environment.

Soviet cartographers involved with the program were culturally predisposed to believe maps available to the public were falsified, since military maps of their own environment were unavailable for public access.

Coming from a culture with this natural assumption caused a cartographer mapping a city to compile a packet of resources that included official state maps, atlases, aerial imagery, guidebooks, and personal reports from military personnel. Each map is the result of laborious data collection for accuracy and reliability that called attention far beyond just the present infrastructure. Soviet cartographers approached any kind of available material as a piece to their puzzle. As a result, a map user became very familiar with the geography and cultural features of a region from this meticulous process on the part of the Soviets, who even included phonetic spelling of regions in Cyrillic.

The mistakes made by Soviet cartographers would be understandable to any local of the region as the Soviets were immersing themselves in the region's geography and culture for a short period of time. When mapping Huddersfield, a town in England known for its role in the Industrial Revolution, cartographers included an important building as object number twenty-three labeled "Institute of Technology," which is unexpected for a small town. Unbeknownst to them, the Soviets labeled the Mechanics' Institute as the "Institute of Technology," a mistake significant to any local eye. The Mechanics' Institute was founded in the mid-nineteenth century for the benefit of workers, providing an alternative to drinking after work at a pub. Soviets were unable to recognize the cultural significance of this institute within the context of the environment. Locals appreciate this landmark for the betterment of the working man because they understand the underlying political, cultural, and economic causes in history that motivated the community to create this educational establishment. These mistakes weren't confined to the United Kingdom; there are a number of small errors in maps produced of cities from other countries.

The cultural misunderstandings in Soviet maps are amusing because Soviet cartographers were removed from the cultures they were writing about, proving that locals interact with their environment in a way only they understand. When mapping London, Soviet cartographers labeled Her Majesty's Theatre, one of the theaters in London's West End, in the index as "Residence of the Queen and Prime Minister." Any Londoner, regardless of their affluence, would know Her Majesty's Theatre as a venue with a variety of entertainment to enjoy. Describing the theater with deep-pocketed sponsors as the Residence of the Queen and Prime Minister is humorous in how far it lands from the truth.

Regarding public transportation and roads, Soviet cartographers had particular trouble without local knowledge. Having only aerial imagery and previous maps, cartographers had inconsistent success with portraying transportation. Any local that utilized public transportation or the roads would've noticed a number of these errors by having personally interacted with the transport links of their environment, including its many complexities that are understood through increased exposure.

The detail present in the maps created by Soviet cartographers as part of a mapping program is still impressive in the twenty-first century. Soviet cartographers made a valiant effort in understanding different geographic regions and the way they've been shaped by human interaction. The incredibly detailed maps as well as the written materials, such as the *spravka*, are still valuable today despite the disadvantages they had as outsiders to the environment.

# TATYANNA WILLS

**GRADE:** Junior

**BORN:** Gaborone, Botswana

**LIVES:** Jamaica, NY

### MENTEE'S ANECDOTE:

Meeting Elizabeth has definitely improved my writing and my ability to speak out as a person. She has not only provided a safe space for me to talk about my experiences, but we have also been able to connect on multiple subjects. Elizabeth has helped me grow not only as a writer, but as a person.

---

# ELIZABETH KOSTER

**OCCUPATION:** Teacher/ESL Coordinator

**BORN:** New York, NY

**LIVES:** New York, NY

### MENTOR'S ANECDOTE:

I've enjoyed our conversations about writing, as well as our in-depth discussions about human nature and human rights. Tatyanna's work is powerful and moving. It has been inspiring to speak with her about her process and see her transform pain into beauty.

# What am I made of?

## TATYANNA WILLS

**Content Warning:** homophobia

*This piece showcases not only the hardships I faced as a queer girl in a Christian household, but how I overcame my self-doubt and learned to accept myself as I am.*

What am I made of? That's a hard question. I am made of sandy beaches and oceans so calming you can fall asleep just listening to them. I am made of festivals and soca. I am made of lights and parades. I am made of music, the kind that fills the void in your heart and gives you a purpose. But I am also made of questions. My body is what Christian men and godly women call a waste. To them my love is corrupting, sinful, a disgrace, a horror story that mothers tell their daughters when they start preferring cars over Barbies, a cautionary tale on what your kids could become if you allow them to stray from God's path. But I can be fixed, right?

This is only a disease that can be cured with prayer and baptism and a god that seemingly loves me but doesn't love me enough to accept me as I am, right? Bullshit. But still, I prayed, I stayed awake at night crying, begging God to rid me of this curse that the devil had laid upon me the day I was born. Longing that one day Jehovah will strike me down before the age of seven so that I can enter heaven with no questions asked. To no avail.

You see, this is what I'm made of. I am made of fear. I am made of prayer. I am made in the image of the Lord himself, crafted with vigorous detail, made with a path that was set in stone as soon as I was placed in the womb. A path that I foolishly refuse to follow. If this isn't the path I'm supposed to take, then why does it feel right? Why does my stomach drop every time I see her? Why does the world stop when I hear her call my name? When she tells me she loves me everything just feels right. Her voice is a symphony and my heart is the metronome. Her soul is like a galaxy and I am merely an astronaut trying to uncover it all. The stars envy her because they too know that they cannot hold a candle to her beauty. I swear I've never loved someone more in my life.

However, according to the church, this isn't what I was made for, this isn't what God planned for me. If this isn't my destiny, what is? What am I supposed to do? What am I made of? That's a hard question. According to the world, I am made of sin. To the Christian men and godly women who once played a significant role in my life, I am a lost cause. But I am made of hope. I am made of questions. I am made of answers. I was made to succeed against all odds, no matter how "sinful" I may be. I was made to follow my heart's path whether that path was looked upon with scorn or delight. It does not matter what the world thinks I'm made of. It does not matter if they believe that I was made to burn in the fiery pits of hell and be tortured for all eternity. Their approval holds no significance to me. Because if there is a god, I am made in his image with this path in mind, with her by my side.

# OLIVIA WRONSKI

**GRADE:** Senior

**BORN:** Queens, NY

**LIVES:** Little Neck, NY

### MENTEE'S ANECDOTE:

Meeting with Jordan weekly these past months has been a fantastic experience. Her bright energy and excitement make every session a place of productive and passionate collaboration. I am so glad and blessed to have met Jordan! Writing together this year has opened up a variety of opportunities for me to not only learn from other writers that Jordan has shared with me, but to also incorporate the styles I've learned from these weekly sessions into my own writing. Brainstorming for the February poetry piece was fun and memorable. I also enjoyed our free-writes and the share-outs afterward.

# JORDAN COWELL

**OCCUPATION:** Senior Project Manager

**BORN:** Kutztown, PA

**LIVES:** Kutztown, PA

### MENTOR'S ANECDOTE:

Wednesday evenings have quickly become my midweek highlight. This is when Olivia and I meet to do creative writing exercises, explore new genres, and workshop pieces. She is a force of a young woman—creative and ambitious, wise and open-minded, kind and warmhearted. I'm grateful to be a part of this journey with Olivia as she finds her voice as a poet. The very fact that we have never met in person (yet have become so close!) only confirms my belief in the power of the written word and its ability to bridge distances and foster deep human connection.

# Stages of Reflection

## OLIVIA WRONSKI

*"Stages of Reflection" reveals the ongoing journey of self-love in three basic stages.*

I.

Why do I continue to look into mirrors
When I know I'll hate what I see?
How could I ever love myself
When I look nothing like the beautiful people all around me?

On my phone in little square Instagram posts,
Posing in front of New York City buildings,
Sprawled on beaches,
Perched on benches.

And they look so gorgeous,
Skinny and shapely,
Small face and small waist,
Which extends to delicate, full curves.

How can I look at them and then at myself
And not see every single one of my flaws
From the dip in my hips to my round face,
To my large arms and tummy
which don't get smaller

no matter how long I starve,
Or exercise
until I'm sweating through my shirt into the carpet.
And even then drenched in sweat,
I was drenched in tears.

I need to hide myself.
Hide these pudgy sides
These pudgy arms
This pudgy face.

So I hide.
Underneath layers of jackets and sweaters,
And long sleeve shirts and baggy pants.

But the layers of clothing build upon my body
Like layers of sediment over eons
Until I feel as big as a mountain
And my sadness collects like snow over my head and shoulders.

It wasn't always like this.
I was happy with myself when I was ten.
When I would wear what I liked
instead of hiding behind dark hoodies and jeans.
I wore fire truck red, tiger orange, sunny yellow.
I wore springtime green, coral reef blue, and grape jelly purple.

I was happy with myself when I was ten.
Until my aunt reached to pinch my stomach
Turning to my mother and laughing
"She's getting fat, how much does she weigh?"

Now at 17
I pinch my own stomach,

Naked before a shower
When I have to be conscious of the space I take up in the small
    stall.
Speaking just as my aunt did:
"You're still getting fat. How much do you weigh today?"

Because my worth is defined by my weight
A woman should be light as a feather
But still have large, soft breasts,
Buttocks and thighs.
But also a thigh gap a train could easily fit through.
And the frame of a child
with no hair anywhere but their head,
But the frame of a child and wide hips.


## II.

I was on the outside looking in
At a world of people who fit these starry-eyed standards.
The beauty of their bodies is a musical piece,
Rolling waves of sound.

Flat stomach hourglass guitars,
Hair strand strings,
Round hipped harps,
A tinkling, sweet sound.

I knew I could be music too—but how?
I looked outwards at others like me.
Confident and beautiful in their unique bodies
Proud of their curves and rolls and roundness
Posing in the little Instagram squares on my phone.
Their happiness encouraged mine.
I looked inwards and pulled the instruments from my body.

My body is also a musical piece
Rolling waves of harmonies.
And suddenly I am in a concert hall
Playing the special sound of my body.

My stomach is round,
Just like a drum.
Meticulously crafted ridges and rounds
I let loose loud, thundering laughs.

My hips that curve in, rather than out
Are the shape of violins,
Delicately curved pieces of art, pieces of me.
A piece in the grand orchestra of my body.


### III.

My legs, long and large
Are what carry me over mountains
Through subway tunnels,
Big, beautiful, and strong.

These broad shoulders,
when I stand tall
block the powerful waves of the ocean
Stone pillars that grow more beautiful as they age.

Why do we reject the bodies
Mother Nature crafted us with?
The body she made by
Twisting locks of vines for our hair
And molding us with the clay of the earth
Filling our mud bodies with beauty

That we've shattered.
We've smashed the hardened clay
Torn the vines from our heads
And from the pieces of our bodies.

This wild jungle of human beauty
Has been deforested.
That wood reaches the factory
And we are manufactured into
Wooden Barbie dolls,
identical and monotone.

If society is a garden,
It is a boring garden.
The same flowers,
Hedges manicured into straight rectangles.

This garden would look so much better
Overflowing with different flowers,
An explosion of color on every bush, in every nook and cranny

If each body was made unique
Why do we try so hard to be identical?
I am worth it.

This body works hard every day.
My body is what gives me life,
It's the reason I can laugh loudly
and the reason I can see sunsets
And sunrises.

My journey
To finding love within myself

Is not an easy task.
It is an enduring process of continuous reflection.

But the present me is not alone.
My future self and I will trudge through snowstorms and sand,
Swim for miles across seas

Until I've returned from my adventures
A source of compassion and beauty,
Smiling at my own reflection in mirrors
Because I am beautiful
Even if I am different.

# JULIA WYSOKINSKA

**GRADE:** Junior

**BORN:** Białystok, Poland

**LIVES:** Ridgewood, NY

### MENTEE'S ANECDOTE:

I always enjoy my meetings with Jamie, as I can be honest and unafraid of my creative side with her. There are no wrong answers and there's always a way out of a sticky situation with her advice. She's always taken time out of her day to impart her wisdom when I've needed it, and I always end up learning something new. I'm looking forward to meeting her in person!

---

# JAMIE DUCHARME

**OCCUPATION:** Correspondent

**BORN:** Manchester, NH

**LIVES:** Brooklyn, NY

### MENTOR'S ANECDOTE:

I am convinced Julia has more than twenty-four hours in her day because she accomplishes more than any human being should be able to and she does it with a smile on her face. I look forward to meeting with her every week because I know she will impress me every time. In ten years, we will all be working for Julia Wysokinska.

# Nervous Scrolling

## JULIA WYSOKINSKA

*A woman dining alone at a restaurant realizes memory doesn't serve her justice.*

I hear utensils clanking against one another, the sound originating from the table near me. A waiter carrying a silver platter almost walks into an unattended chair in his hurry.

How odd it is that I could be sitting alone at a table in a coffee shop and no one would bat an eye, yet here, I feel as though I'm on display. Look at me, restaurant diners! I couldn't find a buddy, so I bare my lonely soul for all to see, for your enjoyment.

Maybe the brunette and the older gentleman across the room are talking about me, exchanging witty, slightly cruel remarks at my expense. Maybe the waiters think I'm being stood up by a blind date, and maybe they'll offer me a free dessert out of pity. Maybe the mysterious figure at the bar is prepared to send a consolation drink my way. But maybe none of them notice me at all.

I still feel their eyes on me. It's almost as though I'm in high school again, reciting a poem in the auditorium as the entire student body stares past me, definitely not paying any attention, my voice threatening to break and shatter if I look away from the text in my hands.

I can't take it anymore. My phone makes its way from my purse to the table. I quickly glance out at the other diners, then look back at the table before me. I knew coming here alone would be a challenge, but this is somehow even more brutal than the worst-case scenario my brain could conjure up. If I pretend I'm busy on my phone, will others think the sight of me is less sad?

Instinct takes over and I click on the light blue link that autofills when I type in the beginning of my email address. I check my work email inbox, then my personal. No new messages have sifted in within the last hour. A crazy idea forms in my head: I'll check my high school email. I discover they've upgraded to online versions of the newspaper and I'm subscribed to their email blasts.

Investigating my former school's website, I realize they've posted many older issues of the school newspaper. My finger hovering over the student work, I click on the collection of sports articles from my senior year. I recognize my own article about the soccer team, complete with pictures documenting the afternoons spent watching games and practices at a nearby park, cheering her on.

She's wearing her soccer jersey, sticking her tongue out at the camera. This was the championship game, and she must have known the hired photographer was taking photos to be published. She was usually so serious around adults, ever the professional. It was only when we were goofing around after school or during free periods that she showed her playful side.

The photo is grainy. It doesn't do her freckles justice. The background washes her out, but the other team's players wearing bright blue jerseys adds some contrast. To the untrained eye, the jerseys are the interesting part of the photo. To me, she's the focus.

I'm surprised to see this photo here. I'd expect to see it taken at a birthday party or weekend trip away, any private affair. She usually would have taken a more appropriate, universal stance. She would have known it would go in the school newspaper for all to see.

A waiter walks over to my table and I set the menu down. He looks at me. I look at him. He smiles and begins spouting off, probably about the specials of the day. I'm his only audience member and yet I can't decipher anything he's saying. His words are like steamed carrots: mushy, unappetizing, and, frankly, confusing. His muffled chatter ceases and he tilts his head. I assume he must have just asked me a question, but I don't know what it was.

"Uh, I . . . I'm going to need more time," I offer hesitantly.

He swivels around and goes to the foyer to send another couple to a table. The string band roars and the conversations around me become unbearably loud. I grab my purse and fumble around, looking for my wallet. After an embarrassingly long attempt, I come across my sage green pocketbook, made out of vegan leather and engraved with my initials. I pry it open, then throw two crumpled twenty-dollar bills beside my empty bread plate. The waiter definitely lost out on tips because of me, so I might as well try to make it up to him.

I grab my coat in my hands, opting to put it on as I rush out of the restaurant instead of taking my time and keeping a semblance of composure. The warm lighting of the eatery recedes into my blind spot, and the honks of taxicabs and cooing pigeons mark my arrival. I find myself on the snowy streets of New York once more.

# ADELLE XIAO

**GRADE:** Junior

**BORN:** New York, NY

**LIVES:** New York, NY

### MENTEE'S ANECDOTE:

Working with Sarah has been such an amazing experience, and I'm really glad that we've been able to connect in the way that we have, even in a virtual setting. Sarah is understanding and supportive, and she continues to challenge me to push myself to not only improve as a writer, but also become more outspoken and confident. I can't wait to see what we'll be able to achieve together in the future!

---

# SARAH A. CUSTEN

**OCCUPATION:** Adjunct Professor

**BORN:** Ogden, UT

**LIVES:** Brooklyn, NY

### MENTOR'S ANECDOTE:

At one point Adelle said to me, reflectively, "I used to think that adults had it all together..."

"—but then you met me?" I offered, and we both laughed. I love that we've been able to honor and validate each other's humanity and complexity, meeting each other where we're at, with an eye towards support and growth.

# I'm Not Hungry

## ADELLE XIAO

**Content Warning:** disordered eating, fatphobia

*A short story about finding my voice.*

I don't remember what I ate for breakfast that morning, the timbre of your voice, or whether the sun was shining. I do remember that we wandered around Central Park, dead leaves crumbling and crunching under the soles of our sneakers, filling the silence with anticipation as I dreaded the questions I knew you would begin to ask. The questions you always asked.

*Do you know how skinny you are? How was your morning? You didn't eat breakfast, did you? Don't lie, I know you didn't eat—can't you at least be honest with me? You have to eat.*

I knew that I was short and skinny, but it had never really mattered to me until I met you—it was all you ever talked about. I mumbled that my morning was good and that I had eaten breakfast—the truth—but you refused to believe me because you *just knew.* I wanted you to like me for who I was, not to judge me for who I wasn't. I wanted you to see more than my skinniness; most of all, I wanted you to believe me.

*Don't wear skinny jeans anymore; they make your legs look like twigs— why would you wear them? God, you lost weight, didn't you? Why can't you just listen to me? Is it really that hard to gain weight? You're hungry, aren't you? Doesn't matter, here, have the sandwich I brought. If you don't eat it, I'll force-feed it to you. You have to eat.*

I told you that I was uncomfortable and not hungry, but I still ate your ham-and-cheese sandwich because that was what you wanted. I knew that I couldn't control the fact that you thought skinny jeans weren't flattering on me, and that you refused to believe that I hadn't lost weight. But when you said it was my fault, I believed you. Your questions pierced me one by one, plucking the words out of my mouth and forcing me to swallow a guilty conscience. I forced the food down with a heavy chest, the weight of wrongness lurching its way through my body and crawling out of my skin.

When I got home, I stripped off the skinny jeans and buried them deep in the closet two rooms away. *You have to eat.* Your voice chased me to the kitchen and delighted in my instantaneous misery as I pulled the fridge door and lost myself in food, rejecting my body's protests as the heaviness threatened to suffocate and consume me alive. *You have to eat.* I willed the crevices between my ribs to disappear, my eyes tracing the outlines of my body with hatred. *You have to eat.* I staggered to the bathroom in a feeble attempt to escape you, steadied only by my reflection in the toilet bowl's blank stillness and the floor's coldness against my bare feet.

The food spilled back out of my mouth and into the toilet bowl, disrupting my stagnant reflection. I sat on the floor, my head spinning as I feebly flushed the toilet. Deep down, I knew that you wouldn't stop telling me to eat, no matter how much I wished for the opposite. I knew that I shouldn't have let your perceptions define me—your words only held power over me because I let them. I finally felt light again. I walked out the bathroom, taking deep heaving breaths, devouring the air that I hadn't realized I was missing.

Shakily, I dug out my skinny jeans from the closet and wore them the next day, ignoring you when you tapped me on the shoulder during history class to demand that I eat. Over time, I learned to not let your perceptions of me define who I was. I learned to mean it when I said, "I'm not hungry."

# MEGAN XING

**GRADE:** Senior
**BORN:** Queens, NY
**LIVES:** Forest Hills, NY

### MENTEE'S ANECDOTE:

My mentor once sent me a *New York Times* article titled "Who Is the Bad Art Friend?" I remember reading it in school and texting her my opinions as they formed and just having such an entertaining conversation about the whole thing. Afterward, she updated me on the Twitter gossip surrounding the subject, and it was a really entertaining experience because I don't know many people who would be as fascinated with writing drama as I am. This just emphasized how good our synergy is and reminded me how lucky I am to have such a great mentor.

---

# SHAYLA LOVE

**OCCUPATION:** Senior Staff Writer
**BORN:** San Diego, CA
**LIVES:** Brooklyn, NY

### MENTOR'S ANECDOTE:

I love to talk about books and writing with others, and so I was delighted to learn that Megan and I have extremely similar taste in literature! We share an appreciation for Japanese translated prose, and angsty, smart essays written by women. I've enjoyed seeing her experiment with her writing— even if at three a.m.—and work with themes and characters that reflect the coming-of-age moment she's at in her life. I've been inspired by her natural spark of talent, and the amount of new material she's produced in a short time that could fuel writing projects for years to come.

# a study in nihilism

## MEGAN XING

*A short story about what happens when dreamers give in to hope-lessness and futility.*

Beth isn't exactly sure when she became a nihilist. When finding her high school friends' wedding pictures on Instagram and promotion announcements on Twitter stopped leaving a bitter taste in her mouth, and her mother's increasingly unsubtle texts stopped making her heart twinge with guilt. When she stopped wearing the cross necklace she never took off throughout high school and donated her Bible to the used bookstore. Probably around the same indeterminate time her impulsive lifestyle settled into dull, pragmatic routine, when the clouds stopped looking like cotton candy and she no longer dreamt of other worlds. She still remembers her bold vow to study creative writing at a reputable university and earn her MFA. To live a life unbridled by routine, basking in the millions made by her numerous bestselling novels. To open a quaint little bookstore, a secret gem nestled between a Brooklyn crystal shop and a cozy cafe, and never worry about profits or the dying industry because of her immense wealth and generationally rich, mostly decorative husband.

At twenty-six, her life is a far cry from her childhood fantasies. Every day, she rolls grudgingly out of bed at eight a.m. and dresses in a nondescript white blouse and black pencil skirt. (She used to make more of an effort—glam it up with jewelry and three daringly open buttons—but she has long since sunk into apathy.) Walks to the subway station from her crappy apartment in increasingly gentrified Brooklyn and tries not to think about how the prices are rapidly rocketing out of her pay range.

(The other day, she walked into her corner bodega to find that a sandwich now costs $6.79.) Pours coffee for tax accountants at her retired mother's old office. Places the same coffee order at Dunkin' Donuts. Wearily says "It's Beth" when her persistent coworker calls "Over here, Elizabeth!" during their thirty-minute lunch break. Fiddles with the Muji pens in her Canada Moose cup holder (she hasn't bought a new one since high school) and reflects on her last disastrous date. Thinks about the high school friends who tearily swore to stay in touch. (The ones who never bothered to check up, or check in, or even text first. The ones she eventually stopped talking to, who might not have even noticed.) Sometimes she thinks every friend is like that, even the ones she thought were different. That's when the depression sets in, and she reaches for the cheap vodka that she suspects is actually just drain cleaner with a home-printed label slapped on.

Same old, every day. Constant. Unchanging. Invariable.

Sometimes she thinks of the dreamer she used to be and feels hollow inside. She stopped thinking she was anyone special long ago—middle and high school thoroughly disabused her of that notion—but she supposes she always held on to that small kernel of absolute conviction that someday, somehow, she would be someone. Not the stereotypical college graduate barely scraping up grocery money. Not the stubborn twenty-something with no hope and no confidence and no faith and constant, borderline suicidal thoughts.

Most days, Beth can't find it in herself to push her hopelessness aside and don the mask of a functioning member of society. Rage surges beneath her skin, bubbling readily beneath the surface like magma in the mouth of a volcano. When her boss makes an unreasonable demand, when her mother phones with another pointless scolding, when her coworkers look at her with poorly masked disdain.

Once, words were her solace. Now, she knows that all they ever are is an unbearable curse. A constant taunt, an omnipresent reminder that the dreamer she once was has settled into a bitter, hateful person. An infinitely recursive mantra, lurking in every corner of her consciousness.

*This is what you could have been.*

# ATLAS YEN

**GRADE:** Junior

**BORN:** New York, NY

**LIVES:** Brooklyn, NY

### MENTEE'S ANECDOTE:

It's absolutely insane how well my mentor and I clicked, even the very first time we met over Zoom. We talked for more than an hour about all our favorite shows, books, and hobbies. We had even gone to the same concert back in 2019 without knowing it! It wouldn't be a mad stretch to say that the Fates themselves brought Arielle and I together—the Fates, of course, being the geniuses at Girls Write Now who paired us up. Arielle is knowledgeable, funny, and kind, and I couldn't ask for a better mentor to accompany me on my journey.

---

# A.N. WEGBREIT

**OCCUPATION:** English/EAL Teacher and Librarian

**BORN:** Plainfield, NJ

**LIVES:** New York, NY

### MENTOR'S ANECDOTE:

The second Atlas and I started bonding about our love for anime, Rick Riordan, and BTS, all my anxiety about being a mentor subsided. Every week, I look forward to our Zoom chats, where I continue to learn so much from Atlas and their experiences, even when we're just nerding out over our shared interests. I'm especially lucky because I get to "fangirl" over the four fantasy novels Atlas has already written. Atlas is naturally gifted with words, and they have already received several writing awards! I am in constant awe of Atlas, and they are truly my role model.

# Mind Your Business

## ATLAS YEN AND A.N. WEGBREIT

*"Mind Your Business" discusses various social justice issues with regard to people involving themselves in things that don't concern them.*

*The characters used here are fictional, and are not representative of the authors themselves.*

### Mind Your Own Business I

---

### INTROVERSION
#### A.N. Wegbreit

"Do NOT Enter!" Can't they read the sign? I even wrote *N-O-T* in huge capital letters with my red Sharpie. But apparently, that is too much to ask in our two-bedroom Upper East Side apartment. My parents must be illiterate, because they turn the doorknob and stand in my doorway without even the slightest knock. My mom asks with her highest voice, "What are you doing up here all on your own?" Like she cares. Like she's not going to scream at me or guilt me for actually *wanting* to stay up here on my own.

*"Mind your own business,"* I want to say. But I know that would never fly. So instead, I look up from my book peeking out behind thick bangs. "Reading," I say, mimicking my mom's high-pitched tone and nodding my book up in her direction.

My dad gives an apologetic smile as my mom loses her cool. "Well, you could spend some time with your family," she says. "It wouldn't kill you, you know."

*It just might,* I think. Doesn't she understand just how much effort it takes for me to be social? It's exhausting. I'm exhausted, and I just want to lose myself in the world of my book for a little while.

---

## ELEVATOR POISON
### Atlas Yen

"Can I touch your hair?" they ask with poisonous curiosity in their eyes. Acid seeps through their teeth.

Looking up at the ceiling of the elevator, I clench my jaw. "No," I say as politely as I can, and hate myself for it. I should be meaner. Crueler. Point out that the venom slipping through their gums smells like the remnants of disease their ancestors spread intentionally to those they drove out of their own homes.

*"Mind your own business."* The words get hung behind my own teeth, which don't stink of poison, like theirs do.

"You should think about styling it *down* more—this is a workplace, you know."

"Maybe," I lie. *No way,* I think. My hair is beautiful—black coils springing here and there, falling over my temples and the back of my neck, like a gorgeous entity of its own, reaching for the sun—and so far it hasn't prevented me from filing paperwork at a desk job. These people must be wearing blindfolds. Someone needs to rip them off—someone like a quick Google search or at least some sense of human decency.

---

## UNPLANNED PARENTHOOD
### A.N. Wegbreit

*Why are there so few Planned Parenthoods in this city?* I think as I fidget with the hem of my shirt on the subway. The pump pop music blasts in my ears as I count down the minutes until I get all the way to the Bronx.

When I get off the subway and walk toward the location using Google Maps on my phone, I'm so focused on the moving blue dot I barely notice the crowd at first. But even through my headphones, the shouts are unmistakable. They shout about SHAME and GUILT and even have the audacity to bring up GOD.

Being female means I have the privilege of bringing new life into this world, but it shouldn't mean I'm forced to. I should have the right to choose. And that's exactly what I'm doing here. Clutching my phone tightly in my hand, I turn up the volume on my music and keep my head down as I pass through the crowd.

I reach the door and pull it open, but one of the women pulls my shoulder, her eyes asking why I'm here. "Mind your own business," I mumble as I cross the threshold.

---

## HONG KONG
### Atlas Yen

Imperialism. It had always seemed like a faraway concept, a series of atrocities committed two hundred years ago, until I saw it broadcasted right before my eyes. A home I'd never visited was being overtaken as I watched helplessly on my couch, where those foreign governments, who couldn't ever seem to simply mind their own business, could never touch me.

I wondered—did anyone who shared my blood get hurt in those protests, fighting to defend their home? Were their screams echoing all the way here, causing that mad vibration deep in my bones—making tears of fire spill from my eyes?

My people sang songs of freedom and whispered rebellious slogans under their breath. Even so, their voices reached me ever so softly, loud as a typhoon, all the way across the sea.

And those who will never understand ask me why I agonize—why I sob for a family I've never met, as the place I'd always heard was vibrant, filled with the clanging of bells, and shouts of food vendors is destroyed, slowly turned to a dystopia where children play with the guns aimed at their own families, and my people lose the war they fought so hard that their voices were lost to quiet rasps.

Somewhere in that city, a gas mask lays on the street beside a can of tear gas, and people will dismiss that, merely, a chemist had been doing graffiti. They're minding the wrong kind of business.

# CLAIRE YU

**GRADE:** Senior

**BORN:** New York, NY

**LIVES:** Astoria, NY

### MENTEE'S ANECDOTE:

Throughout my last year of high school, Jesse's support and advice have been so valuable, especially when transitioning from a quarantined, virtual life to a fully in-person one. Her constant encouragement has allowed me to grow and mature as both a writer and a person, and I always look forward to talking to her! Over the past three years, we've gotten to know each other so well, and I know she is someone I can always depend on in the future.

---

# JESSE CHEN

**OCCUPATION:** Senior Account Executive

**BORN:** Edison, NJ

**LIVES:** New York, NY

### MENTOR'S ANECDOTE:

I've been lucky to work with Claire as her mentor for the past three years through Girls Write Now. In that time, I've gotten to truly know her voice as a writer and have been so proud to watch her grow as a student, writer, and leader. Claire is a fearless advocate, passionate dancer, and vocal activist, and I often feel like I'm learning as much from her as she is from me. I've loved exploring new forms of poetry and finding readings that will resonate with her, and look forward to seeing her continue to grow in college and beyond.

# The Sky's the Limit

## CLAIRE YU

*This is an excerpt from a story about a girl's process of learning to be independent and self-confident after the unexpected loss of her brother.*

### Sky and Wind

*I am Baram,*
*'wind' in Korean*
*My brother is Haneul,*
*the 'sky'.*
*It's strange how they knew,*
*my parents, our names*
*would be exactly what we would become.*

Haneul is perfect—perfect man, perfect son, perfect brother. That list will probably extend to "perfect husband" at some point in the next five years because I don't see how any woman could pass him up. He's a STEM student, like a good Korean son—graduated from college just last week with a degree in chemical engineering, which he did while traveling an hour each way to school and back every day so he could stay at home, cooking dinner for my mother, and impressing all of us with smart-sounding words.

He's tall, and strong, and reliable, the kind of oppa (big brother) everyone wants—the kind who is always there for everyone, with big star eyes.

I'm the sidekick, the Doctor Watson to his Sherlock Holmes. I've always wanted to be just like him, beautiful and intelligent. I learned quickly that I wasn't anything like him. I'm daydreamy and indecisive, constantly blowing one direction and then another, like my name. I'm a sophomore in high school now, and I still have no idea what I want to do with my life. All I want to do is stay a child forever, taking hikes with Haneul and singing to the trees. I'm the nerd, the one who reads books so much that I can quote entire passages from memory. I've texted Haneul so many of my favorite quotes from books and songs that we now insert quotes into our daily conversations, like our own secret language. Haneul is well spoken, always saying the right thing, and I am the opposite. I never know what the right thing to say is, and so I stay silent. I wish I was good at talking, like him, but he always tells me,

> "The ability to keep your mouth shut is usually a sign of intelligence."
> —HOLLY GOLDBERG SLOAN, *COUNTING BY 7S*

I guess I don't like doing anything I'm not already used to doing. Haneul always tries to convince me to try new things as we take our morning hike. He spent most of last year trying to get me to submit to a teen magazine, which I staunchly refused to do. Last week, he said I should join my school's book club. Yesterday, he told me I should enter the talent show. "You should just do it for fun," he said. "For the experience." Smirking, I muttered,

> "Experience is merely the name men gave to their mistakes."
> —OSCAR WILDE, *THE PICTURE OF DORIAN GRAY*

Haneul gave me a look, trying to look stern, but he couldn't hide the smile that was itching to get out from the corners of his lips. "Okay, fine. I had that coming," he finally admitted, grinning. "But seriously. You should go and try stuff out, make new friends. You hang out with your older brother entirely too much, Baram. It's probably not considered 'cool,' you know." I shrugged, and ran up the mountain path ahead of him. At the top, I shouted back, "It's cool with me!" as I watched him jog toward me, his feet pounding on the well-worn trail that Haneul had found in our childhood.

## Eclipse

*funny how an eclipse*
*is anything but abnormal*
*it is just dark*
*just night*
*only*
*at the wrong time*
*something unexpected*
*and we fall apart*

I didn't believe him at first. In fact, I started laughing . . .

# YASMIN ZAYED

**GRADE:** Junior

**BORN:** Brooklyn, NY

**LIVES:** Staten Island, NY

### MENTEE'S ANECDOTE:

As the seasons pass we are always presented with one big question: What are you thankful for? Luckily for me I never had to look far, always thankful for my mentor, Aoife. Aoife has a skill set beyond compare, allowing me to harness mine with great preparation. The capacity to be patient and understanding is limitless, a daunting task to most, especially when working with me. As a true Mr. Miyagi and Daniel LaRusso pairing, our duo has been unstoppable, tackling even the most dangerous writing prompts. The perils of karate are no match for those of your literary quests!

---

# AOIFE SHERIDAN

**OCCUPATION:** Chief Customer Officer—Americas

**BORN:** Dublin, Ireland

**LIVES:** Brooklyn, NY

### MENTOR'S ANECDOTE:

Year Two for the great adventure that is Yasmin and Aoife. Each week I await with eager anticipation, the latest hairstyle, nail design, school story, or work anecdote, but, most of all, each nugget of beautiful, heartfelt, and rendering writing. Yasmin brings such depth of thought, emotion, sass, and care in the craft of each word. It never fails to blow me away. She's mature beyond her years, and it's a joy to see her embracing new genres and formats. The sky's the limit for this Girls Write Now mentee. Watch out, world!

# Tales of Hero and Villain

## YASMIN ZAYED

*A perfect town's decaying world is set in stone; a world unconsented to. It's not the easiest knowing our fate stands between the rich and corrupt, or that there was never any difference at all.*

"Dear diary,"

Today I saved the world again
I'll say deep breath and count to ten
Perfect smile in heaven send.
Graceful poise my hand that waves
my image refracts onto every page
in between those history books
in between those classical nooks
<u>I am found.</u>
oh how lonely it must be
to stay as sharp as one could see
all alone, safe, and sound
may the world rest peacefully.

<u>x Hero</u>

"sorry:/"

i apologize
here's my apology

it wasn't real, nor did it comfort me
sorry i blew up your house
sorry i won cat and the mouse
oh my sincerest to you and your dearest
oh sh\*t i blew up your spouse (my bad).

## Hero delivers their speech at the UN press conference following the incident (2021) This is what the audience hears.

"Escapism"

why couldn't i just leave it alone
you know the saying, when you're in rome
but everyone knows that this isn't fair
the feeling is hard, too great to bear
i've got no time, none left to spare
we're in agony, this is a tragedy
why won't they just let us go
it's a disparity, this is a clarity
you know the saying, when you're in rome
kill and deceive, fight for your home

## Villain becomes a witness, but in today's society don't we all?

"on the ground"

nobody think
nobody move
oh shit it's them
let's just press snooze
we can just stay
turning our backs
they'll get away
amnesiac.

<u>Account by anonymous</u>

"A pep talk"

on your mark, you should get ready
it'll get dark, keep your hands steady
follow through, see to the end
finish your coup, fight and defend
gold, god, and glory, but here's where you stand
blatant outlawry, on my command.

<u>Kagami: the looking glass</u>

"Synchronicity"
**a pen to paper**

                                                    —*a gun to the head*
**a burst fire hydrant**

                                                    —*they left me for dead*
**a critical ache, a burning retire**

                                          —*this feeling of dread, just won't expire*
**the justice unfolds, the one i require**

                                                    —*nothing to lose*
**maybe my way**

                                                    —*they led me astray*
***Just walk away.***

<u>To be continued . . .</u>

# CAROLYN ZHENG

**GRADE:** Freshman

**LIVES:** Millbury, MA

**BORN:** Brooklyn, NY

### MENTEE'S ANECDOTE:

Currie is so patient with me. Even though I often don't see her texts or emails, she's been understanding and telling me not to worry about it. Of course, she's also a great mentor. I've learned how to tighten up my writing by eliminating all the "sludge," how to visualize my settings better, and how to write more consistently by journaling. There was also the time I learned how to be a journalist. I can't forget that. I can't stress enough how awesome Currie is.

---

# CURRIE ENGEL

**OCCUPATION:** *News-Times* Reporter

**BORN:** New York, NY

**LIVES:** New Milford, CT

**PUBLICATIONS & RECOGNITIONS:** Hearst Connecticut, *Time*, *Houston Chronicle*

### MENTOR'S ANECDOTE:

Carolyn has been an absolute joy to work with. She is creative, funny, smart, and a wonderful writer. I will always remember reading one of her stories for the first time. It was so deeply moving that it made me tear up. As I struggled to get through the lines without letting my voice shake, Carolyn waited patiently. Her writing and the tale itself were so thoughtful and wise beyond her years. I carried the story with me for the rest of the week. Carolyn can see things that other writers don't, and she already is a fantastic artist.

# stolen thunder

## CAROLYN ZHENG

*We see these grand beasts working so hard trying to survive and provide for their families, but with one bullet, hunters and poachers can kill them and all of their life's efforts.*

the lion chases the gazelle
powerful sinew and muscles work in tandem
it pounces
kills
and feasts with its cubs
until a man appeared
with a shining metal gun
thunderstruck
leaving scorched black
and cubs
Alone.

# ROOTING YOURSELF IN WRITING

## SEEDING YOUR STORIES

*Have you ever tried to grow your own sunflowers from scratch? Turns out it's a bit harder than one might think, but honestly, so is trying to write a Sci-Fi space opera in thirty minutes. And that is probably just as hard as manifesting your own manifesto in ten minutes. Or penning a poem by grafting Hip-Hop with ooey-gooey love songs before the sun sets! But that is what writers at Girls Write Now do every day. In a world constantly described as "forever changed," mentees become the scribes of what real change sounds like. In this section, the young writers of Girls Write Now share their experiences—and then invite you to join them through some of their favorite exercises.*

## THE SOLACE OF SCI-FI WITH LANI FORBES, AUTHOR AND GIRLS WRITE NOW TEACHING ARTIST

*Reflection by Girls Write Now Mentee Michelle Seucan*

Science fiction is a genre that breathes life into reality, otherwise overlooked. From exploring the blue worlds of *Avatar* to abiding by *The Hitchhiker's Guide to the Galaxy*, I'm drawn to its magnetic pull that gets stronger by the year.

Naturally, I was intrigued by the Saturday workshop, "The Solace of Sci-Fi." There, I got to follow in the footsteps of my favorite science-fiction pioneers and create my own reality with a group of equally passionate mentees. Steampunk, Space Opera, Military Science—science fiction was our oyster!

Eventually, we landed on Military Science, a subgenre that blends history with futuristic elements, a mind-boggling but fascinating contradiction. After deliberating, we combined ideas to create a story we were all proud of: a group of soldiers from World War II stumbling upon a magical artifact on the battlefield that could transport them a century into the future.

I've dabbled in science fiction, from poems about dystopian environmentally damaged futures to screenplays on societies where liquefied emotions are illegally sold. This workshop took me out of my comfort zone to experiment with historical fiction, adding a refreshing dimension to my creativity as a storyteller. With Girls Write Now, there's a surprise around every corner!

## HARVESTED FROM THE WORKSHOP:
### *Create Your Own Sci-Fi Story . . .*

Think about one of your biggest fears or problems—personal or global/cosmic, in the present or in the future. Can you imagine a scientific/technological solution to your fear or problem? (For example, being able to mechanically turn down the chatter in your brain to sleep, or a time-traveling device to solve a problem or learn something.)

Create the outline for a sci-fi story based on that fear or problem and the scientific/technological solution you imagine. Pick your characters, location, and conflict. What's at stake in your story? Develop the plot. Then create a book cover, an opening paragraph, and a back-cover blurb.

# PERSONAL STATEMENTS FOR SCHOLARSHIPS: EASING YOUR FINANCIAL BURDEN WITH AUTHOR, MENTOR ALUM, AND GIRLS WRITE NOW TEACHING ARTIST SUSANNA HORNG

*Reflection by Girls Write Now Mentee Princesa Santos*

You recently applied to a college program, and now you need to write a six-hundred-word essay about yourself to be granted funding for the tuition. You start the process by picking out one of the many prompts given to you that relate to the program's plan of interest. Nevertheless, when you start typing, you realize that you do not know what to say. How can you possibly relay a rich, detailed experience with such a short word limit? How can you make a true story more interesting than the other thousands of essays the program is receiving?

Being part of this workshop on scholarship essay writing allowed me the opportunity to be introduced to professional teachers and editors who provided answers to my questions along with guidance and examples of how to transform my thoughts, ideas, and experiences into a short essay. The teaching artist helped me to use language and sensory details to make my essay my own. Not only did I create a personal statement that has continued to come in handy for scholarship and program applications—I also learned new skills that have bettered my everyday writing.

## HARVESTED FROM THE WORKSHOP:
### *Craft Your Own Personal Statement . . .*

To make your writing stand out, use the following tools when answering scholarship and personal statement essay questions:

- **Hook:** A great opening sentence! Parachute the reader into the middle of the situation.

- **Specificity:** Instead of describing something in general terms, be specific. Show, don't tell. Use your senses.
- **Dialogue:** What people say. Think of how they talk and the words they use.
- **Humor:** In reflecting on your experience, did anything strike you as funny?
- **Point of View:** Ultimately, write from your unique and authentic perspective.

Here are a few popular scholarship essay questions to jump off of. Using the tools above, free-write on the topic for five minutes, then organize your thoughts to begin a personal essay:

- What are some of your academic and long-term career goals? Why are you applying for the scholarship? What do you plan on using the award for if you win?
- How have you had a positive impact on others in your school, community, or world? What are you most proud of? What did you do? What did this teach you?
- Who has been your biggest influence or inspiration? What have they taught you? Explain how that person has values and behaviors you want to have.

## POETRY IN ACTION: CRITICAL RACE THEORY WITH POET, MENTEE ALUM, AND GIRLS WRITE NOW TEACHING ARTIST BRITTANY BARKER

*Reflection by Girls Write Now Mentee Kathryn Destin*

I wrote a lot of poetry in middle and high school. It was a great outlet to channel my ever-changing emotions, using words I rarely used in a fun and rhythmic delivery. In college, I switched to long-form essays, about politics, pop culture, and other topics. It had been a while since I'd written a poem, but this Community Chat got my juices flowing again.

I still wrote about social issues that I'm passionate about, but in a form that was close to me when I was younger. I challenged myself by pulling the main points that stuck out in the critical race theory (CRT) debates. I considered how affected I was by the constant back-and-forth over something that shouldn't be so controversial. I found it key to strike a balance between putting myself into my writing and the concrete realities CRT teaches. Then I came to a sweet spot, writing from my experience and explaining how this topic is something greater than me and should be recognized.

### HARVESTED FROM THE CHAT:
### *Take Action with Poetry . . .*

Write a poem starting with, "If I could change a few things, I would . . ." or "Banning critical race theory is like . . ."

# WORTH A THOUSAND WORDS:
# STORYTELLING THROUGH ILLUSTRATION WITH
# ANIMATOR, ILLUSTRATOR, AND GIRLS WRITE NOW
# TEACHING ARTIST CAMILA TASAICO

*Reflection by Girls Write Now Mentee Celina Huynh*

At first, I was daunted by this workshop, because drawing is not my strong suit, and I had no prior experience with digital art. I was nervous going into breakout rooms, since I didn't know the mentors in my group, but they were kind and encouraging as we shared our ideas. When given the prompt to draw an original character, I was inspired by the teaching artist's characters personifying different foods.

Though I had trouble drawing on the Sketchbook app using my finger, I was ultimately able to illustrate a character personifying an ice-cream cone. She had brown poofy hair, a long beige skirt that resembled a cone, a strawberry sprinkled tube top, and a maraschino cherry hair accessory! I was happy with my drawing and I learned I am capable of bringing my visions to life. I'm thankful for this workshop, for helping me exercise my creativity and inspiring me to enhance my writing by accompanying my pieces with original illustrations.

## HARVESTED FROM THE WORKSHOP:
### *Design Your Own Original Character . . .*

Challenge yourself to look at things in a new way by creating an illustration of your protagonist as you build a story.

Give your original character (OC) a name and build out their background, interests, personality, etc. Sort out elements, by asking questions:

- Where are they from? (It can be real or fictional.)
- What does your character like? (Food, activities, favorite season, etc.)
- Does your OC have a pet? What is it? What is the pet's name?
- Do they have some sort of bag/storage item?
- What's their color palette?
- Do they have a family? Friends? Are they lonely?

Take thirty minutes to illustrate an original character and write a short profile.

# ALL FROM YOUR PHONE:
## CREATING DIGITAL NEWS WITH REPORTER AND GIRLS WRITE NOW GUEST ARTIST MAYA EAGLIN

*Reflection by Girls Write Now Mentee Kathryn Destin*

There is always news, and having our phones with us at all times makes it hard not to be overwhelmed by it. With that said, I do think we can look at this dilemma through a glass-half-empty or glass-half-full lens. While our phone obsession can be too much at times, phones are fantastic tools. Mainstream media is primarily controlled by a few large companies with corporate, profit-driven agendas, but we, the people, have the power to change that by providing nuance to trending topics.

For example: In this Friday Night Salon, I mentioned the Bronx fire of January 2022 and how many leaders, including the new mayor, blamed the tenants/victims. However, the real story was that the landlord, who previously worked for the mayor, ignored hundreds of fire safety and heating complaints. The tragedy could've been prevented if safety were prioritized.

We are more in the know than ever, and with resources to share knowledge. We can all contribute and help change the landscape of digital news by investigating the roots of issues and sharing truths behind the tales, even if it's a simple video or a tweet.

## HARVESTED FROM THE SALON:
### *Amplify Your Own Voice . . .*

Think about the following questions:

- What stories are you passionate about? What makes you a storyteller? How could you use your craft of writing to elevate your community or other voices?
- Think about what makes a good story, news article, or video. What are some of the components of the storytelling that must be

included? What would you like to see change or evolve in the news and media industry?

- What do you think are the benefits of having news and information accessible on social media? What are some of the challenges?
- Think about representation in journalism, media, and writing. Why do you think it is important that writers of color are in newsrooms, telling stories and making decisions on an executive level in the journalism industry?

Consider a current event that you think more people should know about. How can you bring your unique perspective to the world of journalism? Write a news story to bring attention to an important event in your community. If you're feeling brave, record yourself presenting your news story and post it online! Be sure to tag @girlswritenow!

## THE INTIMATE AND THE INVENTED: FICTION WRITING WITH GIRLS WRITE NOW GUEST AUTHOR DAPHNE PALASI ANDREADES

*Reflection by Girls Write Now Mentee Sophia Torres*

As a Baruch student, I was extremely excited to attend the Girls Write Now Friday Night Salon with Daphne Palasi Andreades after the publication of her debut novel, *Brown Girls*. She presented us with prompts that encouraged us to think from multiple perspectives and to explore details that create painted images with words. During the workshop, I started a piece about my grandfather, using words to map out details that captured the essence of his appearance and character.

Then Daphne asked us to write from the perspective of someone who hated them. Hate?! My grandfather? Although incredibly hard, Daphne taught me that fiction writing is not just about the pretty or positive things, it includes everything in between. By pulling those things in, you can place the reader in your work and I think her prompts were a great start.

## HARVESTED FROM THE SALON:
### *Try on a New Perspective . . .*

Think about someone you love (or a character you are working on, whom you love). Write down specific details, images, and memories about this person.

Now write about the same person from the point of view of somebody who hates them. What do they know about the person you love? What do they not know? How have they come to hate the person you love? Write a scene in which the person you love must ask for help from the person who hates them.

## WRITE RIGHT NOW: PROCRASTINATORS WELCOME WITH WRITER, GIRLS WRITE NOW DEI ADVISOR, AND TEACHING ARTIST SHEENA DAREE MILLER

*Reflection by Girls Write Now Mentee Princesa Santos*

Procrastination, a reviled action I take when a task is too hard or too long, and also a summary of my lifestyle. My scribbled-up, packed planner holds all the ways I try to organize my life, and the canceled plans with my family and friends do show I have time to complete my work. Yet, most days, I'm swiping on every TikTok that lands on my "For You" page, and those tasks I spend much effort trying to complete never get done.

Zooming into the "Procrastinators Welcome" workshop, I thought the speaker would give the same cliché advice: Be organized, be disciplined, and just do it. Yet to my surprise, she didn't. She introduced herself as a renowned procrastinator—without shame. She let us know procrastination is a mechanism for avoiding tasks that cause stress and anxiety, and to counteract it by finding enjoyable approaches to those tasks. Her suggestions to minimize the burden included working with a group of classmates or friends, spreading the task out over days, or completing it within a short time frame.

Coming from a place of relatability and humor, the teaching artist turned a sensitive subject into a comfortable one, with solutions we could own.

## HARVESTED FROM THE WORKSHOP:
### Defeat the Dreaded Blank Page . . .

What is something you've put off writing? Set a five-minute timer, and pick one of the following prompts to explore or use that time to work on a piece you've been avoiding. Don't worry about your words being perfect—just get something down!

- Personal Statement
  - ◊ Discuss an accomplishment, event, or realization that sparked a period of personal growth and a new understanding of yourself or others.
  - ◊ Describe a topic, idea, or concept you find so engaging that it makes you lose track of time. Why does it captivate you? What or whom do you turn to when you want to learn more?
  - ◊ Is there an object in your life that holds great meaning for you?
  - ◊ Do you have a favorite book, movie, poem, artwork, music, sport?
- Thank-You Note or Toast
  - ◊ Who is someone who has extended you kindness or support? What do you want them to know?
  - ◊ Who inspires or motivates you?
  - ◊ Who do you think deserves more praise than they've received?

- Wedding Vows
  - ◊ Think of a character you've been working on: What sort of wedding vows would they want or hate to hear? What sort of wedding vows would they write?
  - ◊ Think of someone or something you love, and write something that reflects how you feel.
  - ◊ Is there a couple from a book, TV series, or other media you're intrigued by? Imagine and write their vows.

*In closing, we hope you not only read through all of the inspiring pieces in this anthology, but create your own inspired work too. Consider this a gentle nudge to take these pickings and let your imagination run wild!*

—SAMANTHA ARRIOZOLA,
*GIRLS WRITE NOW FELLOW*

# ABOUT GIRLS WRITE NOW

We are a powerhouse of voices that have been ignored or silenced for too long. We are a pipeline of talent into schools and industries in need of new talent and different perspectives. As a community, we follow our hearts and—through bold, authentic storytelling—inspire people to open theirs. We are Girls Write Now.

For nearly twenty-five years, Girls Write Now has been breaking down barriers of gender, race, age, and poverty to mentor the next generation of writers and leaders who are impacting businesses, shaping culture, and creating change.

Girls Write Now matches female and gender-expansive young adults from systemically underserved communities—over 90 percent of color, 90 percent high-need, 75 percent immigrant or first-generation, and 25 percent LGBTQIA+—with professional writers and digital media makers as their personal mentors. Mentees' multigenre, multimedia work is published in outlets including *Teen Vogue, LitHub, The New York Times,* and *The Wall Street Journal;* is performed at Lincoln Center and the United Nations; and wins hundreds of writing awards. One hundred percent of its seniors are accepted to college—equipped with confidence, portfolios, and lifelong bonds.

In addition to being the first writing and mentoring organization of its kind, Girls Write Now continually ranks among the top programs nationwide for driving social-emotional growth for youth. Girls Write Now has been distinguished three times by the White House as one of the nation's top youth programs, twice by the Nonprofit Excellence Awards as one of New York's top ten nonprofits, by NBCUniversal's 21st Century Solutions for Social Innovation, by Youth INC for Youth Innovation, and as a

DVF People's Voice Nominee. Reaching more than 50,000 youths, Girls Write Now is a founding partner of the STARS Citywide Girls Initiative.

## TEAM

Samantha Arriozola, *Fellow*

Terence Diamond, *Grant Writer*

Ariah Dow, *Senior Community Manager*

Shira Feen, *Graphic Designer*

Spencer George, *Special Initiatives Assistant*

Gabriella Gomez, *Senior Development Manager*

Dacia Green, *Fellow*

Margery Hannah, *Community Manager, Writing Works*

Vahni Kurra, *Fellow*

Kelsey LePage, *Development and Operations Manager*

Molly MacDermot, *Director of Special Initiatives*

Natalie McGuire, *Controller*

Emily Mendelson, *Community Manager, Publishing 360*

Sheena Daree Miller, *Diversity, Equity, and Inclusion Advisor*

Maya Nussbaum, *Founder and Executive Director*

Erin O'Connor, *Fellow*

Daniella Olibrice, *Talent Director*

Lisbett Rodriguez, *Senior Community Coordinator*

Erica Silberman, *Director of Curriculum and Engagement*

Richelle Szypulski, *Senior Editorial Manager*

## BOARD OF DIRECTORS

Ellen Archer, *Board Chair*

Bruce Morrow, *Vice Chair*

Lynda Pak, *Secretary*

Mustafa Topiwalla, *Treasurer*

Ahu Terzi, *Partnership Committee Chair*

Cate Ambrose, *Finance Chair*

Joy Altimare

Judith Curr

Gati Curtis

Maya Nussbaum

Stephanie Gordon

Dacia Green

Dr. Emily Green

Wendi Gu

Haydil Henriquez

Christina Hogrebe

Susanna Horng

Candice Iloh

Maggie Iuni

Elle Johnson

Julia Kardon

Stephanie Kariuki

Vahni Kurra

Dr. Janet Lefkowitz

Laurie Liss

Amy Maclin

Ivy Mahsciao

Jasmine Mans

LaTonya McQueen

Lynn Melnick

Emily Mendelson

Maya Millett

Mareesa Nicosia

Janice Nimura

Christina Olivares

Daphne Palasi Andreades

Cynthia Pelayo

Andrea Plasko

Angelica Puzio

Megan Reid

Sherese Robinson

Misako Rocks!

Rebecca Scherer

Nic Stone

Carina Storrs

Camila Tasaico

Kiki T.

Eliza VanCort

Arriel Vinson

Qian Julie Wang

Samantha Wekstein

Abby West

Diana Whitney

Ashley Woodfolk

Liza Wyles

## GIRLS WRITE NOW CIRCLE

### Honorary Chairs

Ellen Archer and Jeffrey Gracer

Ann and Bob Hammer

Maja Kristin

Jane Lauder

Amy Morrill

Susan Sawyers

James M. and Margaret V. Stine

Kate Stroup and Matthew Berger

## Co-Chairs

Cate Ambrose

Judith Curr and Ken
   Kennedy

Rebecca Gradinger

Andrew Guff

Agnes Gund

Kate Levin and Robin
   Shapiro

Suzanne Levine

Maya Nussbaum and Todd
   Pulerwitz

Lynda Pak

Alina Roytberg

Mustafa Topiwalla and
   Melissa Connor

## Vice Chairs

Marci Alboher and Jay
   Goldberg

Rachel Bloom

Josephine Bolus

Rachel Cohen

Lisa Gardner

Catherine Greenman

Janice Horowitz

Bruce Morrow

Hope Pordy and Bob
   Osmond

Nicolas Rohatyn

Elaine Stuart-Shah

Ahu Terzi

Lisa and Frank Wohl

## Patrons

Nisha Aoyama

Stuart Applebaum

Tamara and Theodore
   Becker

Amy Berkower and Dan
   Weiss

Daniel Brodnitz

Marie Capasso

Veronica Chambers

Jill Cohen

Brian DeFiore

Lynn Feasley

Melissa Febos

Jon Fine

Elizabeth Frankel

Anne B. Fritz and Libbie
   Thacker

Lisa Gardner

Forsyth Harmon

Carol Hymowitz

Robert Koroshetz

Mollie Meloy and Jeff Fitts

Natalie Nussbaum

Danae Prousis

Molly Pulda and Gary
   Sernovitz

Linda Rose

Liane Roseman

Zoe Rosenberg

Alanna Schubach and Scott
   Kilpatrick

Amy Singer

Gail Stuart

Ann and Tom van Buren

## Members

Joy Altimare

Christine Ambrose

Maria Aspan

Paul Aspan

Steven Baum

Jillian Berman

Lisa Chai

Seth and Lynn Cohen

Marya Cohn

Ken, Emily, and Lisa Connor

Andrew Delveaux

Ritik Dholakia

Jamie Ducharme

Renee Dugan

Andrew Ertman

Sandra E. Garcia

Scott Gerber

Megan Giddings

Keli Goff

Tia Hanke-Hills

Laura Hankin

Jennifer Harlan

Forsyth Harmon

Courtney Hartman

Michael Hirschhorn

Jackie Homan

Eliza Karp

Claire Karwowski

Joyce King

Kelly and Chris Koenig

Amalie Kwassman

Jeffrey LaPlante

Wendy Lauria

Hilary Leichter

Robert Levin

Erica Lubetkin

Meghan Louttit

Tara McCann

Ciara McCarthy

Gregory McGillivary

Amy Padnani

Chelsea and Harish Rao

Leslie Riedel

Terry Rieser

Andrea Rizvi

Michael Rogan

Lilli Ross

Jennifer Schuessler

Lisa Schwartz

Katy Staples

Caryn Summer

Thomas Urbain

Vivian Wang

Lesley Ware

Bess Wohl

Nicholas Zeltzer

## AGENTS OF CHANGE CORPORATE PARTNERS

### Game-Changer $100–200K

Estée Lauder Companies

The Upswing Fund

### Leadership $75–95K

BBDO

BIC Corporate Foundation

HarperCollins

News Corp

### Visionary $50K

EHE Health

Kickstarter

Macmillan

WarnerMedia

### Innovator $25–35K

Mattel's Barbie Dream Gap Project

NBCUniversal

Penguin Random House

RBC Foundation

Scholastic

### Champion $10–20K

Adobe

Amazon Literary Partnership

Bloomberg

Bloomingdale's

Dotdash Meredith

Estée Lauder Foundation

GFP Real Estate

Twitter

### Creator $5K+

Fletcher & Co

Forbes

Minute Media

Nike

ViacomCBS

The Feminist Press

Piccolina

Jane Rotrosen Agency

Spotify

Oracle Corporation

Workman

## FOUNDATION AND GOVERNMENT SUPPORTERS

### $100K+

The New York City Council and the Department of Youth and Community Development

### $40-$50K

Blanchette Hooker Rockefeller Fund

Harman Family Foundation

New York City Department of Cultural Affairs

### $15-$25K

Charles Lawrence Keith & Clara S. Miller Foundation

Costas Family Foundation

The Nancy Friday Foundation

National Endowment for the Arts

Poetry Foundation

The Rona Jaffe Foundation

### $10-14K

Berger Family Foundation

Find Your Light Foundation

Malka Fund of Jewish Communal Fund

New York State Council on the Arts

### $5-$9K

Blue Hill Road Foundation

Cowan Slavin Foundation

The Diller–von Furstenberg Family Foundation
The Lotos Foundation

## $1–$4K

DuBose Family Foundation
Fondation Femme Debut
Holidays with Heroes
Marshall-Freimanis Family Giving Fund
Oracle Corporation
The Raymond and Gloria Naftali Foundation
Robert & Mercedes Eichholz Foundation
The Starbucks Foundation
The Strand Book Store

# ANTHOLOGY SPONSORS

We are grateful to the countless institutions and individuals who have supported our work through their generous contributions. Visit our website at girlswritenow.org to view the extended list.

Girls Write Now would like to thank Dutton, including Christine Ball, Maya Ziv, Lexy Cassola, Susan Schwartz, Claire Sullivan, Dora Mak, Sabrina Bowers, and Amy Brosey for their help producing this year's anthology, and Amazon Literary Partnership, which provided the charitable contribution that made this book possible.